T0375661

Reconciliation in Trans Mara

THE ODYSSEY OF A FAMILY

CARL E. HANSEN

WESTBOW
PRESS®
A DIVISION OF THOMAS NELSON
& ZONDERVAN

This book is a work of non-fiction. Unless otherwise noted, the author and the publisher make no explicit guarantees as to the accuracy of the information contained in this book and in some cases, names of people and places have been altered to protect their privacy.

WestBow Press books may be ordered through booksellers or by contacting:

WestBow Press
A Division of Thomas Nelson & Zondervan
1663 Liberty Drive
Bloomington, IN 47403
www.westbowpress.com
844-714-3454

Because of the dynamic nature of the Internet, any web addresses or links contained in this book may have changed since publication and may no longer be valid. The views expressed in this work are solely those of the author and do not necessarily reflect the views of the publisher, and the publisher hereby disclaims any responsibility for them.

Any people depicted in stock imagery provided by Getty Images are models, and such images are being used for illustrative purposes only. Certain stock imagery © Getty Images.

All Scripture quotations are taken from the Holy Bible, NEW INTERNATIONAL VERSION®, NIV® Copyright © 1973, 1978, 1984, 2011 by Biblica, Inc.® Used by permission. All rights reserved worldwide.

ISBN: 979-8-3850-1249-7 (sc)
ISBN: 979-8-3850-1251-0 (hc)
ISBN: 979-8-3850-1250-3 (e)

Library of Congress Control Number: 2023921695

Print information available on the last page.

WestBow Press rev. date: 11/30/2023

A Development Commission

The Spirit of the sovereign Lord is upon me,
because the Lord has anointed me
to preach good news to the poor.
He has sent me to bind up the broken hearted,
to proclaim freedom for the captives
and release from darkness for the prisoners,
to proclaim the year of the Lord's favor
and the day of vengeance of our God,
to comfort all who mourn,
and provide for those who grieve in Zion,
to bestow on them a crown of beauty instead of ashes,
the oil of gladness instead of mourning,
and a garment of praise instead of a spirit of despair.
They will be called oaks of righteousness,
a planting of the Lord for the display of his splendor.

Is. 61:1-3 (NIV)

CONTENTS

DEDICATION

In memory of the late J. Paul and Erma Lehman, unsung heroes whose lives reflected the genuine, humble, self-giving spirit of the Christ they served. This beautiful couple consistently exuded gifts of hospitality, kindness, understanding, and generosity, providing comfort and rest to weary travelers, a listening ear and encouragement to the discouraged. They provided a nourishing home away from home for my family and me as well as for so many others who entered their doors.

Petition Denied

A simple prayer wings its way swiftly to the throne
of grace.
And the reply as quickly flies back to its place:
"Your petition is denied!"
    "But go on out, and in your seeking find.
    You will be a blessing to humankind!"
                – Carl E. Hansen

ACKNOWLEDGEMENTS

I dare not take credit for a photographic mind that retains all the details recorded in this book. Nor did I have access to a well-kept diary, for I failed to keep a diary during those busy years. However, I did possess one filial virtue. I wrote letters to my mother regularly, at least once a month. My mother, Elizabeth Hansen, treasured those letters and wisely saved them for many years. When the time was right, she returned them to me.

Those old letters plus others we wrote and articles and reports that were made, stirred up old memories grown dim with time, joined together to form the basis upon which this book has been written.

I owe a debt of profound gratitude to our eldest daughter, Cindy Kreider, who, while undergoing the discomfort and distraction of chemotherapy for colon cancer, showed her love and devotion by reading and meticulously editing my manuscript and advising me on many points. This is a much better book because of her.

In addition to Cindy's good judgement, our second daughter, Karen, contributed her professional skill, honed to perfection through thirty years of experience as a middle school English teacher, laboring over this manuscript, correcting my notorious spelling, grammar, punctuation, and word usage.

Also, appreciation goes to my faithful partner and companion, Vera. She not only lived out those Maasai years with me, but also read my manuscript and helped me to remember more details. Two witnesses are always more reliable than one.

I must also make special mention of our daughter, Kristina, whose keen memory and personal experience refreshed my mind on many points.

ACRONYMS

AIC	Africa Inland Church
AMBS	Associated Mennonite Biblical Seminary
CBHC	Community Based Health Care
CHAK	Christian Health Association of Kenya
CMF	Christian Missionary Fellowship
CPK	Church of the Province of Kenya
D.E.L.T.A.	Development Education Leadership Training Activity
EMBMC	Eastern Mennonite Board of Missions and Charities
EMM	Eastern Mennonite Missions
EMC	Eastern Mennonite College
GSU	General Service Unit
ICMT	Institute of Christian Ministries Training
LWR	Lutheran World Relief
MCC	Mennonite Central Committee
MDS	Mennonite Disaster Service
MEDA	Mennonite Economic Development Associates
MKC	Meserete Kristos Church
NGO	Non-Government Organization
OSP	Ogwedhi Sigawa Community Development Project
RVA	Rift Valley Academy
STAT	Summer Training Action Teams
STU	Stock Theft Unit
WV	World Vision

FOREWORD

Being endowed by our Creator with a lifelong bent towards enjoying history, it has been one of my goals for my retirement years to record some of the highlights of my life and reflect upon what has given it meaning and purpose. I want to leave a historical record for future generations who might have a similar interest in the story of their ancestors from whence they have sprung.

Such a record would never be complete without including the vital roles my family played in it. Hence, I am putting together a series of books that record something of the odyssey of our family. These might be of interest to our descendants and perhaps a much wider world.

The events recorded in this book took place between August 1985 and June 1991. This record reflects something of the odyssey that my wife, Vera, our two daughters, Sheryl and Kristina, and I experienced among the Maasai and Luos in southwestern Kenya. We fondly remember that period of time as "our Maasai years."

INTRODUCTION:
THE MAASAI DILEMMA

An ancient legend holds that when *"Enkai"* (God) made the world with all the animals and people, He made the cattle special and gave them to the Maasai. So, when the young warriors go on cattle raids among neighboring tribes, they are not really "stealing," but simply bringing home their "strays."

While their neighbors may not share that particular theological perspective, they do recognize the Maasai first and foremost as cattle people. For hundreds of years the Maasai have moved their large herds of cattle and goats back and forth across the vast central plains of the Great Rift Valley in what is now called Kenya and Tanzania in East Africa. While their lives as nomads demanded that they live a simple lifestyle in terms of few material comforts, they did develop a culture rich in poetry, songs, legends, proverbs, and wisdom, and a profound sense of identity in community.

It was this sense of satisfaction or pride in their identity as strong and independent nomads as well as their legendary ability as warriors that motivated and enabled them to resist the pressures for change brought upon them by the colonization and subsequent westernization of East Africa. From ancient times up until the 1970's they remained an island of traditional conservative resistance in a sea of change. The colonialists and the missionaries together tried to bring them the benefits of schools, clinics, and churches just as they did to the tribes surrounding them. The Maasai just as steadfastly resisted. They, like the Amish in America, were satisfied with their way of life and just wanted to be left alone.

It was the young men, such as these "Il moran," the warriors,
that kept the Maasai proud and free for so many centuries.

Most of the Maasai were quite well to do. The size of their cattle herds indicated the balance in their "bank accounts." Living as nomads, their lives were simple and their needs few. Whenever they did need money, they would take a few steers to the market to sell.

Unlike that of their settled modern agrarian neighbors, the Maasai communal land was still covered with grass and a scattering of small trees and bushes. It was open, without barriers such as roads, bridges, fences, or cultivated fields. There were no electric or telephone lines marring the landscape. The Maasai had no schools, churches, or clinics, or any other sign of modern civilization. Most were illiterate. Child mortality was about 50%. Although there were attempts by many different Christian missionary organizations to convert the Maasai to their way of faith, most still adhered to their ancient traditional views of the spiritual realities.

In Kenya the situation changed. As the colony developed into a modern nation state, with a citizenry that was capable of recognizing and capitalizing on good business opportunities, and as the population grew from about three million in 1903 to near eighteen million in 1975, the traditional pastoralist peoples faced irresistible pressure from their neighbors who saw the commercial potential in their "unused" lands.

Mostly illiterate and lacking in understanding of land ownership laws or of the commercial value of land, or of how modern businesses operate, the Maasai found themselves at a distinct disadvantage. Bit by bit their lands were being taken by others. At this point the government put additional pressure on them to divide and privatize their communal lands. The nomadic way of life was doomed.

More specifically, in the Trans Mara region of Narok District of Rift Valley Province in southwestern Kenya, the Wuasinkishu, Siria, and Moitanik Maasai clans were living on high potential land that has adequate rainfall to sustain a two-crops-per-year farming cycle. They were surrounded on three sides by industrious, populous, subsistent agricultural societies who exerted tremendous pressure to find land for their landless offspring.

The Maasai population was light, and they knew they could not keep all this valuable land for grazing much longer. Already, many of these landless people had been making private arrangements with individual Maasai to farm small plots in Maasailand. At first these squatters were just a few, but then their relatives each wanted a piece also. They were soon perceived as a threat.

In the 1970's the Maasai elders, with some pressure from the government, decided they would leave their nomadic way of life, demarcate, and privatize all their communal lands, and become farmers, thus joining the mainstream of Kenyan life. In other words, they were now willing to completely change their way of life, and this would have a profound effect on their culture, and they knew it.

The squatters, being residents, also hoped, upon demarcation, to get a share of the land. The *Il moran* (warriors) in the Sikawa location were aware of this danger. In 1977, without consulting their elders, these brash young warriors launched a surprise attack and killed more than fifty Luo and Kisii squatters, burned their houses, destroyed their crops, and drove the rest, fleeing in terror, out of Maasailand. This act of "ethnic cleansing" created a climate of fear, mistrust, and hostility among the peoples on both sides of the border.

The Maasai elders were embarrassed by their sons' aggressive tactics. They met with Luo elders and their chiefs to discuss ways they could work together for peace and reconciliation between their two tribes. The Maasai elders acknowledged that they were changing and wanted to join the mainstream of modern Kenyan life. This meant they wanted to settle down, become farmers, keep improved cattle, have schools for their children, accept Christianity, and have better health care for their families.

As a result of these talks, with the encouragement of the Luo Chief, Wilson Ogwada, a Mennonite from Osingo, the Maasai requested the Kenya Mennonite Church to launch a development project to help them start schools, churches and hospitals, and to teach them better agricultural and animal husbandry practices.

Their choice of inviting the Mennonites to come to their aid was not only because the Luo chief was from that persuasion, but also because the Mennonites were reputed to be a non-violent people of peace. Which Christian denomination would be more qualified to assist in bringing about reconciliation and peace in the larger community? It may seem amazing that a people known for their warrior-like behavior would choose a church known for its strong pacifist principles. Yet, it was not so strange as it may seem. They had decided that they would become "Christians," although they did not know all that would entail. However, they had been exposed to some Maranatha Christians before who espoused non-resistant principles.

It seems the Maasai believers in this area had more or less accepted a non-resistant or a non-violent gospel largely due to the influence of the Maranatha believers, promoted by a pentecostal type of mission from Finland. Of course, the position is plainly backed by the life, teaching, and example of our Lord as found in Scripture. Therefore, the Maasai had little difficulty, once they have accepted Christ, to accept his peace teaching as well. The Mennonite stance on peace simply confirmed what they knew about the Christian way.

The Maranatha believers were living in three locations, twenty-five- or thirty-kilometers east, near Kilgoris. They had been severely tested when there was an outbreak of war between the Maasai and the Kisii. The Christians there refused to pick up weapons and go to battle. They were bitterly despised as cowards. Also, the Maasai converts in the Church of God took the same non-resistant non-violent stance as the Maranatha believers. They were very few in number, but their stance confirmed that of the Mennonites and strengthened the unity of the believers on this issue.

Some in the Maranatha group insisted that a Christian should not even take a job as a watchman because he must carry weapons and be prepared to defend property and even inflict wounds or death upon an aggressor. In that war with the Kisii, the brothers even refused to allow their wives to scream the traditional war cry because that would be contributing to the war effort, by calling people to go and kill and/or die.

Now, at Ogwedhi, to facilitate this plan, the Maasai set aside one hundred acres of land just 200 meters north of Ogwedhi shopping center, about twenty-eight kilometers east of Migori town, in the Trans Mara Region of Rift Valley Province on the boundary with the Upper Suna, Suba East, Migori, in South Nyanza Province, between the Maasai and Luo peoples. This borderland location was chosen so that the project could reconcile and benefit both communities.

The little town of Ogwedhi was spread out on both sides of the provincial boundary between Maasai and Luo tribes. The Maasai shops and houses were on the Trans Mara side to the east and the Luo shops and houses were on the South Nyanza side to the west. At the south end was an open marketplace. The center's claim to fame was mostly its well-known cattle market, the meeting point for distant cattle buyers who come to purchase cattle from local sellers. At that time the center had neither telephone nor electricity. A small government clinic was out of service. A small police station made the government's presence known.

During colonial times, the boundary between South Nyanza and Rift Valley Provinces was marked by an "elephant ditch", a one and one-half meter deep and one and one-half meter wide ditch that kept the elephants from crossing from Maasailand to destroy the crops of the sedentary Luo farmers. Only traces of this ditch remain as a road now marks the boundary and the elephants have long disappeared from the area due to extensive poaching.

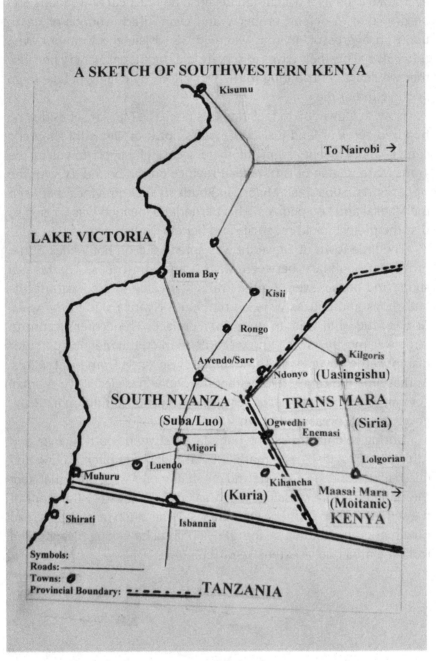

A SKETCH OF SOUTHWESTERN KENYA

Kisumu

To Nairobi →

LAKE VICTORIA

Homa Bay

Kisii

Rongo

Awendo/Sare

Ndonyo

Kilgoris

(Uasingishu)

SOUTH NYANZA

(Suba/Luo)

TRANS MARA

(Siria)

Ogwedhi

Enemasi

Migori

Luendo

Lolgorian

Muhuru

Kihancha

Maasai Mara →
(Moitanic)

(Kuria)

KENYA

Shirati

Isbannia

Symbols:
Roads: ———————
Towns: ●
Provincial Boundary: ▪ ▪ ▪ ▪ ▪ ▪ TANZANIA

Sketch of the southwestern Kenya project area

Launching the Ogwedhi Sigawa Community Development Project (OSP)

In 1979, the Kenya Mennonite Church (KMC), in cooperation with Eastern Mennonite Missions (EMM), responded to the elders' invitation by launching the Ogwedhi Sigawa Community Development Project (OSP). The name *Ogwedhi Sigawa* is derived from the names of the two places, the village of *Ogwedhi*, the name of which in Luo means "blessed" and *Sikawa*, a hill about four kilometers north inside Maasailand, which means "peace" in the Maasai language. At the same time, the government officials, in cooperation with local elders, began the lengthy process of land demarcation.

OSP's overall objectives were (1) Peacemaking. To work at reconciliation and creating a sense of community between the sometimes-hostile Maasai, Luo, and Kuria tribes. This area, which had experienced war and bloodshed, should become a place of peace and blessing for all; (2) Development. To be a resource and a catalyst that would encourage people to utilize their resources more appropriately so that they could better their lives economically, educationally, spiritually, physically, and socially.

These objectives were to be realized through launching programs in five areas:

1. Education – To provide primary education for community children of all tribes where Luo, Maasai, and Kuria children can learn and play together.
2. Health – To provide basic health care through operating a dispensary and through providing preventive measures such as vaccinations and prevention education for people on all sides.
3. Evangelism – To promote the Christian religion by teaching and establishing congregations throughout the Maasai and Luo areas.
4. Animal husbandry – To help Maasai and Luo farmers to improve animal health and productivity by introducing improved breeds and better techniques of animal husbandry.
5. Agriculture – To improve farming practices and increase productivity.

A community-based board of governors known as the "Management Committee" was formed to give OSP overall direction. It consisted of nine members of which Ole Kitiyia, Ole Sikawa, and Paul Ole Sankei were appointed by the Maasai community; George Obute, Barack Ochanda Ogola, and John Odongo by the Luo community; and Chief Wilson Ogwada, Jackson Owilo, and Charles Oluoch were appointed by the church. An evangelist couple, Paul and Siprosa Otieno, were also appointed by the church to give leadership in church matters.

OSP Chairman, Ole Sikawa and wife, Noonkipa, at their home

At first, many of the church leaders were afraid to visit the area because of fear of the Maasai. However, as this spirit of cooperation between the leaders of all sides persisted, the level of fear diminished as the level of trust grew. Jerry Stutzman, an EMM missionary stationed in Migori, was sent to build the first church building and two staff houses, one for the director and one for the pastor on OSP property.

In 1980, Leon and Lou Ann Ressler from Pennsylvania, USA, were sent by EMM to give leadership to OSP. Barack Ochanda Ogola was hired as manager a year later. The Resslers began work immediately, clearing the bush, building fences, plowing fields, and building the first classrooms of the Ogwedhi Sigawa Primary School.

Over the next few years, other buildings such as a dairy barn, a goat barn, water tanks, and a storage facility followed. Better strains of cattle, especially dairy—mostly Ayrshire and Sahiwal—were introduced. Artificial insemination was made available for crossbreeding and upgrading community cattle. Basic veterinary supplies and medications for the treatment and prevention of cattle diseases were made available. Improved methods of plowing by oxen and seeding were demonstrated. Ox carts were built and introduced to the community. Farm workers were trained.

While the OSP buildings were on the Maasai side of the road, the primary school was divided with some of the classrooms built on the Luo side and other classrooms on the Maasai side. The road and the provincial boundary ran through the middle of the school land.

Basic medical care was introduced by hiring a medical practitioner who operated a reliable dispensary from a small room just next to his house. Construction of a dispensary building was underway, and Mennonite churches were started among both tribes. World Vision International agreed to fund OSP for the first six years.

Leon and Lou Ann came as a young couple brimming with energy, enthusiasm, and dedication. Leon was a recent graduate from Penn State with a degree in agriculture. He picked up the Swahili language and communicated fluently. Lou Ann had training as a nurse, but, after assisting her husband in building fences and clearing the land, gave priority to birthing and raising their first two children at Ogwedhi.

Under their energetic and wise leadership, the Ogwedhi Sigawa Community Development Project developed from an idea to become a highly admired and successful community-based ministry of the Kenya Mennonite Church. It laid the foundations for promoting peace, reconciliation, development, and spiritual growth among the Maasai, Luo, and Kuria peoples in the Southwest corner of Kenya.

*Arial view of the Ogwedhi Sigawa Community
Development Project, 1989*

CHAPTER 1

Orientation to Our New Home

After pioneering this Ogwedhi Sigawa Community Development Project (OSP) for five-and-one-half years, Leon and Lou Ann decided to terminate their services with Eastern Mennonite Missions (EMM) and settle in their native Pennsylvania. EMM recruited us to take Leon's place as director of OSP.

Vera and I had served with EMM for eight years in Ethiopia between 1967 and 1975. There I served, first as a high school teacher, and later as director of the Wobera-Garamuleta Rural Development Project, and Vera birthed and mothered three of our four daughters. Then, in 1975, we had gone home to Alberta, Canada, to raise our daughters and pastor the Salem Mennonite Church at Tofield for nine years. After spending one year in Pasadena, California, studying missiology, we accepted this new assignment in Kenya for a three-year term.

A New Country

We arrived in Nairobi on August 6, 1985, with our two youngest daughters, Sheryl, age sixteen, and Kristina, age thirteen. Our two eldest daughters, Cindy and Karen, remained in the USA enrolled at Eastern Mennonite College. We spent that night at the Mennonite Guest House in Westlands, a suburb of Nairobi.

The next morning, the director of the Mennonite Board in East Africa, Maynard Kurtz, drove us to Kijabe to introduce Sheryl and Kristina to the Rift Valley Academy (RVA). This was the missionary children's boarding school operated by the Africa Inland Mission

(AIM). Our girls would return there in September to pursue their studies.

On the second day, Maynard presented us with a map, instructions, and the keys to a rented car, and sent us off to find a tiny remote place called Ogwedhi, eight hours away, in southwestern Kenya. There, we were to meet Leon and Lou Ann Ressler, who were strangers to us. We were to live with them for a week while Leon would orient us to the new job and living situation. Then Leon would return the car, bringing his family to the city.

I had only been in this strange country for two days. I did not know any Swahili. I had never driven on the left side of the road. I had no valid Kenya driver's license, no cell phone, no credit card, no AAA membership, and no GPS. I was following a map to a place I did not know, with a wife and two teenage daughters who were skeptical of my driving ability on the "wrong" side of the road. I knew I was once again a "missionary"!

We arrived on time at the appointed junction at Awendo Sare where we met a green Toyota Hilux single-cab pickup with a happy, smiling, bearded *mzungu* (white foreigner) waving his welcome to us. Leon led the way over a rough, potholed trail through many kilometers of sugarcane fields that gradually gave way to small farms and then brushland, to what would be our next home.

For the next six days, the four of us were guests in the little two-bedroom house, eating, sleeping, and living with the Ressler couple and their two small children, Lynn and Lee. Leon eagerly devoted the days and the evenings to giving us an extensive introduction to the history and workings of OSP. His introduction included an enlightening exposition and evaluation of the personalities connected in the community, as well as the larger church, their failures and successes, their conflicts and resolutions. He also shared his hopes and the unfinished vision that would challenge us in the days and years to come.

Our house and vehicle at the Ogwedhi Project, 1985

Security Concerns

To make us feel more secure, Leon proudly showed us the recent fortifications he had added to the house. On the inside of each of the two outside doors, he had installed three sliding, two-inch-diameter steel pipes that fit into steel rings embedded in the masonry walls. With the door closed and the three bars slid into place across the top, bottom, and middle, it would take a huge battering ram to break into his fortress/house. As a final inner line of defense, he added a steel door in the concrete hallway, also reinforced with three sliding pipes, protecting the bedrooms.

Also, at his request, the government had relocated a small police station just outside the compound with two officers available, just in case. This was to supplement the security services of OSP's own night watchmen.

In justification for his, perhaps seemingly excessive, security precautions, Leon related a horrific story that had occurred in Migori the previous year. One night, thieves broke into the home of his friend, a Maranatha missionary, in search of four million shillings that the missionary was rumored to have received from outside to construct a church building. In the vain search, the missionary was murdered, and his wife wounded. Apparently, some thieves were not

3

aware that wise people keep their large sums of money in banks, not under their mattresses at home.

Living with a defenseless wife and two small children, in a remote bushy place, in a house shielded only with flimsy wooden doors and cheap locks, and without telephone or radio, gave enough justification for Leon's concern. Further, surrounded by needy neighbors and traveling vagabonds of unknown character, being the "rich" foreign outsider in charge of an institution with a perceived huge budget, Leon felt a bit vulnerable. Hence, this extravagant outlay for security.

A New Community

On our first day there, we were introduced to a Maasai friend of Leon's who wanted to negotiate with me for cows to marry one of my daughters. The next day we were all invited to another Maasai home for a meal. That man also suggested that, since we had daughters, he would be glad to negotiate marriage with their Maasai sons! It was their way of welcoming us to the community.

One afternoon we all went to the home of George Obute, a Luo and a committee member, for a meal. He had two wives. One wife, Yunia, was a high school graduate and worked in the dispensary. George was a merchant and a farmer. He had a grade-ten education and spoke English. Their hut was neat and clean in comparison to the Maasai home we had visited, which smelled of urine and was inhabited with plenty of flies.

The Maasai custom was to keep the small animals like calves, goats, or sheep in their living room over night for protection, while the family slept in the crowded kitchen. In the morning, when the animals went out to pasture, the women cleaned the dung and tidied up the space for their living room. It did have a peculiar odor somehow attractive to flies.

Chief Wilson Ogwada had invited Leon's family and us to his house at Osingo for a feast that was meant to say farewell to Leon's and to say welcome to us. Sunday evening, Leon and Lou Ann set out, with us in the back of the pickup, on a three-hour journey over a very rough road, twenty-eight kilometers west to Migori and about six more to the northeast to reach the Ogwada estate.

4

There we were introduced to the finest hospitality befitting a Luo chief. Wilson had two wives, so the home had two houses and was occupied by eleven children, all of whom welcomed us with considerable curiosity, while showing proper respect.

Wilson shared his deep concern for the many widows and orphans in his community and his interest in building a church at Osingo. He also shared their involvement in a recently established polytechnic institution for training needy youth. He was obviously a chief who cared about his community.

On our way home in the dark, the truck engine started missing. We reached Migori and tried to find a mechanic. It being Sunday night, no mechanic was to be found.

Rather than risk being stranded with a vehicle breakdown and spending the night in the back of a pickup on the dark, empty road somewhere between Migori and Ogwedhi, we found a hotel where we spent the night. Vera had a bad asthma attack in the less than spotless hotel. She had left her medicines at home. It was hot, so we had the window open. Beside mosquitoes, a bat entered the room, provoking an added level of sleep-depriving excitement. Thus, she had a miserable night in the not too pleasant hotel. The next morning, the truck drove like a charm. Perhaps it just did not like to work on the Sabbath!

A New Mode of Transportation

OSP's only mode of transportation was this old, dark green, single-cab, four-wheel drive Toyota Hilux pickup. It was a strong, useful vehicle for those road conditions but very small for carrying passengers in comfort. Leon had made a pillow "seat" for his eldest son between the bucket seats in the front, and Lou Ann held the baby in her lap. All other passengers had to ride in the rear, where two side benches were installed that could carry up to ten people comfortably, or many more uncomfortably.

A metal frame with wire cage material on the inside and a removable canvas tarp gave protection from rain or sun but also obscured the vision of the passengers unless rolled up. The seats were padded, but the only back support was the wire cage material. Consequently, while bouncing along up and down and from side to side on those road conditions, riding in the back offered the passengers rather limited comfort. However, it was a preferred alternative to walking!

For the driver and his companion, this was not bad, but for our teenage daughters, remembering the nice comfortable cars and vans we used to drive in Alberta, my heart ached. In accepting this assignment and bringing them to this remote place, what had we done to them? That was a question that haunted me for the months and years to follow.

A New Home Lifestyle

In my first letter to my parents, written on August 15, 1985, I attempted to describe something of our new surroundings and the challenges to which we were committing ourselves.

> Here we are at our new home in Ogwedhi, Kenya. Today is our twenty-first wedding anniversary. We had a nice supper of pizza and cake. Now I'm sitting under a kerosene pressure lamp on our shabby couch. Vera just sat down beside me. The girls are in their bedroom getting ready. They are tired after a hot day.
>
> We just had a nice, refreshing evening thunder shower, and lightning is still flashing in the otherwise totally dark cloud-covered African night.
>
> On the more usual cloudless moonless nights, it is really nice to go outside and stand in complete darkness. No city lights or even neighbors' fires visible. Only the stars and are they ever clear. We think we will love it here!
>
> We found the weather almost perfect. I even questioned whether heaven could have it much better. The days were generally sunny and warm. Direct sunlight around noon could be uncomfortably hot but move into the shade and it felt just right. The air tended to be dry and humidity low. We never felt cold. Even at night we kept the screened windows open and never wore a sweater.

Our house is a simple structure. The outside looks rather drab and unfinished, the walls being made of cement blocks sealed with a thin slurry of cement and water that is left unpainted, kind of ugly!

But the inside is painted and quite cheery. A fiberboard ceiling forms an attic which allows some protection from the midday heat of the tin roof. Floors are of concrete. It has a living room, dining room, study, two bedrooms, and a tiny kitchen with inadequate cupboard space. We have a small kerosene fridge and a small propane stove.

The house is about six years old, has nice louvered windows with screens, a porch, and a tiny shower room outside the back door with one cold water showerhead, faucet, and a washstand. Our water supply comes from the roof and is stored above ground in a large round cement storage tank just beside the back door and shower room.

Yesterday Leon and Lou Ann Ressler and their children left, in the rental car, for Nairobi and America. So now we have the house all to ourselves ....

We enjoyed the close intimacy of sharing this new experience with our daughters those first three and one-half weeks in August. There was little to do in the evenings except to enjoy each other's company while reading, writing letters, or playing games. I suspect they were a little bored at times. On the other hand, I think they felt real release from the social pressures they had been living under back home.

One day they swept out the cobwebs and painted the inside of our toilet, a brick and cement outhouse, making it a lot more inviting and hospitable. Unfortunately, the paint didn't eliminate the sometimes-foul odors emanating from the five-meter-deep pit latrine beneath!"

In another letter a week later, I continued describing our new life together:

This is another nice quiet evening at home. There are some real advantages to living out here in the wilderness. There are no telephones to disturb, not even committee meetings to attend! As darkness creeps over the land, everyone goes to their home. There is no television either. Great for family togetherness. But the girls are getting batty at times because of having no place to go.

Here we sit in our usual places for this time of day in the living room when we light our one kerosene lamp and relax around it writing letters or reading. The gas light is quite good, only confined to one room at a time.

The windows are open. Screens keep out large insects. Besides emitting a steady hissing noise and a faint odor of burning kerosene, the gas light attracts hundreds of God's little creatures which squeeze through the screen. They fly, with suicidal intent, directly to its light only to get burnt by its heat and fall in a steady slow drizzle on our coffee table and our writing or reading material. Vera is quick to sweep them up first thing in the morning.

Outside on the window screens the geckos eat the big ones who can't get in through the screen to incinerate themselves in the irresistible all-attracting light.

Today Vera and Kristina were sewing some place mats. Sheryl was sewing name tags on her school clothes. Both girls are cheerful and happy most of the time. Kristina really likes it here. Sheryl misses her friends and heavy social involvements in the "real world." She finds African culture rather primitive and uninteresting. Kristina is interested in the Maasai morans (warriors). The morans are the age group of young men who serve as warriors for a number of years before marriage. They sometimes paint themselves, their hair and clothing with red ochre mud, and their half-naked bodies smeared with the same oily substance, rather sensual. Kristina thinks they are attractive!

RECONCILIATION IN TRANS MARA

A New Church

On that first Sunday, Leon's had introduced us to the little church they had started southeast at Osero near Enemasi. This consisted of about sixty to eighty Maasai women and children (mostly children) meeting under a tree. They sang a lot of Maasai songs, listened to a Bible teaching on tape, took an offering, had prayer, and served us rice, boiled potatoes, and tea. It was very interesting. However, we were disappointed that there were no Maasai men present.

That week, Ole Sikawa, a Maasai leader and the chairman of the management committee, requested us to start a church at his place. Leon and I responded with a visit. He showed us the "holy" tree he had selected for that use. Leon made him promise that if we started a church, he would take leadership to see that the men also attended. He agreed, so we decided to meet at that place the following Saturday at 8:30 a.m.

That Saturday, after Leon's had left, our dispensary assistant, Francis Ole Sire, a young Maasai who knew English, accompanied me to the site designated by Ole Sikawa to start the new church. Francis served as translator. Only three women and seven children came. Ole Sikawa came too but didn't stay for the message.

We were using cassette tapes with lessons in Maasai about Christ and the Christian faith and Christian Maasai songs. I felt rather helpless in meeting this challenge not knowing the language at all.

This was a new experience for me. Back at Salem Mennonite Church in Tofield, Alberta, I was a pastor for nine years. It was a mature congregation of firmly established believers who knew their Bibles from cover to cover and were articulate in expressing their theological convictions. With the added benefit and sophistication of a seminary degree, I was accustomed to preparing and delivering challenging sermons to encourage and stimulate the faithful, rather than simply to inform.

Here, things were quite different. Instead of an architecturally and esthetically well-designed sanctuary with comfortable padded pews, we sat in the partial shade of a "holy" tree and struggled to stay balanced on improvised tree-branch pews. Instead of a congregation of 250, my congregation consisted of three illiterate mothers and their likewise illiterate children. They had no biblical background at all. I could not refer to any biblical character or situation, not even Moses or Adam or Peter, without some simple explanation.

Instead of speaking in lofty, eloquent, measured phrases, expounding profound thoughts through a finely engineered sound system, I was speaking outside in the open air with occasional goats or sheep wandering nearby, or local dogs who insisted on accompanying the family members and occasionally attracting attention by scrapping with one another. I was speaking in the simplest English possible to a grade seven student who translated into the Maasai language. I often wondered what the congregants really heard of the message I intended.

I had to forget all I knew about rhetoric, homiletics, three-point sermons, clichés or idioms and get down to basics. I had to simply tell stories and answer questions, and most importantly, build relationships.

The next day, Sunday, we went again to the church under the tree at Osero. There were at least ninety women and children there this time. The women were enthusiastic and eager for more teaching. How I wished we could speak their language. What a joy it would be to pastor a church of eager learners! Besides the tiny babies at their mothers' breasts, no one in this church fell asleep during the service.

A life saver for me was the cassette tapes Leon left for us to use. These were a series of about forty tapes prepared in the Maasai language by missionaries of Christian Missionary Fellowship (CMF) who worked among Maasai in other parts of Kenya. Besides a tape or two of Christian songs sung in their language, the tapes were teachings on various topics designed to root and ground new believers in the Christian faith. Leon was using these tapes with a hand cranked cassette player to give a lesson in each Sunday service.

I arranged to have these tapes used while we were in language school. I felt this was the time to reach the Maasai. They were a people group one soon learned to respect and, in many ways, admire.

A New Career

One early morning, as I was exiting our gate on my way to Kisii to buy lumber, someone flagged me down. A man asked me to take a sick woman to a hospital on the way. She was pregnant and bleeding and seemed to be having a miscarriage, so I made space for her. The doctor gave her medicine and sent her back home with me. Thus, I was introduced to my undesignated career as the unofficial Ogwedhi ambulance service provider.

In line with our commitment as agricultural development workers, we had come prepared with a selection of vegetable seeds. We immediately planted a vegetable garden before we were to leave for language study.

A New School Experience

After being oriented to life at Ogwedhi for three and one-half weeks, it was time for our daughters to be enrolled in the Rift Valley Academy in Kijabe and for Vera and me to engage in learning Swahili.

Eastern Mennonite Missions had arranged for Vera and me to enroll at the CPK Language School for three months. The school was held in the compound of the Anglican Church of the Province of Kenya (CPK) in downtown Nairobi. We were to lodge at the Mennonite Guest House where we also would be provided with our meals. We would commute each day.

So, on Monday, September 1, 1985, we left Ogwedhi and brought our girls to their school in Kijabe. Kristina was accepted into eighth grade and Sheryl into eleventh grade.

We spent the rest of the week shopping, getting drivers' licenses, securing alien registrations, applying for dependents' passes, and getting acquainted with Nairobi. Perhaps most important of all, we spent time learning to drive safely in a congested city on the left-hand side of the road.

CHAPTER 2

Life in Language School

An Oasis in Nairobi: The Mennonite Guest House

"And what denomination/organization are you serving with?" This question inevitably came after preliminary introductions that happened dozens of times at the Fuller School of World Missions where over 500 seasoned missionaries and church leaders from eighty different countries of the world met for an extended time of study.

When I would reply, "Mennonite," almost inevitably the next statement would go something like, "Oh, really? I met some Mennonite volunteers working in Bangladesh ..." (or anyone of fifty-three other countries), or "Are you connected with the Mennonite Guest House in Nairobi?"

Located in the beautiful middle-class suburb of Westlands, The Mennonite Guest House was well known among international and domestic travelers of many denominations as a welcome oasis offering shelter, food, and fellowship at the end of a long and tiring journey.

Its reputation for excellence was second to none in East Africa. The food was good. The beds were clean. The buildings were adequate. The compound was secure. The yard was spacious and offered a nice place for children to play. The staff was friendly and efficient. Tasty meals were served on time, and the hospitality was warm and genuine. The whole atmosphere was peaceful, quiet, and soothing, and let me say in the best sense of the term, "Christian."

The sixteen rooms were almost always full. Travelers came from all over the world. Certain rooms were reserved for regional Mennonite workers at special low prices. There were other prices for those from other missions and churches, and higher, but still modest, prices for tourists and others who were fortunate enough to find an empty room.

Missionaries came from remote places like Wajir, Shirati, or Soroti, often tired, lonely, and sometimes sick. They found a refuge here, a place to detach, catch one's breath and rest awhile. It was a place for quiet, uninterrupted, spiritual reflection and renewal. It offered opportunities for fellowship with their own kind, or a home base from which to do their city business. How often they thanked God for the Mennonite Guest House.

Then there were the local church workers needing a place to stay while in the city. Occasionally, former missionaries returned for a visit, sometimes bringing their grown children to remind them of bygone days. Sometimes the parents or family members came to visit their loved ones in service.

Others came too: the tourists, the adventurers, the "See-Africa-on-thirty-dollars-a-day" types. Some of them were young and inexperienced; some were naive and gullible; and some were experienced and knowledgeable. Almost all of them were exuberantly excited to share what they learned or experienced and were often curious to learn more.

Meals were served family style. The great and the not-so-great, the novices and the old-timers, mixed together and shared their stories and learned from one another. Acquaintances were made and friendships deepened. Ideas were shared, and inspiration stimulated. These were the moments of nourishment: physically, mentally, socially, and spiritually.

The beautiful flower bedecked and well-manicured yard, the clean rooms, and the excellent meals did not just happen by themselves. A loyal and dedicated staff of ten men worked quietly and harmoniously, each doing his part without waiting for orders, giving the impression that these services just happen. Some of these men had been working since the Guest House opened back in 1965. Their commitment had made their service outstanding.

Paul and Erma Lehman, host and hostess
of the Mennonite Guest House

At the very heart of the success of this Mennonite oasis was the skillful management and gracious hospitality provided by Paul and Erma Lehman. For most of two decades, this older couple gave themselves wholeheartedly to add a touch of excellence to the work they were called to East Africa to do.

Paul and Erma originally came from Virginia to Ethiopia where they served for nine years as house parents for boys boarding at the Good Shepherd School for missionary children. Now in Kenya, it was gratifying for them to meet many of those "boys," now also missionaries or world travelers and forever a part of the Lehman's extended family.

As host and hostess, Paul and Erma made a conscious effort to know and remember the names of their guests and something about where they lived and what they did. This gesture of concern and care enriched their lives immeasurably. It won them many friendships, much respect, and deep gratitude from the thousands of guests who passed through their doors. It certainly helped to make the name of the Mennonite Guest House one that evoked appreciation wherever it was mentioned around the world.

Now, we counted it a distinct privilege to be welcomed into this oasis of hospitality and to make it our home for the three months we attended the language school.

We enjoyed the spacious green lawn with generous patches of shade provided by the huge jacaranda trees which, when in full bloom, dropped their petals forming lavender circles on the green carpet below. The gardeners tended a great variety of flowering shrubs and flower beds, adding their respective hues to this amazing environment.

On a typical Sunday afternoon, we would sit out in the yard enjoying the warmth of the sun and the coolness of sporadic shade cast by passing clouds. Surrounded by the singing of birds, the humming of bees and the chatter of children playing, it was an ideal environment in which to write letters or read a book.

Social life at the guest house was most interesting, very different from what we would experience in Ogwedhi. It was a pleasure to interact with the many guests. Each one had a unique story to tell, from which, if one took the time to listen, a person could learn something more about the broader picture of human nature and its interaction with the worldwide Christian movement.

An Ethiopian Connection

We met several guests from Ethiopia. It was good to catch up on the news from there, but most of it was depressing—civil war, famine, Marxist oppression, persecution, and economic collapse.

At that time, Nairobi was a favorite destination for Ethiopian refugees who were fleeing from the oppressive Dergue regime. They tended to gravitate to the Eastleigh slums where the rent was cheaper. These thousands of refugees created their own community in exile with a variety of churches, several Ethiopian restaurants, as well as other businesses. Desperate to eke out a living, some opened their tiny, rented homes to serve the public their tasty Ethiopian food. The environment was exceedingly humble, but their food was tops. Many a delicious meal was enjoyed by adventurous expatriates who valued it as a privileged treat.

Since Paul and Erma Lehman had spent many years in Ethiopia, they interacted with this diaspora community and occasionally served their guests with Ethiopian cuisine. One night, after serving Ethiopian food, they sent a love package of the surplus to Sheryl and Kristina at RVA with someone who was going there. All our children loved Ethiopian food.

One of the Ethiopian diaspora churches worshipped in the upper reading room of the Mennonite-owned Eastleigh Fellowship Center in the Eastleigh suburb. Their loud enthusiastic worship almost drowned out the competing English/Swahili service held at the same Sunday morning hour in the adjacent chapel.

I found it interesting, maybe a bit nostalgic, to visit the Ethiopian church from time to time. I liked their enthusiasm, and, although I never understood it all, it was good to hear Amharic again. I didn't know many of the Ethiopians there, but I must admit I liked them as a race and as a culture.

A few years later, one of my former students of the Bible Academy days, Paulos Gulilat and his wife, Tigist, came to Nairobi with their four sons and served there as a pastor of that church.

Language Learning

Language learning at any age can be tedious and boring, and at our age, it was not easy. Living in Nairobi, and particularly at the Guest House, was not a conducive environment to learn Swahili. We found it very difficult to get the practice time after school hours. The guests conversed in English. The Kenyan staff either talked in English or in Kikuyu or Luhya. When we tried out our garbled Swahili, they would smile and answer in English.

16

I will admit, when we came home each day from classes, we were a bit tired, undermotivated, and a bit lazy. We found other things to occupy our after-work hours. The guest house had a tennis court, so Vera and I began to learn to play. It was good exercise. In the evenings, Vera took to reading books, lots of books. She had no cooking or house cleaning to occupy her time. Life at the guest house was like being in paradise. However, we would definitely not recommend lodging at the guest house if seriously trying to learn Swahili in Nairobi.

On Sundays we usually attended either the Swahili/English service at the Eastleigh Fellowship Center or the English service at the Nairobi Baptist Church on Ngong Road. Since the service was conducted in English, we went there when our girls were with us. The western-style program was well organized, and the preaching was good. They had three services every Sunday morning with 300-400 attending each time. This church was very popular with middle-class Kenyans as well as the large international community.

After six weeks, students at RVA were allowed to go off campus for a mid-term break, either to be with their parents or with other parent-approved arrangements. Sheryl and Kristina came to spend their first weekend break with us at the Guest House.

They were adjusting to the new reality, but it was a lot harder than they expected. They missed their friends back home. They were making new friends and getting along okay, but they still didn't like the school. But then, there are not many high school-aged kids who will admit to liking school anywhere.

We took them on a four-hour guided bus tour in the Nairobi National Park just outside of the city. We saw a lot of animals including zebras, giraffes, wildebeests, gazelles, antelopes, ostriches, two buffalos, a rhinoceros, a lion, and a hippopotamus.

We had supper with the John and Helen Miller family at an Ethiopian restaurant that Friday night and then saw a remarkable rendition of the musical "Jesus Christ Superstar" put on by the Kenyan Boys School. We had known John and Helen as fellow students during our Eastern Mennonite College days. Now they were serving with our mission as teachers at the Rosslyn Academy, a day school for missionary children. John was a music and drama teacher.

Every two weeks we had "Menno Meetings." All foreigners connected with Mennonites were welcomed to get together on a Sunday evening for a supper and then an hour of singing with Mary Oyer in charge.

The famous ethnomusicologist and music professor from Goshen College in Indiana was working in Kenya in the music conservatory for a two-year assignment. She was also working on a new hymnal for the American Mennonites and the Church of the Brethren, which was to be released in 1992. We enjoyed her song leading, her enthusiasm for music, and her knowledge about the various hymns.

One early morning I indulged in a phone call to our daughters, Cindy and Karen, in the USA. The half hour cost us nearly $3.00 per minute! On a missionary support allowance, that could have been considered an extravagance. I considered that they were worth the outlay, and besides, it was my birthday. They left the impression that they were adjusting to college life quite well.

However, it was only many years later that we learned that that impression of well-being was a cover-up. Was it pride, or a healthy sign of maturity, a spirit of self-reliance? They would not complain or let their parents know anything of how much they suffered, especially Karen as a freshman. Left as orphans, without resources or home or parents to coach them in their adjustments and meet their financial and emotional needs, they would never burden their parents by divulging their personal sufferings.

On Thanksgiving weekend, we received a pleasant surprise, a telephone call while we were at breakfast. It was Cindy and her boyfriend, John Kreider calling from John's home near Lancaster, Pennsylvania. She seemed very happy about John. He was taking the same academic program as she and shared the same classes. He had the same goal as she, to be a missionary in some underdeveloped country. They would both be graduating in April. He was twenty-three years old, the son of a Lancaster County Mennonite farmer—an "authentic" Mennonite pedigree.

On the last day of November, we went to RVA and brought Sheryl and Kristina and their things to the Guest House to be with us during the last week of our language school.

Following that, they accompanied us to the MCC and Mennonite Mission workers annual retreat held at the Brackenhurst Conference Center (Baptist) near Limuru about twenty miles north of Nairobi.

This retreat center is situated in a beautiful spot in the highlands surrounded by luxuriant green tea plantations and dairy farms.

We enjoyed ten days of relaxing, fellowship, and inspiration with about 120 expatriate colleagues including children from surrounding East African countries such as Ethiopia, Tanzania, Somalia, Djibouti, and Sudan. There was much to learn from their diverse experiences.

Our Swahili lessons were over, but we were still not fluent in the language. We understood the grammar quite well and knew a lot of words, but it was hard to hear it and understand when people talked fast, and harder yet to answer in an intelligent manner. I hoped that it would come with practice, but for us, it did not. We reminded ourselves that we did not learn English in three months either.

CHAPTER 3

Settling in at Ogwedhi

We could hardly wait to get home to Ogwedhi. Our daughters, released from their exile in "prison," were overly eager to enjoy some home life and anticipated celebrating Christmas as a family, as truncated as it was. Vera and I were eager to get to work for a change. While studying the language, I made many plans for all the things I wanted to accomplish.

We found everything at OSP in good shape. The little rains had been excellent, and the crops looked good. The field corn was about ten to twelve feet tall and had nice full ears. Field beans (kidney) were being harvested. Workers were making bricks. Other workers were installing barb wire fences around the school and church yards.

For some reason though, the garden we planted in August didn't do so well. Our favorite sweet corn seed we brought from the USA did not flourish in equatorial Africa. Potatoes were poor but ready to eat. Carrots never appeared at all. There were a few cabbage heads, but they were over-ripe and split. Cucumbers, melons, and cantaloupe were all over-ripe and rotten. Pumpkins didn't grow. Peanuts looked excellent. Tomatoes were ripening. Pineapples were growing. Peas were eaten by insects. The beans were ready but turned out to be the stringy kind, which we found uninteresting.

I found farming was different where two crops can be grown per year. You just finish harvesting, take a deep breath, and start plowing and seeding again. There was no time for rest.

An abundant fall crop had left a surplus of corn in Kenya. When the crops in the region are good, prices go way down, and if the crops are poor, the prices go up. Either there is a famine, and the price is high, and the farmers have nothing to sell, or there is a good crop, and the farmers have lots to sell, but the price is unbearably low.

Of course, as every farmer knows, that is nothing new. It seems the farmer is predestined to be poor.

We were shocked at how dirty our house was after three and one-half months of being empty. Spider webs, roaches, bugs, and salamanders messed it up, and layers of dust covered everything. Vera immediately went to work with broom, dustpan, and mop and about wore herself out by the time she could judge the whole domicile fit for human habitation.

To assist her, we hired Pilista, a Luo widow about our age. She was very poor, having been expelled from her home by her brothers-in-law after her husband died. She had worked for the Resslers before us. So, we sort of inherited her with the house and job. She was a good woman!

We brought a few Kenya-style improved beehives from Nairobi. They were not as complicated as our beehives in Canada but were recommended by the Canadian Aid (CIDA) experts for Kenyan farmers.

We bought a new treadle sewing machine from Nairobi. When I put it together, I found the belt was missing and four screws were too big. So, I had to wait, hoping to find them the next chance I would have to go to the city. The machine was a "Janome" made in Taiwan. It had a zig zag stitching feature which Vera liked.

That chance to go to the city came soon enough. As soon as the family was settled, Barack, the OSP Manager, insisted we drive to Kisumu to attend a five-day seminar organized by World Vision for project managers and treasurers. That trip provided an opportunity to stock up on medications and supplies for the clinic. Also, I was pleasantly surprised to find the much-needed parts for Vera's Janome without having to send an order to Taiwan.

A Family Christmas

Sheryl and Kristina were happy to be home with us for the month. They both did okay in their first term in school. Because Sheryl had done well in her Canadian grade nine, she was allowed to skip grade ten and was doing well in grade eleven. Kristina and Sheryl spent some days baking and decorating Christmas cookies. Kristina was

21

quite cheerful and seemed to like living in Ogwedhi. They found it interesting that the dog gave birth to a lone baby pup while we were away.

To celebrate Christmas, a small tree was cut, and Sheryl did the decorations while Kristina spent many of her days in the kitchen developing the fine art of baking Christmas specialties. Before coming home, she had asked Vera, "I want you to teach me to cook." So, we gave her the kitchen and she went to work. We bought a cookbook as one of her gifts.

On Christmas Eve, Vera and I attended the church service on the compound. The girls, not understanding the language and not knowing the people, preferred to stay home to make the final preparations for our Christmas celebration. When we returned from the service about nine p.m., we found snack things spread out on the table, candles lit, and Christmas music playing. Beautiful!

Just as we were opening the last of the presents, a knock on the door stopped us. It was around ten p.m. There was an accident, a Land Rover overturned full of people and at least four were seriously hurt. Would I take them to the hospital in Migori?

This brought back memories of the Bedeno years. One cannot say, "No," so off I went and returned at 2:00 a.m. No one was killed, and the wounded were all in the hospital. I could sleep well.

Suddenly, it was Christmas morning. There was to be another service in the church, and I was to preach at eight o'clock. But the owner of the wrecked vehicle was knocking on my door. He had just heard about the accident (he wasn't in it) and came to ask me about the passengers and wanted me to drive him to see the vehicle. So, I took him.

Then he wanted me to take him to Migori to see the patients and bring a police inspector to the accident scene to take care of the legal work. Well, I told him I had to preach in church first. So, by 10:00 a.m., I was done, and we left for Migori, saw the patients, brought the police, towed the vehicle to town, took the police back to Migori, and got home at 5:40 p.m. Such was our Christmas day. We had our Christmas dinner on the 26th. In time, all the patients were released from the hospital and the vehicle was repaired.

Too soon it was December 30th 1985, and time for the girls to return to school. After a morning of shopping in Nairobi, we took them back to RVA in the afternoon. We spent a few more days doing business and returned home on the third of January.

Again, we were alone. With all the children gone from the nest, their absence filled our home with a deathly silence, a silence of loneliness and longing that cried out for what had been and what would be no more—the empty nest syndrome.

Marriage Prospects

While in Nairobi, where we had access to a phone, we had talked to Karen and Cindy on New Years' Eve. Although they were not ready to make a public announcement yet, they shared their secret that Cindy and John Kreider were making tentative plans for marriage, likely in the fall or late summer.

Although we had not seen this "knight in shining armor" yet, we heard from other sources that he was a very nice fellow. He had taken training as a mechanic in high school. He was preparing to graduate with Cindy from the same agriculture program. He had been in Paraguay for a few months of mission exposure and was interested in missionary service in the third world. He was a deeply committed Christian and was a member of the Masonville Mennonite Church. He was planning to start a two-year master's program in Economic Development near Philadelphia at Eastern Baptist College the following year. He was six feet and one inch tall and not bad looking according to Cindy's unbiased opinion.

Guests Are a Blessing

Agroforestry, afforestation, and reforestation are all important components of a balanced approach to economic and environmental development. To advance those enterprises in our community, we started a small tree nursery beside our house. Then, we invited a young MCC volunteer couple, Tim and Elaine Gammel, whom we had learned to know in language school, to visit our project and give advice on how we can use trees more effectively to transform

23

the community. They were in Kenya on a forestry assignment. With them, we visited some government tree nurseries in the vicinity.

The Gammels brought along some friends including Pearl Gamber, who had taught school in Bedeno, Ethiopia, long before we lived there. She and her husband, Henry, had been with the Peace Corp teaching in Yemen for the last eight years. She was retiring and going to the USA. Henry had stayed on teaching one more term before he would go home too. Our guests stayed for two days.

In February 1986, Edgar Good, a member of my Salem congregation in Tofield, Alberta, came to Kenya with a "learning tour," a group of MCC supporters who were visiting projects in Africa. After their tour, he stayed on to visit us for a few days. Before he went home, we took him on a one-day safari to the Maasai Mara National Reserve, the famous game preserve just fifty kilometers southeast of Ogwedhi. Seeing all the African animals in their natural habitat was a highlight for Edgar.

Then in March, I drove to Migori to collect Nathan and Arlene Hege, old friends from our Ethiopia days. They were on a four-month tour of some African countries where EMM had workers. Nathan, trained as a journalist and experienced as a missionary and a bishop, was writing reports on his findings for the mission. They had just arrived from completing a month-long visit among the churches in Tanzania,

They stayed with us for a few days until we took them to Kisumu to visit the church leaders in that sub-diocese. We stayed together in a hotel that night, then parted ways. Nathan and Arlene stayed to visit that day, then took a train east to Nairobi. We headed south to Ogwedhi.

Mission as Business

In response to the Maasai cattlemen's need for veterinary supplies such as antibiotics and cattle dip, acaricide, to treat their cattle for parasites and tick-borne diseases, Leon had been shopping for them while in the city, bringing the needed items home and being paid by the users.

This need developed into an income-generating retail trade in agricultural inputs and veterinary supplies. Using balances in the project's bank accounts, we were able to expand the inventory to include such items as cattle salt by the truckload, and later barb wire and cement by the truckload, iron roofing sheets, and nails. This trade helped the small farmers and the cattlemen, as well, and earned OSP a nice income. It also became a major burden replenishing the inventory. Finding and purchasing and transporting the materials took a lot of our time and energy whenever we travelled to Nairobi or Kisumu.

Vera Finds a Niche

When EMM commissioned us to serve in Kenya, they gave me a job assignment, but, as they often did with the female spouse, they didn't specify any particular job or role that Vera would be expected to play.

It didn't take long after our arrival at Ogwedhi that the headmaster of the Ogwedhi Primary School invited Vera to teach. She was not a trained teacher, so she hesitated. She tried teaching English, but the students complained; they did not understand her American accent. Kenyan use of English was learned from their former British colonial masters.

In mid-January, Vera started teaching the grades seven and eight home-science class. The home-science classroom did not have a roof on because they ran out of money. We sold some cows and an oxcart to get money to put a roof on and to finish the room.

Home science was a basic introductory course that was required for all students which included mother-child care, health, cooking, and home care. In the home-science classes, Vera included sewing. With donated funds we purchased four treadle sewing machines, and Vera tried to teach the students to sew. With about thirty-five to forty students in a class and four machines, this was rather difficult.

Lessons were taught in English, but the students' level of English was not so good and with Vera's American accent, they found it hard to understand. Often the testing was more on how well they understood English than on whether they knew the subject material.

Vera found it difficult to teach when the students didn't have their own textbooks. She had to write notes on the blackboard, and they copied them in their scribblers. The school was very basic. Besides lacking textbooks, the little tots in grade one had few desks. Most of them sat on rocks on the ground. One class met outside under a tree.

In February, Vera offered sewing classes for community women. Imagine her consternation as well as joy when thirty-six women signed up! She had only four sewing machines. So, she broke these up into six groups and taught two groups on Wednesdays and Fridays. After teaching these for two months, she offered the next two groups to come to learn sewing.

She found it difficult to teach sewing without patterns, which were not readily available. The local tailors found a picture from a catalogue and cut and sewed copies visually without a pattern. Vera did not know how to do that, so it was a challenge for her to teach these women.

She also helped the school acquire some used books to start a small library where students could spend one forty-minute period a week reading books or looking through magazines. She was usually in charge of the library period for the two classes.

Vera taught in the school for five years. During that time, she also tried to teach some women child health care classes, but through lack of interest, that attempt faded out. Like her attempt to launch an adult literacy program, the adults wanted to learn but found it difficult to maintain the commitment required to attend regularly. The life of a rural African mother and homemaker was demanding.

CHAPTER 4

The Kenya Mennonite Church Connection

Historically, the Kenya Mennonite Church had its origins as an extension of the Tanzania Mennonite Church. After national independence in 1961, members of the Tanzania Mennonite Church, mostly of the Luo and Suba ethnic groups, migrated north into Kenya for various reasons, mostly economic in nature. There, they formed communities of like-minded people. In some of these communities located along the shores of Lake Victoria, they formed congregations.

At the time we arrived, there were about fifty congregations with around 2,500 members in Kenya. They were still under the leadership of Bishop Zedekiah Kisare of Shirati, Tanzania. Zedekiah Kisare was the first African to be ordained as bishop by Mennonite missionaries in East Africa in the 1960's.

At this time his diocese included all the congregations in the North Mara Diocese in Tanzania and the congregations in Kenya. In 1986, the Mennonites in Kenya were divided into two sub-dioceses, the Kisumu Sub-diocese which included three pastors, Musa Adongo, Naaman Agola, and Eliphaz Odundo and their congregations, and the Southern Kenya Sub-diocese which included Pastor Joshua Okello Ouma and his congregation in Nairobi as well as Pastor Nashon Adera Arwa in Migori and his twenty-six congregations spread out from Ogwedhi to Muhuru Bay on Lake Victoria.

As the churches in Kenya matured, and as the bishop in Tanzania aged, the three pastors in the north demanded the formation of a separate diocese for the Mennonite churches in Kenya. Bishop Kisare delayed action for certain reasons, unclear to those who wanted to proceed. The two other pastors supported Kisare with his "wait" strategy. It seemed to me that there was a feeling of competition.

Which of the five pastors should be chosen to be the first bishop in the soon-to-be-formed Kenya Mennonite Church?

That became a church problem when the leaders of the Kisumu Sub-diocese basically rejected Bishop Kisare's leadership. The leaders of the Southern Kenya Sub-diocese saw that as a kind of rebellion and supported Bishop Kisare.

This state of division among the Kenya Mennonites presented a quandary to EMM which was financially subsidizing some programs and was supporting missionaries like us to work with the church in Kenya. Were they to support the "rebellion" by recognizing the de-facto two dioceses in Kenya? What about their historic ties to the church in Tanzania and its leadership? They looked for a peaceful resolution and transition to form a united Mennonite Church in Kenya.

Our appointment with EMM came at an awkward time. Were we being sent to serve at the invitation of the whole Kenya Mennonite Church or to serve the Southern Kenya Sub-diocese, thus recognizing the schism? For us, we wondered, "Were we invited? Or were we being imposed?"

Without this issue being settled, we just came out to Ogwedhi to get oriented to the Ogwedhi Sigawa Project on our own. Mission board leaders, Harold Reed and Hershey Leaman of Salunga, Pennsylvania, were coming in mid-September to talk with the church leaders. We assumed they would get the issues settled while we were studying Swahili, and that we would be returning to carry on the work at Ogwedhi in December.

At Ogwedhi, we found the Luo church in a sad state of neglect. Nashon Adera Arwa, the pastor of the Migori District, had twenty-six congregations under his care. He, being of limited ability, tended to appoint people less competent than himself to leadership in the congregations. The evangelist, Paul Otieno, appointed to be in charge at Ogwedhi seemed uninterested and had moved back to Muhuru Bay with his family and was fishing to support them. The congregation as well as the Maasai outreach existed like sheep without a shepherd. Some were finding homes in other denominations such as Pentecostal, Catholic, Salvation Army, Seventh Day Adventist, and Anglican churches in the area. Others were abandoning their faith.

Harold Reed and Hershey Leaman from EMM came all the way from the USA in mid-September to try to resolve the church division.

However, the "rebel" leaders in the Kisumu Sub-diocese found it "inconvenient to come to the meeting at this time," so they returned to Pennsylvania disappointed—precious time and expensive air fare wasted.

Based upon their report, EMM decided to cut off funding for the Kenya Mennonite Church. Maybe after a few months they would be more willing to talk? Where all this would leave us, we were not sure, but we were not worried either, as, perhaps "walking by faith," or perhaps simply naive, we believed something would be worked out!

Upon our return to Ogwedhi following language learning, I spent a couple hours in Migori talking with Pastor Nashon and the now ex-chief Wilson Ogwada about plans for the future.

In the conversation, Pastor Nashon considered that the church problem was solved because the bishop dissolved the Kenya Mennonite Central Committee. He perhaps naively assumed that, since the members of the congregations respected the bishop, the other three "rebel" leaders would be on their own without a following. He reported that he and the bishop planned to ordain three more pastors. They envisioned starting a Bible institute at Ogwedhi in conjunction with OSP as a training center for complete ministry in spiritual as well as physical betterment. Perhaps it was a bit ambitious considering the realities on the ground at that time.

I didn't say anything, but I was skeptical. Maybe it was because of the added workload it implied for me? I was concerned about the apparent ease with which he dismissed the loss of the Kisumu Sub-diocese. I thought of a saying my teacher had repeated, "It is easier to be a big fish in a small pond where there are a few fish than to be a big fish in a big pond where there are many fish!" This man seemed perfectly happy to move on alone with a few less-competent subordinates. I found myself uneager to be one of those subordinates. I didn't say anything, but I wondered what EMM's position would be on this when Harold Reed would make his next visit the following month?

The Kenya Mennonite Church seemed to be permanently divided. The Migori District was planning to make itself into a separate conference. They wanted to set up a separate office and administration. I felt sad about it. When splitting becomes the accepted way to solve personality conflicts, there will be more divisions in the future!

The second week in March 1987 we were ordered to take the pastors to Shirati, Tanzania to visit Bishop Kisare. They held a one-day meeting to decide where to place the three newly ordained pastors.

Among their appointments, they gave the pastoral oversight of the Ogwedhi Sigawa District to the newly ordained Pastor Paul Otieno. They told me, that since I was also a pastor, I should train Paul. My job, being a foreigner, was "to raise funds for church projects."

I felt devalued and humiliated by this job description but didn't say anything. They did not consult me either, to see how I felt about it. Why did they call me, a person experienced in ministry, teaching, and leadership and trained in Biblical theology and missions to be their missionary? Why didn't they call a banker or financial administrator "to raise funds for projects"?

To train Paul in the fine art of being a pastoral leader was another challenge. The first time I noticed Paul taking an action in his congregation that I saw as possibly counterproductive; I called him aside in private and suggested an alternative. His reply was simply, "You foreigners have your ways, and we Africans have our ways!" That was the end of his training experience.

L to R, Paul Otieno, pastor, & Barack Ogola, OSP manager

A Cinema at Osingo

Vera and I were invited to visit the home of Wilson Ogwada on the following Saturday evening. We were to show some film strips, stay overnight, and preach in their church the following morning.

Wilson and his large family welcomed us warmly. They showed us their church building under construction on their land. Their preacher was a Luo woman who used to preach in the Anglican Church but then joined the Mennonites.

First, we were served a scrumptious dinner which wasn't ready until around 9:00 pm. The time was close to 10:00 p.m. before all the adults and children crowded inside the house to see the cinema. It was good entertainment for them. The show went on until 11:30 p.m.

Vera and I were ushered to a small empty house where we both slept on one single bed, really cozy. The next morning, I preached in the church that was mostly made up of the Ogwada relatives. After another fabulous Luo meal, we returned home.

A Visit to Muhuru Bay

Still being a newcomer in Kenya and quite unfamiliar with how the Kenya Mennonite Church culture functioned, it was of considerable interest to Vera and me to be invited to the home of our recently ordained pastor, Paul Otieno. It was in April 1987, and the occasion was the installation of Enos Mang'ira as the new pastor there.

Paul and Siprosa and their family lived in Muhuru Bay, a small fishing village on the southwestern most point of land jutting out into Lake Victoria. It was near the border of Tanzania and about twelve kilometers north of Shirati, across the bay.

We drove 130 kilometers west from home on a Friday afternoon. We brought our tent and mattresses along. When we arrived, we put up our tent, ate a late supper, and had some devotional time at Pastor Paul's house, then went to bed.

The next morning, Saturday, there was a church service which started at 11:00 a.m. and went on until 2:00 p.m. The pastor who was to be installed was sick, so we had baptisms, baby dedications, and communion without him. After the three-hour service, the women prepared lunch which was served around 4:00 p.m. This was deep in Luo country and the language of the day was Luo.

Then we drove about twenty kilometers back east to Bande, another church where we again pitched our tent behind the leader's house. We were served a tasty dinner there around 9:00 p.m., after which there was another devotional time. It was almost midnight by the time we went to bed.

According to their schedule, the Sunday morning service was to start at 9:00 a.m., but it really only got started at 11:30. It was 3:10 p.m. before we got back from church to the host's house. Then there was a wait for lunch to be prepared and shared. We arrived home at Ogwedhi around 8:30 that evening.

All in all, although we did not know a word of the Luo language, we learned a lot about their culture and their devotion to their church. Their hospitality to us as strangers and to their other guests was outstanding. Their food was delicious and unforgettable. We enjoyed this experience immensely. To us westerners, it became obvious that punctuality and respect for time had a different meaning in the local culture.

CHAPTER 5

Family Time

As much as possible, our work schedule at Ogwedhi was shaped around the demands of our daughters' school calendar. The academic year was divided into trimesters of three months each, separated by one month vacation between each trimester. Every six weeks, the students were expected to leave campus for a long weekend or mid-term break. This meant that in a given year, there would be twelve times students would either come to or leave from the school. For most parents, that meant twelve trips to RVA to either pick up or to deliver a child. Some of the older children were trusted to find their own way to or from school by bus, taxi, or carpooling with friends.

For us, this meant we, as parents, were to be on hand at the beginning of the break to receive our children from school and to return them at the end. We usually had them come home for the months off. For the mid-term weekends, since it was far and the time short, we usually tried to find something that we could do together with our children in or near Nairobi.

A Weekend in Mombasa

When it was time for the February 1986 mid-term break, Vera and I drove to Nairobi a few days earlier so we could complete the purchases for ourselves and for OSP by Thursday noon. Then, we hurried back to Kijabi, picked up the girls at RVA, and took them to the train station in Nairobi. There, we boarded the night train leaving for Mombasa at 5:00 p.m.

For a family, the night train was a fun way to travel. The second class provided closed compartments that could sleep four, just right for us. This being the first time to travel this way, our girls were excited. After a good sleep, we woke up facing a bright rising sun as the train was entering the sprawling town of Mombasa.

After disembarking at the busy station, we took a taxi to the Shelly Beach Hotel where we had rooms reserved. The hotel sits on the shore of the beautiful turquoise Indian Ocean. We liked the hotel, the warm water, and the cool ocean breeze. But the white sandy beach, for which Mombasa is famous, was missing. The shore was just plain sharp coral—no sand. This was our first time, so there were things to learn. On later visits, we chose hotels that had those magnificent spreads of white sandy beaches.

Being at sea level and near the equator, Mombasa was known to be quite warm. However, a brisk ocean breeze and the shade of occasional coconut palm trees made our stay at the hotel quite pleasant.

This precious time together gave us the opportunity to catch up with what was going on in our children's lives. Sheryl was maturing, thinking about going to college, something she would never have admitted to a year earlier. She decided to make the most of her time, and her grades were showing it.

She was keeping in touch with her boyfriend, Len Ricci in California. They were making plans for him to visit her in April, something we had misgivings about. She also was having doubts as to whether she wanted to be tied down to a guy yet. A part of her wanted to be free to look over the field. We were committing it to God to work out everything.

Kristina informed us she had just broken up with a boy and was feeling relieved. So were we. That was her second romance in six months at RVA—not bad for a thirteen-year-old. They would learn from such experiences, we hoped.

We took the Sunday night train back to Nairobi, completed our business on Monday, and returned the girls to their school that evening. RVA had a guest house to accommodate parents such as us, so we spent the night there before driving home the next day.

Special Guest from California

Six weeks later, we again made our way eastward, stopping in at RVA to eat supper with our girls before going on to Nairobi to take care of our business. The girls were to get out of school on Saturday morning, March the 29th, for their April vacation.

Len Ricci came from Pasadena, California, to spend a four-week vacation in Kenya with Sheryl. On March 28, we met him at the Jomo Kenyatta International Airport in Nairobi and took him to RVA to see Sheryl and her school. The next morning, we returned to pick up our girls and celebrated Easter with them in Nairobi. We brought Kristina home with us while Sheryl and Len went with a group on a four-day hike to climb Mt. Kenya.

Kristina had become a good baker and cook. She was getting a bit bored sitting around with us old folk but seemed glad to be home. Since there was no place to go in the evenings, we sat in our kerosene-lit living room and wrote letters, read books, or put together a 1000-piece jigsaw puzzle.

Sheryl and Len returned from their Mt. Kenya climbing adventure, along with Leona, a friend of Sheryl's from RVA. They came to Migori by bus where we met them. They stayed with us for a week.

We all took a two-day trip to the Maasai Mara game preserve about fifty kilometers, southeast of Ogwedhi. We took lunch, a tent, and blankets and camped in the park overnight. Hyenas and zebras prowled around our tent throughout the night. The next morning baboons tried to steal our breakfast. They were real pests. One even feigned to attack Len. He was so surprised; he instinctively backed away, stumbling over a lump of uneven ground. We all laughed as he fell, defenseless on his back, in front of the advancing menacing baboon.

This being his first African safari, Len brought along a video camera. He had ideas about how to make a sensational video to show his friends back home. Out in the tall savannah grass, we came upon a family of elephants. Len asked us to stop for a photo opportunity.

He gave his video camera to Sheryl while he climbed down off the back of the pickup, pulled out his eight-inch hunting knife, and approached the big male elephant while Sheryl was filming. The bull elephant faced Len as he was holding his miniscule blade and facing the elephant. Then the elephant flopped his huge ears and began approaching.

Len had not calculated this action in his script. What should he do now? At that moment, wisdom finally prevailed over Len's macho instinct. The "brave hunter" lost his cool, turned, and ran towards the truck.

At the same time, the elephant lost interest and turned his tail towards Len. Both the "brave hunter" and the "victim" elephant turned their tails toward each other in the tall savannah grass! I caught that scene on my 35 mm camera. Unfortunately, Sheryl, out of concern for the safety of her man, lost her cool, and forgot to focus the video camera on the dramatic scene. The opportunity was lost forever. We all had a good laugh at Len.

Later we learned that it was illegal for any person to get out of his/her vehicle within the park boundaries. It could have been a sudden and perhaps final disaster for the novice tourist, and for the rest of us, had the bull elephant decided to charge. Lucky for Len and us, the elephant failed to see that a small California tourist with an eight-inch knife could pose a serious threat to the security of his family!

We liked Len. He was twenty-three years old, short, and very handsome. He was Italian from eastern Pennsylvania. His father was a nominal Catholic, and his mother was a serious follower of the Worldwide Church of God (Armstrong's group). They had recently divorced.

With that background, Len was kind of turned off on religion, cynical, and afraid of being misled into another cult. Yet, he had a lot of the values of a religious upbringing. He was old enough to be serious about finding a mate. Sheryl was still a growing kid with a year of high school ahead and plans to go to college. She warned him that she was not in a hurry to commit herself, that he must give her time. She was only sixteen when they met a year earlier. She had already changed a lot since that time. She would change a lot more in the next few years.

After a week, we took them with Kristina to the bus in Migori and sent them to Nairobi. They all went on to Mombasa for five more days before Len left. Sheryl and Kristina remained in Nairobi until school started at the beginning of May.

Adjustment

It is amazing what a difference one year can make in the development of a teenager. The year began with the expected trauma of culture shock, of being uprooted, of dealing with a gnawing homesickness and loneliness for familiar places and old friends. The girls had to go through the pain of adjusting to strange, and sometimes disgusting, experiences and situations. They both matured a lot. Sheryl wrote the following poem expressing her tumultuous feelings as she transitioned. It was published in the January 1987 issue of the *Missionary Messenger.*

Ask an M.K.

By Sheryl J. Hansen

Oh, how I fought it! How I struggled!
And still there lingers a bit of rebellion in me,
a refusal to accept my situation.

How ironic, on the latest Kenya newsreel,
A scene of women and men raking garbage,
part of a sanitation program.
They step in it without shoes.
People walking, wandering along the road, wearing away the path.
The poverty, the hopelessness, the aimlessness;
    no plan in life.
A man lives in the middle of a round-about,
    burns garbage by day, sleeps in it by night.
Aw, yes, "Plenty be found within our boarders."

Where I learn, we complain.
Mold in the showers, moths on the floors, walls, everywhere,
dorms need paint, and we eat from WWII
    US army trays!
"Justice be our shield and defender!"
God sent us here; I must deal with my nausea.
Yes, Lord, I did struggle!
Loneliness saturated my heart.
My aching tears for my past life and friends
    fell nightly.
I longed, above all, for a one-way ticket home,
a way out.
    I needed an attitude change.

You changed it!
I opened my eyes and looked around, beauty!
The variety of peculiar animals,
unique to Africa!
Such a contrast in splendorous colors,
    from lush green of the forests to the
    scarlet in the desert sunsets!
The Rift Valley in its dry splendor!
And a true friend whose selfless love has been an example to me.

I am not here to live in wealth, to associate with high society
    and the elite.
No, Lord, what you said about
helping the poor, giving to the needy.
I remember what you did for me.

And I remember, Lord, that there is a beautiful message
    waiting to be told:
    Every tribe, every nation
    must come to know
    the God of all creation.
--written in Kijabe, Kenya

Sheryl and Kristina did a lot better in school in the second term. We noticed a marked change in their attitudes, a change for the better. Sheryl, especially, was much more pleasant to be around, and it made our lives a lot easier.

Before the first year was up, Kristina asked us to come back to Kenya after our furlough. She liked living in Kenya and wanted to finish her high school at RVA. That was quite a switch from the previous fall. We attributed the change to God who is good in answering prayers. It was comforting to be able to commit our children to his care and watch him work in their lives!

CHAPTER 6

Planting a Maasai Church

The English word, "church" translates the Greek word, *ecclesia,* which means "a gathering of those summoned or called out." In our experience, the Maasai used the word "church" to include a small group that gathered, whether in a building or outside under a shady tree, and sang together, had prayer, a sermon or teaching from Scripture, or a pre-recorded cassette tape teaching in their language, and an offering. It did not necessarily mean a building or organization like a denomination, nor any commitment to a set of doctrines, beliefs, or practices.

In the years before our arrival, Evangelist Paul Otieno and Leon Ressler had been gathering these groups of interested Maasai in different locations and teaching them as best they could. There was a certain fluidity in their composition as the Maasai were still following a nomadic lifestyle.

Upon our arrival, Leon introduced us to two such churches. One met in an Africa Inland Church's primary school at Sikawa in the north. The other met under a tree at Osero in the southeast. At that time, there were only three baptized women.

When we returned from language study four months later, we found some changes. Several Luo volunteer evangelists were trying to keep four Maasai churches going and growing. Altogether nine Maasai were baptized by that time. These groups called themselves "Mennonite," although they had little knowledge of what that meant. Most of the adult attendees were not-yet baptized women.

A fifth church started at Keshuek near the project in February 1986, when two teenage boys gathered approximately forty-five children and ten women and taught them what they knew.

It was a joy to teach since those who gathered were eager to learn. I preferred to work through one translator if he could translate directly into Maasai. Therefore, we hired a young Christian Maasai man, Joseph Nairenke. He was twenty years of age and just finished high school. He was to work as a teacher at our primary school and as an evangelist to help build up the congregations.

We hoped this young fellow could gain the respect of the men and have some men's meetings during the week. But that didn't happen. In that traditional culture, it was not likely that a twenty-year-old youth would be considered to have anything worthwhile to say to the more senior adult males.

Joseph Nairenke teaching the congregation.

On many occasions I did not have a Maasai able to translate my English. In that case, I depended upon an elementary school student to translate my English into Swahili, and a Maasai student would translate his Swahili into the Maasai language. These young students were not very immersed in Biblical knowledge nor Christian doctrine themselves. I often wondered what they actually communicated and what the hearers grasped from what I intended to say.

These developments were interesting and kind of scary as we realized that this was a historic moment, a foundation-laying period for the emerging church. The people could go one way or another. What happened now would determine their future. Since the men were not yet involved, it fell to women and boys to lead the churches, and it could take some strange forms.

The Maasai community was still following its traditional religion, but with their new interest in changing towards Christianity, the more established denominations among the neighboring tribes took interest. The Catholic Church had established a hospital and school at Kilgoris and had a missionary presence at Oyani. Some of the Maasai claimed allegiance to that expression of Christianity. The Seventh Day Adventists had a strong presence among the Luo in the Ogwedhi area. There were also Africa Inland initiatives and Pentecostal contacts from outside the area. At one point, the Maasai elders said they all wanted to become Mennonites because "The Mennonites taught us that God loves cows."

When the Maasai elders agreed that they would leave the nomadic life and settle into a sedentary rural lifestyle, they had also agreed that they would become Christians, whatever that meant. To make that change, they tended to allow their wives and children to attend the new church groups, but they, themselves, preferred to stick to their old traditions.

For us, this was a problem. How can you build strong vibrant Christian communities without the men being involved? We prayed that men would hear the call of Christ. One day we were surprised when ten men came to the service in time to listen to the sermon. At the end, we learned they came to get a ride in our vehicle to a wedding after the service. Disappointing. One hoped that sometime someone, a Maasai "Saul," would be touched.

One Sunday in June 1986, we visited two churches. At eight a.m., we left for the new church nearby in Keshuek, the one started by the two boys. That day there were six women, the two leaders, and twenty-two children. They had it quite well organized including a "choir." I preached, then ran off to Osero, the other church we often went to on Sunday mornings.

We were late. They were all singing. I preached there also. There were seventy people present altogether. The day before I had preached at our Saturday church, the one we started in January. There I had turned the leadership over to a young Luo schoolteacher who wanted to preach the Gospel.

A Maasai choir, a synthesis of traditional costumes, Maasai tunes, Christian lyrics, modern western accompaniment

Outreach among the Siria Maasai was started at Enemasi when Samson Ole Masake, an older Christian Maasai, visited Pastor Paul Otieno, begging him to come to Enemasi to start a church. Samson had experience in the larger world for many years as a truck driver, and sometime before had become a Christian. He wanted the same for his family and community.

Paul, Vera, and I went to his appointed place and found Samson with his two Kisii wives and his children, along with about a dozen others gathered for worship under a tree. A regular meeting led to the allocation of land for the Mennonite Church at the site which was demarcated to become the town of Enemasi.

We had many more such invitations from different communities to come and help start churches, invitations which we had not had time to respond to yet. It is one thing to go and start a church where there is an invitation. It is quite another thing to keep it going. It means travel and time committed every week. It also means helpers are needed—leaders, teachers, preachers, pastors, and/or translators.

Beautifully attired young women

These churches usually had two or three core believers who were exposed to Christianity or had become Christians somewhere in their previous nomadic wanderings. The rest were people interested in becoming Christians including those who thought they were Christians because they took a Christian name or because they came to church or because they wanted to be "modern." We accepted them all and taught them, and slowly, one by one, they asked for baptism.

Most of them were illiterate, so a cassette tape ministry was very helpful. We provided seven hand-cranked cassette players and distributed them among the church groups. We could have used that many more. We gave them a few cassettes with songs or teachings in their own language to listen to for a few weeks. When they were finished, they would return the cassettes, and we would give them a few more. Bible story pictures were also very useful for teaching illiterate people.

We also found that, though the men did not come to church, some of them eavesdropped on the cassette player at home. Altogether, we were ministering to about as many people in our churches as we had at the Salem congregation in Alberta, but they were in quite a different stage of spiritual development, and behind them, they represented a community of several thousand who had yet to hear the Good News. Our prayer was that we could find good leaders and teachers so this work could grow.

On the first Saturday in October, Vera and I went up to Ole Ng'ong'ote about fourteen kilometers into Maasailand where we arranged to start a church the next Saturday. This would be our seventh church. Actually, that did not include one of the two original ones that were active when we arrived a year earlier. They had decided that they wanted to be associated with the Africa Inland Church instead of the Mennonites, so we did not go there anymore.

One Sunday, we visited a new church for the first time. This one was started about four months before by David Ole Shaai, a twenty-year-old illiterate boy who led it. He used to attend Leon Ressler's church which had been closed about two and one-half years previously. He apparently had a dream or vision in which he was told to start a church. So that Sunday, he had twelve women and twenty-five children gathered for a very nice service. I preached and asked for testimonies. One woman shared how it took children to draw their mothers to church, and now she said, "We women will draw our husbands to church!" She sounded very optimistic!

*The Luo congregation at Remo standing
in front of their church building.*

On November 9, 1986, we visited the Maasai church at Oyani or Oloonkoijoo. I preached, and we had a child dedication or blessing service afterwards. There were fifteen mothers with their children and about three men besides us. This was the church that was started the previous January. Several of the women were strong Christians and were being prepared for baptism. John Ndege, a Luo schoolteacher, became their leader. There were a few Maasai men involved.

A year later, the land demarcation team granted their church a nine-acre plot of land upon which to build a church and a school. OSP donated seedlings and a perimeter row of trees were planted on the land. The congregation built a temporary shelter for worship with a grass covered roof.

Pastor Paul baptizing by pouring at Osero, 1986

To encourage the development of our leaders, we sent six young Maasai men to a leaders' seminar at Narok for one week. This Maasai church leaders' seminar was conducted by the Christian Missionary Fellowship (CMF) group.

The CMF had a strong core of committed missionaries who had been working for many years among the Maasai over a large area in the central Rift Valley Province. They used a Maasai translation of the New Testament and produced a book of Maasai spiritual songs. They had prepared the set of over forty teaching tapes which we were using in our work. At this point in time, they had initiated many congregations of Maasai Christians.

We were deeply disappointed in the young man, Joseph Nairenke, who was my mouthpiece, my translator in Bible teaching and our song leader. He suddenly left his work and disappeared. We had noticed a lessening interest in his roles as a teacher, in the project, and in the church. He had also expressed a desire to marry a Maasai girl.

He returned from Christmas vacation one evening in January 1987. We thought he had returned to start teaching the next morning. However, he got up at six o'clock and walked out of his residence without saying goodbye to anyone. He just disappeared without informing us of his intentions or whereabouts.

We wondered what was happening to him emotionally, mentally, and spiritually? A nomadic trait? We never heard from him again.

I really missed him. He had gifts of leadership, teaching, and song leading. He used to travel with me as my interpreter, so I was rather handicapped, depending mostly on Swahili translators instead of Maasai language speakers.

One day, I called a meeting with our church leaders. Six came, four Maasai and two Luo. They each shared their spiritual pilgrimage. They were all so young and weak and yet strong. The two Luos were converted from lives under the curse of heavy drinking. One was making his own booze, dealing in contraband and stolen cattle before he was converted in 1982. Now he was leading a Maasai church!

The four Maasai were still youths, between nineteen and twenty-two years of age. They had all been Christians for a few years. Two of them were called of God through dreams. They were all leading churches they started within the past year.

After our meeting, I was asked to take a sick Maasai to the Tabaka Catholic Mission Hospital, fifty-seven kilometers north in Kisii land. It took me four hours to go and return. It was a very nice, well-managed hospital.

While waiting there, I met an old Irish monk who worked as a nurse. He was very friendly and invited me to share tea with him and then introduced me to several other white staff members, mostly Italians. God has all kinds of saints—unknown, unsung heroes, in the most remote places, quietly doing his work, answering the cries and prayers of the sick, the suffering, and the needy in his world. May he bless these dear monks for their lives of sacrifice and self-giving!

CHAPTER 7

Missionary as Ambulance and Hearse Driver

One of the duties not included in my job description was that of ambulance driver. Since OSP had the only functioning vehicle in the Ogwedhi community, since OSP was a Christian charitable institution devoted to enhancing the welfare of the community, and since I was the only licensed vehicle operator at the time, it was my unwritten duty to serve the community as on-call ambulance service driver. This meant I would be experiencing a lot of unexpected and inconvenient adventures at a moment's notice.

I accepted this service as a part of my ministry. I felt I was assisting God in answering the many prayers of suffering people who had nowhere to turn for help but to God as they understood him. I believe I received much benefit from all the deeply grateful people who wished me, "God bless you!" in return for this vital service. As I served, I felt the blessings stacking up!

For example, one Sunday in July 1986, we arrived home after church to find a man waiting for us to take his two-month-old child to the hospital. I skipped lunch and rushed off to the hospital in Migori. When I returned about three hours later, I found another person waiting for me to take a sick man who had urinary blockage. So, off I went to Migori again.

It was getting dusk when I returned only to find a party of Maasai waiting for me. One of our church women's nine months-old baby was very sick. Could I please take them to the hospital at Kilgoris? I was quite tired after the rough journey, and the car was low on fuel, so I could not go to Kilgoris, which is farther away and has no petrol station open at night. I persuaded them to go to Migori instead. I got home after 11:00 p.m. I was ready to sleep!

At times, my service was extended to that of an undertaker as well. A memorable case occurred when I took a prominent Maasai elder's ten-year-old daughter to a clinic nearby. Due to her condition, she was transferred the next day to Migori Hospital, and I was asked to take her parents to see her. It was Sunday afternoon, and we got back late in the evening.

Then, on Tuesday, I went to Kisumu to replenish our supply of medicine. There, I met Harold Reed and brought him along back with me. He was making his annual visit to the area. The next day we took him to a church leaders' meeting in Migori. After the meeting, he left for Shirati, while we had plans to drive to Nairobi.

However, we were informed that the little girl had died. Her father was at the hospital. He had no other way to take the body home, so we changed our plans.

The Maasai traditionally did not bury their dead. Since they were nomadic, they simply put the body in the bush and moved away. Now they were settling and burying their dead, but they did not like to see or get close to their dead. When we went to collect the body, this father took only one identifying glance at his dead daughter and walked out of the morgue.

I and an attendant put her in a coffin, a rough wooden box that was six inches too short. We had to break the lower end of the box to let her dead feet stick out. Then we carried it out and placed it in the back of our pickup.

When we got to Ogwedhi, the father hired a man of another tribe to bury his dead. This grave digger and I took the body out to the bush where a place was selected by a friend of the father. We unloaded the coffin, and I left it there for the other man to bury all alone. The father did not even see or select the place.

When I got back to town, I found the father waiting. He asked me if the job was being done; then he went home to inform the mother and family that their daughter had passed away and was gone.

Whereas most African cultures make a big thing of funerals, the Maasai are very uncomfortable with funerals and prefer to stay as far away as possible from the dead. They may even burn or destroy any photo, clothing, or anything that would remind them of the deceased and never mention his/her name again.

Another time, there was a combined worship service with the various congregations, Luo and Maasai, coming together at Ogwedhi.

After the service, they held a fundraising activity known as *harambee*, which means "to pull together." This activity made giving into an exciting game involving singing, dancing, and worship. About 6,000 Kenyan shillings (Ksh.) was raised for constructing church buildings. This could pay for the bricks for a small church. The *harambee* went on for three hours. Then, a light dinner was served, after which I was asked to drive the honored guests to Migori.

We set out with the guests at about 5:00 p.m. Just as we were leaving the church yard, a Maasai man flagged us down, pleading for help to take a sick woman to the hospital in Migori. The young woman had given birth six days earlier and now had serious abdominal pain, indicating a bad infection.

This was a priority, so we asked our guests to get out of the truck and wait at Ogwedhi while we went driving in the bush looking for the sick woman. We found her lying in her hut about nine kilometers away. We seated her and another woman in the cab with me and returned.

By that time, it was about 6:00 p.m., and a dark threatening cloud appeared on the horizon moving in our direction. We hurriedly picked up our guests and headed out for Migori.

Imagine the scene: a little green Toyota pick-up truck with me at the wheel and the sick girl with her mother, I presume, both occupying the other bucket seat. On the open back are the eight guests, mostly women. We are racing down the dusty, rocky, eroded, rutted, back country African trail with a huge, black, threatening, storm cloud chasing us in hot pursuit, while we are frantically dodging potholes, boulders, gullies, cows, and people, trying to stay ahead of it!

Well, it caught up with us about halfway to Migori with a torrential downpour of rain and hail. The road turned into a rushing stream as the floods poured down the hills in the wheel-rut channels. The low places became a sea of mud and water. The rain continued its deluge, pummeling us the whole way to Migori. We dropped off the patient, her mother, and the wet husband at the emergency entrance to the Migori Catholic hospital and then took the soaked, shivering guests to their respective homes seven kilometers beyond Migori.

Then, I returned to the hospital, picked up the husband and

mother of the patient and returned to Ogwedhi. I took the long way around to avoid the bad road scene and arrived safely at 10:00 p.m. I was disappointed to discover we had less than one-half inch of rain at our place.

One of our neighbors, an older, respected, Maasai elder, known as Oleng'ayo Ole Momposhi got sick. This man was wealthy, had four wives and many children. He was reputed to own about 2,000 head of cattle. His family members asked me to take him to a hospital. It was rainy weather.

When I reached his home, the family stopped me from getting close to his house. The wet, partially decomposed manure surrounding his house was soft and so deep, the truck would get stuck. So, we carried the man out through the deep muck, put him in the truck, and took him to the hospital. Days later, we heard that he had died.

Now Ole Momposhi was a traditional Maasai. His 2,000 head of cattle was his bank account. Being an established livestock businessman of his time, whenever he sold a bunch of steers in Dagoreti, Nairobi, he would bring the money as much as Ksh. 200,000 home in a paper bag and hand it to one of his wives and tell her to hide it until he would "need it someday."

Ole Momposhi, was a respected, wealthy and peace loving elder at Ogwedhi Sigawa community. He was one of the founders of OSP, and an official who was a member of the land demarcation board.

Well, this man had very few needs. He lived in a simple old mud hut in the midst of a manure pile, wore a few different sheets and plastic sandals, and ate the traditional food. The "someday" with its need never came. Later, I was told that his firstborn son, William Sankei Momposhi, being educated, went around to the various widowed mothers and collected the money stashed away in the aging huts. Some of the money had been eaten by rats, some had gotten wet and had rotted. Some had turned moldy. The son gathered what was left and took it to a bank for deposit.

Another time, early one rainy Sunday morning, someone came for help. A lady was in labor. Could I please rush her to a hospital? I had other plans, so I sent our new driver, Caleb.

Well, the roads were soaked, and the vehicle got stuck. While Caleb was desperately trying to extricate the vehicle from the mud, the baby proceeded to extricate herself from her mother. When Caleb finally got the vehicle out, he just turned around and brought the mother and child home. In a pinch, this versatile vehicle could even serve quite well as a delivery room!

CHAPTER 8

An August Wedding Interlude

We began hearing the distant chime of joyful wedding bells ringing in our daughters' communications from across the vast ocean. It had been only seven months since we had bid them farewell in Virginia. At that time, we were assured there were no immediate prospects of matrimony on their agendas.

But now, in March 1986, Cindy was excitedly sharing her latest wedding plans. She and John were favoring an August wedding. Would we be able to come? Up to then, we had planned for our daughters to visit us in our Kenya setting during the summer. Now there was a conflict.

Cindy and Karen insisted it was possible to do both. They would visit us in Kenya in May through July, and we would come to the USA for the August wedding. Very simple and doable!

We protested that it was too extravagant in time and money to have both their visit and the wedding in the same year. It must be either/or. Communicating and making plans by letter was frustrating. John was in Israel doing his cross-cultural requirement, so Cindy had to communicate both ways by letter. The official engagement announcement had not yet been sent out.

In the end, as usual, the girls won. By April 6th, they had decided that Cindy and Karen would both be leaving for Kenya on May 17th. They would live and work with us until Cindy would go back on July 11th, and Karen would remain with us until we all could go back together for the wedding. We debated long and hard with them about these plans, and now it looked like it was going to be their way.

Cindy was completely determined to come and visit us even if it meant postponing her wedding for a year. She felt this would be her last chance to live with her family as a single person and felt the need to get in touch with her African roots.

We didn't think Cindy and John should delay their wedding for a whole year either, so we finally acquiesced. We agreed to fly home for the wedding in August. The wedding would be held in Lancaster, Pennsylvania. Then, we would all fly to Alberta for a reception at Salem Mennonite Church, where we had lived and served for nine years.

The tentative date for the wedding was August 9th. The reception would probably be a week later. So, we would be in Alberta for two weeks.

The Mission did not send missionaries home for weddings, so it would take some doing to gather the funds. It seemed rather extravagant, but it was a once in a lifetime thing for Cindy. We felt right about doing it and trusted it would work out.

Cindy and John both graduated on May 4th with outstanding academic achievements. Then, according to plan, Cindy and Karen arrived at the Jomo Kenyatta International Airport in Nairobi on May 19th.

Of course, it was exciting to see them again and to introduce them to our new home in Ogwedhi. They were very excited about being back in Africa. It was not quite the same as the Ethiopia they remembered leaving as children, eleven years earlier, but it was still Africa.

In Ogwedhi, with some assistance from her mother, Cindy gave herself to sew her wedding dress. She brought the materials with her, expecting her mother to make it. Vera wisely told her that she would gain more satisfaction from making it herself, so Cindy spent most of her days on the treadle sewing machine. Finally, after laboring over each stitch and button, she had a gown of which she could be proud.

After all the labor and love she put into that dress, it really bothered me to see her carefully, and lovingly press that finished masterpiece with a live charcoal heated iron! Amazingly, it did come out "without spot or wrinkle." Perfect!

Karen enjoyed the challenge and opportunity of helping her mother teach some classes until the end of the term. She enjoyed teaching and was a big help. She of course had an eye for African boys, too. "What else is there to do to keep from being bored?"

She bought herself a complete Maasai woman's costume and really impressed the men.

We took them on a camping trip through the Maasai Mara National Reserve and spent a night at a young CMF missionary's house on the east side of the park. David Giles had been a missionary kid in Ethiopia and had attended Good Shepherd School. He and his wife were our neighbors in Pasadena the previous year. In fact, Karen and Sheryl often babysat for them there.

The next day, we drove on to Kijabe and took our younger girls out of school for a long weekend of camping at a YMCA campground on Lake Naivasha for three days and nights. It was fun doing a bit of what we used to do as a family in Ethiopia in old times.

After returning the girls back to their school, we went to Nairobi where Cindy and Karen purchased souvenirs. They took the night train to Mombasa for a three-day holiday on the Indian Ocean coast while we returned to Ogwedhi. Upon completing their holiday, they returned by bus to Migori, where we picked them up.

Two weeks later, we took Cindy and Karen along on a short trip to Kisumu to re-stock our dispensary's supply of drugs. While we were eating lunch in a restaurant, thieves broke into our truck and stole everything from it. Barack, our manager, lost his bag with 1,800 shillings in cash, all checkbooks, keys for the whole project, mailbox keys, and all the mail for OSP and the primary school children. Karen was the other victim, losing her $150 camera and her jacket with $70 cash in the pocket. It was the same place we were robbed of our overnight bag the last time we were there with the Heges.

Later, while we were walking down a street in Nairobi, a thief grabbed Karen's gold chain, ripped it off her neck, and ran away with it. It had four gold ornaments on it. They were memento gifts from her friends, including a heart with a pearl and a "World's #1 Babysitter" pendant from a grateful mother in Pasadena. This was a big loss for her since she, as a student, was already financially strained. So is life—disappointing if our treasure is "where thieves break in and steal"!

We were having a delightful time with our two oldest daughters. The youngest two missed out on a lot of what we did since they had to be in boarding school during the months of May, June, and July.

Time passed so quickly. Apart from our camping trip and visit to the game park in Maasai Mara and their three-day trip to the coast at Mombasa, the older girls had been with us at Ogwedhi the whole time. They enjoyed Kenya. It was a sort of homecoming for them, though they wished they could have stopped over in Ethiopia.

Cindy returned to the USA on July 11th. We sent her off alone by bus from Migori early Friday morning. She arrived safely in Nairobi and found her way to the airport on time and flew out late that evening. In retrospect, knowing what we know now, I certainly would not recommend such a tight one-day travel schedule, as an African proverb says, "A journey is never known!"

A week later, Vera, Karen, and I followed, leaving Ogwedhi on July 17th. We stopped in Kijabe to take Sheryl and Kristina out of RVA and spent Friday and Saturday in Nairobi.

The plan, then, was that Vera and the girls would board a plane on July 20th and fly to Harrisburg, Pennsylvania. I was to travel back to Edgerton College for a two-week course on goat and sheep raising and then fly out on July 31st, arriving in Pennsylvania on the same day.

As their departure date neared, both Karen and I started feeling sick. Since it was time to fly, Karen, sick as she was, boarded the plane. She had a miserable ride. I remained behind at the Guest House.

The next day, I felt worse, and decided I must visit a clinic before proceeding to the workshop at Edgerton. The doctor's diagnosis revealed that I had malaria. So, I cancelled my plan to attend the workshop and nursed myself with medication at the Guest House. I was a little delirious one night but soon got better.

Karen was not so fortunate. She suffered on the plane trip and was taken to a hospital in Pennsylvania. Unfortunately, no one there had any experience with malaria, so they failed to diagnose what was making her sick.

After receiving my diagnosis, I phoned Vera and informed her that I had malaria and suggested that Karen's illness was probably the same. Since malaria was largely unknown to medical professionals in Pennsylvania, this was a rare case for them that attracted a lot of attention. They made a celebrity case out of her. Many medical students came to see and interview her. Even two years later, she was still getting phone calls and follow up questionnaires from people studying malaria.

Despite these challenges, we both eventually got well again, and I was able to attend and officiate at my eldest daughter's wedding. It was held outdoors by the Mill Stream at Lancaster Mennonite High School on August 9th. A week later, there was a big reception at Salem Mennonite Church in Tofield, Alberta, Canada, for Mr. and Mrs. John and Cindy Kreider. About 300 people shared a potluck dinner and program there.

Two weeks after the wedding, I had a reoccurrence of malaria. This time I was referred to a doctor in my small hometown of Brooks. Fortunately, he was an East Asian doctor who had grown up in Kisumu and knew all about malaria. He gave me a shot of quinine which cleaned my body of the nasty parasite completely.

At the end of our stay in my parent's home in Duchess, Alberta, I was too relaxed and failed to take note of our departure date. One morning, the thought occurred to me that perhaps I should look at our itinerary. Imagine my horror when the itinerary indicated that our flight was already in the air at that moment, without the four of us!

Immediately, we got on the phone with our travel agent and rescheduled our flight. The revised flight involved changing planes at JFK Airport in New York and again in Madrid, Spain, before going on to Nairobi.

That was okay, but for some reason, our plane was delayed a whole hour on the tarmac at JFK Airport. This meant a late start across the Atlantic, and a late arrival in Madrid. This also meant that by the time we got to the departure lounge in Madrid, our plane to Nairobi had already departed, again without us.

Now what? The Iberian Airline, which got us to Spain late, graciously booked us on the next flight, which left three days later. They put us up in a nice hotel for the wait, along with several other travelers.

Two of those others, a talkative Texan and another American, approached the four of us and suggested we pool our resources and hire a taxi. They wanted to take a tour of Toledo, a few hours' drive from Madrid. So, we had a memorable tour of the historic site and the landscape between. It was an unplanned cheap break which we enjoyed. Sometimes there are unforeseen benefits in not looking too closely at one's itinerary.

In planning, we knew we could hardly afford the cost of the four of us flying this above-budget wedding trip. However, in the end, different friends of ours gave us gifts amounting to $2,900 which covered 3/5ths of the total cost.

Various people gave us monetary gifts to assist in the work in which we were involved. In the months that followed, we bought three tape players for evangelism, a set of the Maasai New Testament on tapes, and one more sewing machine. We also painted the home science room, made two tables and four benches for that room, made thirty desks for grade one that could seat four students per desk, made two blackboards, eight tables and stools for teachers' desks in eight rooms, and a bookcase. Quite a bit of this money came from Karen and Cindy's tithes.

We carried back two guitars and an accordion, gifts from some people in the Salem Church. The church in Ogwedhi was happy for these musical instruments to enhance their choir.

All the above were superlative blessings, byproducts of our daughter's wedding. Of course, the biggest blessing of all was that our family gained an outstanding and much-loved son-in-law!

CHAPTER 9

Resumption of Routine Service

After enjoying an exciting five weeks of travel and festivities centered around our daughter's wedding, we found ourselves back in Kenya on September 6, 1986. The social interchange with old friends and relatives, plus a final unplanned vacation in Spain, made it difficult for our daughters to return to "prison" at RVA. This time Sheryl was starting 12th grade, and Kristina was in 9th grade.

Back in Ogwedhi, after expecting us a week earlier, the staff greeted us with considerable relief. With no phone and no communication, apprehension had been increasing day by day. They had the house and yard in top shape awaiting our arrival. We felt warmly welcomed.

An Agricultural Show

We arrived back just in time to enter competitions in the Annual Fall Agricultural Show in Migori. On Monday and Thursday, we went to Migori to build a booth and get ready. The show's managers arranged for a truck to come on Thursday night to pick up three selected cows and a goat from OSP for the show on Friday and Saturday.

The goat, a Toggenburg (Swiss dairy) male won the distinction of being a champion. In all honesty, I must admit that he was the only goat in his category. The cows won first and third prizes.

The truck driver refused to bring the cows home before Sunday morning. So, I got up that morning and left by 6:00 a.m., dismantled our booth, returned by 9:00 a.m., shaved, washed, ate breakfast, prepared a sermon, and arrived at church at 10:30. What a sermon it must have been!

The next morning, I returned to Migori to do some banking.

Banking can be a pain. That day, it took over two hours, mostly waiting in line, to complete our transactions. Antiquated bureaucracy. The following day we returned to collect some cattle feed. In between trips, I helped plant some beans in our demonstration/test plots. We had 150 plots of ten square meters on which we planted a lot of different varieties of vegetables and cereals to test and demonstrate.

That evening, we harvested the first honey from our bees. We only got one small incomplete piece of honeycomb, rather disappointing.

A week after the fair, we were informed that a grade eight schoolboy who was riding on the back of our pickup after the show in Migori, had jumped out near Ogwedhi in the dark. It was about 9:00 pm. He was found by travelers on the side of the road at 1:00 a.m., unconscious. They picked him up and took him to the police station. He couldn't talk. His mouth was cut, and three teeth were knocked out. They couldn't identify him until a teacher was called at 3:00 p.m. the next day. His face was scratched and swollen. Several days later, his mind was still not working right although he was awake. Apparently, he jumped while I was going quite fast. Other kids riding along saw him jump, but it was dark, and they assumed he was okay.

Accolades for the Primary School

Vera went back to teaching at the school. This time, they were studying cooking and nutrition, which she knew something about. Vera said she sort of enjoyed teaching. That was something I never thought I'd ever live to hear her say. She was still stretching towards her potential.

As the Ogwedhi Sigawa Primary School was being established, its reputation in the larger community was growing, and more parents were having their children transferred to it from other schools. The campus was becoming more crowded. More classroom space was needed. Fundraising efforts in the community were undertaken. At the close of 1986, as funds came in, the foundations and walls of two more classrooms were under construction. As funds were depleted, construction stopped. It would take years before the roof and floors would be completed. Classes were often held outside in the shade of a tree.

Ogwedhi Sigawa Primary School

Drought

Farmers in Trans Mara expect to grow two crops per year, and September is the appropriate time to seed for the fall rains. This year, 1986, the farmers around Ogwedhi had a lot of seed in the ground, but the rains failed to come as expected. Storm clouds appeared on the horizon, hopes arose, but were quickly dashed as they kept bypassing us and dumping floods on our neighbors. So often this is the farmer's story.

We were about out of water. Our cisterns were almost all dry. The water level in the well was down to the bottom, and we were contemplating how to haul water from the river for all the cattle. The pasture grass was grazed down to the bare brown earth, and we were hauling feed from thirty kilometers away in our little pickup truck. Although eight new calves were born, milk production was way down due to the stress of drought.

Finally, in October, some nice rains came just in time to turn our fortunes around. Our crops, which had begun to germinate then shriveled, were beginning to look much improved. However, it turned dry again, and the crops stagnated. It seems normal for farmers everywhere that nothing works out "normal."

The weather turned around in November, giving a little rain

almost every day. The grass grew, and the cows produced more milk. The crops grew towards their maturity, although the germination rate had been far below normal.

We had to re-seed some of the napier grass. Napier is a special grass that grows in a clump like sugarcane but looks like sorghum. It can be cut for cow feed every six months or so and grows for five or six years. We needed more cattle fodder and wanted to get a few acres of this planted. To propagate napier, a dry mature stalk is cut into three-inch pieces, with at least one nodule on each piece. These pieces are planted in rows. If conditions are right, the nodules grow into mature plants. If it is too dry, they rot, or termites eat them.

When we first arrived in Ogwedhi, our yard was undeveloped. The house was not fenced, so cattle and goats roamed at will. Neither vegetables, flowers, shrubs, nor trees could thrive in their presence. During that year we fenced off the house and yard with barb wire reinforced on the front with a cypress hedge and a gate. We planted trees. These additions set our yard apart and gave us a sense of privacy that we liked.

We hired a talented young Luo man, Robert Opanga, to make a tree nursery right next to our yard. By March 1987, he had about 8,000 seedlings ready to be sold and planted during the April rains. We sold them to the people for twenty cents (two cents USA) apiece. The tree nursery became very popular.

At the Cinema

We had a few old-fashioned film strips that we sometimes showed, with a projector and a car battery, to teach people in the isolation of their rural communities at night. These depicted Biblical stories or development or health education themes.

Generally, in a rural community devoid of electricity, let alone television, movie theatres, or smart phones, the people found these nocturnal shows fascinating and educational, a major to-be-gossiped-about community event. Large neighborhood crowds would gather when this rare opportunity was presented.

One night, we were showing Bible story film strips at a nearby Maasai church. That night there was no moon—that means dark! As we were showing pictures, a young Maasai came running out of the dark, bursting into the group, screaming in a strange manner. In the commotion, he bumped our electric wire, and the lamp went out. We were left in confusion, not knowing if our attacker was one or many, armed or unarmed, playing or in earnest. It turned out, our attacker was a young fellow who had been drinking too much.

After the show, we had to stay for tea and rice. Then, we had to go to another home for more tea and rice. After visiting for an hour or more, sitting around a smoking fire in the little dark hut, we set off for home.

On the way, I took a short cut trail through the bush I thought I knew and promptly got lost. With no roads and no road signs to guide us, we drove around among clumps of bushes seeking some familiar markings in the dark pasture.

Suddenly the motor stopped. There we were at eleven p.m. out in a Maasai bush, lost and broken down. One of the girls prayed and I jiggled a certain safety switch and the truck started.

However, while I was out looking under the hood, I inadvertently stood in the way of some busy safari ants, who promptly swarmed up both my legs under my pants. They do bite. There I was out in the wilderness dancing around in the dark with "ants in my pants!" A dramatic climax to our cinema night in the Maasai bush! Darkness was a mixed blessing as I modestly attempted to remove the biting critters from my most private parts in the presence of all the women in the truck. We survived and got home by 11:30 p.m. Such are the adventures in the lives of some missionaries.

Illegal Alien

One time we were asked to take a group of pastors to Shirati for a seminar. I thought we needed to go to Isbannia to enter Tanzania legally at the official border. The accompanying pastors had a different idea. They assured me that it would be simpler to cross the border near Muhuru and Shirati. That was the way they usually did it. Apparently, for the locals in that part of the country, the Kenya/Tanzania border security was very lax.

Following their advice, we went to Muhuru for the night. The next afternoon, we took a back road across the Kenya/Tanzania border to Shirati, which is only about twelve kilometers down the Lake Victoria coast.

There was no immigration or customs office at the crossing, but the pastors knew there was one in Shirati town. So, we went to the immigration office when we arrived. The young officer decided this was a good opportunity to pull rank and declared that we were in the country illegally! He said we had to get our passports stamped at Isbannia (near Migori) before entering Tanzanian soil. He said he would see us in the morning about it.

With that assurance, we went to our place of abode and were eating supper when one of the church leaders interrupted us. He informed us that we were being asked to leave Tanzania tonight, or we would be arrested and confined to jail as illegal aliens. We went back to the officer right away and pleaded our case. But he was adamant. Here was his golden chance to expel a white man, and since no bribes were forthcoming, nothing could dissuade him.

Apparently, the order only applied to the white man and his vehicle. The Kenyan pastors stayed on, while Vera and I drove back to Kenya that night. We spent the night at somebody's friends' house who had a spare bedroom. We slept well and returned to Ogwedhi the next day. I hoped the immigration officer slept well also. Two days later, I drove back to the border to pick up the pastors. They had had a nice seminar.

A Welcome Break - Family Time

The daily grind of our hyper-busy lives, meeting the demands of the project, plus the duties imposed by unplanned emergencies wore on us. It seemed we hardly had time off as I was often gone even on Sunday afternoons or evenings. It was always refreshing to get away and be with our kids for a few days. Again, the RVA mid-term break in October afforded such an opportunity.

This time we travelled by night train to Mombasa for the weekend with the girls' two best friends. Sheryl's roommate, Leona DiVries, was from Calgary. Her parents taught at Rosslyn Academy. Kristina brought a friend, Norma, a pretty girl from Senegal. Her father was a minister in his government, and her mother had a big job in the UN. Norma was stuck in RVA with no plans nor place to go for mid-term break. She was happy for our invitation.

We rented a cottage one hour south of Mombasa at Diani beach on the Indian Ocean. It was a lovely place where we could do our own cooking.

This was a timely break. Both our girls were feeling depressed and having a hard time enjoying their lot in life. They both wept when we came to see them this time.

Kristina was struggling with science courses, and felt she had a hard time making solid friends. She wanted to come home to live with us and take correspondence. Sheryl had been through about as much stress as she could handle and just felt she needed her parents to listen. She did not want us to give advice or answers, just love her, listen to her, and bear with her.

Sheryl was struggling with who she really was. She decided to break off her relationship with Len, as much as she hated to do so, "at least for the time being." She felt he was pressuring her too much, so that she couldn't be a normal teenager. She was determined to finish this last year of high school, graduate in July, and follow her sisters to Eastern Mennonite College.

She was doing a major research paper on non-resistance, pacifism, and nonviolent resistance. She wasn't satisfied to just inherit her beliefs or to accept what some church taught her. She wanted to find the truth for herself and come to an understanding how that impacted her life.

The emotional swings of a teenage girl. A few weeks later, an upbeat letter from Sheryl indicated she was a lot happier, enjoying "freedom," didn't want to get tied down to a boy for a while. She was enjoying her studies more. She reached the high honor roll for the first time. She was still focusing on entering college at EMC in the fall.

From Pennsylvania, Cindy wrote and was elated that she finally landed the job she wanted with Catholic Social Services to work as a career counselor for the Southeast Asian refugees in Philadelphia.

While driving in the city, a bee got into their car. In their distraction evicting the bee, they collided with another car. Their car was totaled. The insurance company gave them $1,500 and let them keep the car. John fixed it up for $10 and drove it for several more years. So, they made out pretty well. Even their accident turned out to be a blessing.

Once again it was December, the major vacation month in Kenya. When their school was closed for the month, Kristina came home with us, but Sheryl stayed in Nairobi with her roommate for the first week. She was to be coming by bus to Migori the following Friday. Having Kristina with us somehow made our home more complete. She was rather quiet by herself, into baking and cooking.

When I went to Migori on Friday to meet Sheryl, I waited about four hours for all the Nairobi buses to get in that evening. No Sheryl. Disappointed, I drove home without her. Then, I got up early and drove back to Migori to check the arrival of the night buses. Still no Sheryl, so I went to a friend's house and phoned.

The people where she stayed told us the situation. She had planned to come by bus, but it was a big weekend, and the buses were all booked several days in advance. We had no phone for her to contact us, so she gave up and decided to stay there until we got to Nairobi a few days later. On December 13, we drove back to Nairobi, picked Sheryl up, and drove on to Limuru to attend the annual MCC and EMM Workers Retreat at the Brackenhurst Conference Center.

Academically, Sheryl and Kristina had done well in the fall term. Sheryl had attained a place on the high honors list. There was still another special list of highest honors which she had not yet attained. Kristina's grades had improved, and she found herself on the honors list as well.

Kristina told us stories about her friends. Some of them, including her roommate, Iryne Kamau, were from wealthy African families. Kristina learned a lot about the children of the rich and famous. She planned to share a room with Norma next term.

Upon arriving home from the retreat, we had a leader's seminar on the 24th, followed by church Christmas programs that evening and all the next day.

After everybody went home Christmas night, we were left alone to celebrate our own Christmas, in our own way. We also had Boxing Day mostly to ourselves. We gave each other gifts, mostly souvenirs for parents and perfume, cosmetics, and decorative accessories for our beautiful daughters. Kristina baked a lot of her specialties and Sheryl decorated the house. Each contributed in some way to making it a special occasion.

CHAPTER 10

Funding the Ogwedhi Sigawa Project

World Vision International had been funding OSP for six years. Early on, they informed us that their contract with us was about to expire and that we would need to find new donors. According to their policy, World Vision would not renew the contract.

Therefore, being forewarned while still in language school, I contacted several donor organizations that expressed interest. We needed to present a well-thought-out proposal that fit their criteria to convince them that our project was practical, workable, and worthy of their supporting partnership. Since these agencies had slightly different criteria, I would have to make several editions of the proposal, tailoring each one to meet the specific agency's requirements in a convincing way.

One of the first challenges I faced upon returning from language school was to draft several such proposals for funding OSP for the next three years. I submitted them to several organizations that like to give money for such projects.

Three of these organizations, Catholic Relief Services, V.A.D.A., and Lutheran World Relief, showed interest. A planning dialogue was initiated and progressed over the next several months. Then, we got an unusual invitation from our current sponsor, World Vision, to come to discuss a new proposal.

Responding to the invitation, one Monday morning in early November 1986, I got up at 4:00 a.m., picked up Barack, and drove over to Osingo. There, we roused the Vice Chairman, Wilson Ogwada, out of his bed, ate breakfast, and took him with us to Eldoret, about five hours drive from Migori, to visit the World Vision Office.

There, they informed us that they had unilaterally decided to fund our project for another five years! We had not even applied for it. They would give about 440,000 Ksh., or $40,000 Canadian, to our project for the coming year. This would go towards hiring a community nurse, buying a motorcycle, hiring a bookkeeper/social worker, keeping the dispensary going for another year, paying the manager, buying a few tape players, organizing three youth camps and three conferences, giving away ten pairs of oxen, 300 bags of seeds, and five milk cows to needy people, helping twenty students in high school, digging ten wells, and other things.

We found this troubling. We did not want money to dictate our priorities. We did not plan to do all those things. World Vision had told us the previous year they were phasing us out at the end of this year. We never asked them for any of the money. Now they came with this package. Much of it was for handouts. So, we still would need a lot of money for the things we felt we should be doing. We did not believe in handouts. We felt we should be doing things that help the community help themselves. So, we had to go and negotiate some changes to try to fit it into our program.

There is sometimes a certain advantage in not having a telephone in one's home, the advantage of no spam calls, no unsolicited advertising, and no unnecessary interruptions. At other times, it would have been so much simpler if there was a way to contact someone when plans change. We were expecting three guests from V.A.D.A. one evening in November. V.A.D.A. was one of those organizations that provided money to development projects. We had made an application to them, and they were interested enough to come out and take a look.

We were expecting their arrival that day. They would be coming by car. We had been having good rains, and the roads were in a mess, so we wondered whether they would make it. Without a phone or radio, there was no way they could let us know if plans changed. So, we just got ready, then waited and waited. Finally, we went to bed. They never came.

In late January 1987, we were informed that Mr. Bob Cottingham from the Lutheran World Relief headquarters in New York was passing through Nairobi and would like to see me. With some anticipation, after having a committee meeting at home, I rushed to Migori and caught the night bus to Nairobi. After sleeping for three hours and getting up in time for breakfast, I rushed off to meet him. After speaking with him, I was disappointed to be told there was still no final word on the status of our application with LWR. They would decide sometime in mid-February. The dim ray of hope would have to flicker a little longer in my breast.

It had been more than a year since I started these applications. My finite patience was running low. I confided in a private letter:

> Perhaps by the time my term expires, and I leave this project, there will be plenty of money to work with. Anyway "knock and the door shall be opened, seek and you shall find!" And also "Thy kingdom come; thy will be done!" If God is behind this program it will succeed, and if not, then we do not want it either.

In February, the OSP made and distributed school uniforms for 300 "poor" children thanks to the World Vision give-away plan. We also provided school fees for eleven "destitute" secondary school students. The Committee refused to give away the thirty oxen, five cows, and three hundred bags of seeds and fertilizer that World Vision wanted OSP to give to the destitute.

The Committee felt that OSP was a development project and not a relief agency, and it didn't want it to become a relief agency when the people are not desperate. It would only foster a beggar mentality. Handouts invite the danger of making people into beggars who would come to expect handouts and who would hate the provider when the handouts stop coming.

Instead, we asked World Vision to let us use the money to build a dormitory where the Maasai children could live and learn. Giveaways feed for a day, but buildings can help from fifty to one hundred years or more.

In March, World Vision informed us they would fund OSP for another three years at the same rate as last year. What happened to their five-year promise? They seemed to change their minds every time they had a meeting, making arbitrary decisions without consulting us. Anyway, we were grateful, but still needed funds from another organization. Now both those other organizations informed us they should have an answer by the end of March. It was January, then February, now it was March. We were getting skeptical.

World Vision gave us permission to use 122,000 Ksh. to build a dormitory to add a boarding component to the primary school. This was deemed important for certain Maasai children. World Vision would also give money for equipment but not over 300,000 Ksh. We estimated we would need about 600,000 Ksh. so would have to find other ways to finish the boarding facilities. At least, we planned to build as fast as we could for as long as the money lasted. I went to Kisii and bought enough tin for the first roof.

World Vision also designated funds to dig ten water wells before the coming October. In March, we selected most of the sites, places like school yards, marketplaces, or any place where the public should have access to clean water. We contacted another organization about helping to install pumps and cement tops.

Then, at the end of April, while passing through Nairobi on a brief vacation to Malindi, I stopped by the Lutheran World Relief office to see if there was any movement on our application for funding. They had just received a telex from New York saying our project was approved. Wow!

They agreed to back our project by giving us $155,000 to be used over the next four years. Needless to say, that made our day. I had applied about fifteen months previously. Now when there was only one year left to my term, the funds came through. "Better late than never!"

This good news meant that our next year would be very busy trying to spend that money wisely. That money, on top of what we were getting from World Vision, would be adequate to keep OSP going and would enable us to expand our program by adding a community-based health program, hire two development extension workers, start a serious dairy goat program, launch a model farmer program, a water development program, plus expanding the farm work at the center and keeping everything else going.

It would also buy a new truck and two motorcycles and keep them running. It would also provide some much-needed tools and improvements around the center. Expanded activities would also increase our staff to twenty-seven people.

The promised World Vision funding was geared more for handouts and for support items in evangelism, education, and administration. They promised to help start a theological education by extension program (TEE) in the fall. This would give training to all church leaders in the diocese on a study-as-you-minister basis. There would be one-day seminars every three weeks for the leaders. Participants would be given study assignments to work on before the next meeting. World Vision also wanted us to help some of the poorest people to enable them to support themselves and to help them educate their children. So, there was a lot of work to be done!

CHAPTER 11

Challenges Along the Way

Dawning of a New Year

Vera and I welcomed 1987 by driving the now familiar eight-hour trek back to Nairobi on New Year's Day. We had come to Nairobi, at this particular time, to bring our girls back to school. It was a long holiday weekend.

That Sunday morning, we were still lying in bed at the Guest House when Karen phoned from Pennsylvania. It took precious minutes (at $3.00 per minute) for the office help to rush over and call us through the open window. We were surprised, scrambled out of bed, put on appropriate attire, unlocked the door, and rushed out down the sidewalk to the office to the phone. It was good to hear her voice again. She was at Cindy's place over the holiday. She wanted us to hear her out as she struggled to make some academic decisions.

Should she sign up for the Middle East tour next fall like Cindy and John both had done or not? It would mean extending her time in school by another semester because she didn't need the credits for her education degree. As it was, she was already needing four and one-half years at EMC to graduate with a B.Ed. degree. This would extend it to five years and add more to her college debt. We listened, and in the end, she came to her own conclusion. Much as she wished to go, economic realities forced her to decline the semester abroad opportunity.

That afternoon, we had time to relax sitting in the shade of a frangipani bush on the green lawn of the Mennonite Guest House with our feet in the sun. It was one of those perfect Nairobi days with quiet blue sky and a few small white cumulus clouds gently floating by.

In the distance we could hear the occasional truck roaring up the hill on the main road, an airplane, a dog bark, somebody sawing a tree, a lady practicing piano in the house next door, birds chirping or singing or whatever birds do. A little child, Sarah, was playing about three feet above my head in the frangipani and chattering with all her four-year-old wisdom and vocabulary. She lived here because her mother, Dr. Esther Kawira, was resting here trying to save her pregnancy to full term. Her home was in Shirati, Tanzania.

While in Nairobi, we needed to do a couple of days' worth of business, but everything was closed for the holiday and weekend, so we had ample excuse to wait till Monday and Tuesday to accomplish that. Some of the major items on our "to do" list included the purchase of a motorcycle for the community health program, and the purchase of a microscope, some dental forceps, and ear syringe for the dispensary.

God Bless Volunteers

On January 10th, Gary Roth, a twenty-five-year-old farmer from Oregon, came to live and work with us for two months. He came at his own expense to experience Africa and especially missionary Africa firsthand. He helped us with any kind of work we could find for him to do.

One of his lasting contributions was to renew the crumbling cement floor of our milking parlor, which was a simple set of five stanchions, and re-build a holding pen. He also built a large worktable and shelves for our shop. It was nice to have this young fellow with us. It relieved the loneliness for us, although I can only imagine it must have been a bit boring for him at times!

In the Shadow of Death

On one of our trips home after completing our business in Nairobi, Vera and I stopped to visit our daughters at RVA. We had arranged overnight lodging at the AIM guest house, just across and down the road from the girls' dormitory. After an enjoyable evening eating dinner and visiting with the girls, it was time for the nine o'clock curfew. The girls persuaded their mother to spend the night sleeping with them. Men had to leave the girls' residence. Instead of going the long way by lane and road, I took a shortcut, walking down a path alone in the dark, to my room at the guest house.

The path was dark, and I had no flashlight. However, the light from the dorm was behind me, so I could see some of the tops of the taller grass along the edges of the path. Otherwise, all was dark in front of me. I was carefully searching, finding my way.

Suddenly, out of the darkness, I heard a commanding voice in Swahili ordering me to stop. The command was coming from the darkness down the hill in front of me. I paused, peering into the blackness before me. I could see nothing, so I continued on. Again, the command, this time louder, "Stop!" Then another command, "Come here, or we will shoot!" I replied in English, "I can't see you!" Then one of the two policemen turned on a flashlight indicating where they were.

When I got closer, seeing I was a white foreigner, they switched to English and said, "You are a lucky man. There was a robbery in the station office about three hours ago, and we are looking for the suspect. We were going to shoot you, but then we saw you stumbling around like you might be lost or didn't know the path, so we called out for you to stop." With the light of the dorm behind me, I was completely visible to the men with the guns hiding in the darkness before me. An easy target.

I was appalled. Would these police actually shoot someone without warning, based only on suspicion? I replied, "It would be a very foolish thing for you as policemen to shoot someone when you don't know who you are shooting. Then I explained that I was just a parent, a guest, who wanted to take a shortcut down to the guest house for the night.

I did not fall asleep right away that night, as I usually do. For a few hours, possible scenarios and questions kept going over and over in my mind, thinking about what could have happened; what that would have meant for my wife and daughters up in the dormitory if I had been killed, or even wounded; what it would have meant for the two policemen and their families if I would have been killed. How would the Kenyan government explain the killing of a Canadian citizen to the Canadian Embassy, and on and on.

However, in the end, I thanked God that I did not have to find answers to all those questions. I was very much alive, in good health, and safe in his powerful loving protection. Yes, safe, even in the "valley of the shadow of death." Then, as I usually do, I slept well.

Purpose-driven or Crisis-driven Management?

I found myself continually frustrated. The demands placed upon me by my role in the project and in the community were almost equal to the demands I placed upon myself. While I desired to lead by systematically pursuing the goals I set for the project and for myself, I was, instead being led by the emergencies and demands of others that imposed themselves upon me. It seemed I was busy all the time, going here and there, and yet getting little of what I intended done. While my intentions were goal-oriented actions, too much of my actual activities were crises-driven responses.

For example, on Monday, I was in Migori to take care of some business. Tuesday, I went back to Migori to catch the bus to Nairobi. I spent Wednesday in Nairobi shopping and visiting several offices on project business. Then on Thursday, I caught a ride back to Migori with a Tanzanian car that was passing on to Shirati. After spending the night at home, other unfinished business demanded another trip to Migori. In summary, I had been in Migori on Monday, Tuesday, Thursday, and Friday of that week alone, not to mention Wednesday in Nairobi. The next week I went to Kisii on Monday, Migori and Luendo on Tuesday. and then ...? It seemed I almost lived on the road. No wonder I got nothing done at home.

It got about as bad as it could get during the month of February when I was home all day for only two days. I couldn't say that I did anything significant; I just seemed to be going somewhere for some important reason every day. The time away that month included one week we spent in Nairobi, which included a long weekend with our girls. We were back home in time to take a trip to Tanzania. We got back Saturday, the 28th, then I left for Nairobi the next morning for a short meeting with World Vision officials. Vera stayed home, and I got back Tuesday, March 3rd. Too often this was the reality in contrast to what is often idealized as the life of a missionary.

CARL E. HANSEN

A Short Look at Theological
Education by Extension (TEE)

Vera, our volunteer Gary Roth, and I took a short journey to Tanzania from February 24 to 28, 1987. We visited the missionaries at Shirati and Musoma. I was particularly interested in their theological education by extension program (TEE) at both centers. Bishop Kisare had included a similar TEE program in his wish list/job description for our involvement in South Nyanza. Hence my interest.

Victor and Viola Dorsch, a missionary couple from Ontario who had been in East Africa for thirty years, were teaching over 300 church leaders by this method. They divided the churches in this region into ten centers. Church leaders studied lessons on their own, at home. Then, every three weeks, Victor and Viola would visit each center and hold a one-day class for all the students in that area. The Dorsches covered five centers per week for two weeks, then took the third week to correct papers and prepare for the next lessons. It was a tiring schedule for these sixty-year-old missionaries. They were planning to terminate in September and take on a pastorate in Ontario.

The TEE program was started in Tanzania after the Bukiroba Bible Institute was closed. TEE seemed more appropriate for the need to train grass-roots church leaders in the Tanzanian situation. It spread the teaching to a lower level so more active leaders could benefit. It seemed so much more practical. Some of these leaders had no formal training beyond their own catechism when they were baptized. The church in Tanzania was growing. Its southern diocese had between 10,000-15,000 members and the northern diocese had about 6,000.

At the conclusion of our visit, I realized that to start a similar program in South Nyanza would require a whole package of resources including a full-time teacher, a vehicle, and a budget to meet all expenses. This was more than the Kenya Mennonite Church or OSP or World Vision was prepared to provide at that time.

Innovations

The role of a development agency includes, among other things, the role of innovator. New ideas must be tested and tried before being introduced to the public. It is not always as easy as it first appears. Among the many innovations that we introduced; the sunflower business was a flop.

In 1986, we introduced sunflower growing to the farmers and also introduced the community to an oil seed company in Nakuru which supplied free seed. So, in the fall, a lot of farmers started growing sunflowers. They grew well.

However, at harvest time there was no local representative of the oil seed company to purchase the farmers' crops. They were very disappointed. Finally, the company asked, or begged us to be a purchasing agent for them. That took a lot of work, arranging cash to purchase the crops from the farmers, providing sacks and storage, and a weigh scale.

In the end, we collected about 300 sacks of sunflower seeds and sent two truckloads to the factory in Nakuru. OSP made a modest commission for our efforts. It showed potential to become a successful business.

The following year many farmers took free seed supplied by the company and grew sunflowers. However, the local birds discovered this new delicacy and developed a craving for the goodness of sunflower seed. They beat the farmers to the harvest, and the farmers were left with the ugly empty stalks to dispose of. The birds were the only beneficiaries. The oil seed company, the farmers, and OSP were the losers. Not all innovations are as suitable as they at first seem.

Conflicting Values

One Saturday, upon returning in the late afternoon from a church organizational meeting in Migori, I was approached by a group of Luo neighbors awaiting me. Some cows had been stolen the night before; they had traced the footprints to a certain Maasai community. Now, would I take the police to that spot to put some pressure on the elders so their boys would return the stolen property?

I found such requests very distressing. As a non-violent Christian missionary, how should I respond? Cattle-stealing happened often, every week, perhaps. I had the only available vehicle to transport the sick, or the police, or whatever. Now my Luo neighbor, a poor man, had all his cattle stolen. In one fell swoop, his life savings and source of livelihood were gone. The ones who stole them were the teenage or young adult sons of the Maasai, the ones to whom I preached the Gospel.

If I take the police to help my neighbor in need, to the Maasai village where the cattle tracks disappeared or dispersed, the police will call the elders and question them, and demand that they return the stolen goods. The elders, if they know where the stolen cattle are, may promise to return them to the police station the next morning.

If they do not know, of course, they cannot say where the cattle went. The police may beat them, thinking they are lying, until they confess where the cattle are. The police assume the fathers should always know what their sons are doing, and therefore, beat them to the point at which they will cry out and promise to give of their own cattle to the man who lost his.

A few weeks earlier, one of our Maasai church elders was beaten in just such an incident. He came to our dispensary for medical attention. He didn't know where the stolen goods were. Later they found the tracks again and followed them into a different community where they recovered the lost animals. That recovery did not address the injustice nor mitigate the suffering of our falsely accused Maasai brother.

With this painful memory fresh in my mind, I faced a dilemma. Do I help my neighbor in distress by bringing the police to a community who knew me as a Christian missionary? In doing so, the police may harass, beat, or maybe even kill, whether they are thieves or not, the very persons to whom I preach the peace and love of Jesus.

I told the police and the people how I felt about getting involved. The policeman assured me that there would be no beating this time, so I finally gave in and hauled them to the Maasai village in time to meet the elders before dark. The elders were nice and cooperative and served us tea and assured us the cattle would be returned in a few days, so we went home.

In retrospect, it turned out to have a positive outcome. At least the police knew how I felt about them beating innocent, and not-so-innocent, old men. Also, the leading elder of that village invited me to come back and start a church there. He said he would even give land for the church and school. Another challenge.

*Young Maasai "il moran" (warriors) were
quite adept at stealing cattle.*

The next day, we visited two Maasai churches where I preached. Before I got home, a Maasai man stopped me and begged me to take his two wives to Komotobo Hospital, a Catholic mission about fifteen kilometers south in Kuria land. So, I missed lunch and took them. The wives were two young girls, sixteen and eighteen years old. One had miscarried, and the other was pregnant and had malaria.

The next morning, I got up and thought, "Maybe today I'll be able to stay here and get some real work done." Such a vain thought! After breakfast, some Maasai men asked me to go to Kilgoris Hospital about forty-three kilometers away to bring Magdalena back to her home from delivering twins. She was one of the leaders of the church at Osero. So, my morning plans were changed again. Aaron and Anna were the cutest little babies.

CHAPTER 12

Family Vacations 1987

Once again, April was a vacation month for all schools, so we took our daughters on a trip to Malindi on the shores of the Indian Ocean. We took the night train from Nairobi and arrived in Mombasa on Thursday morning. From there we took a bus for the two-hour ride north along the coast to Malindi. We had reserved a cottage with four beds, a bath, kitchen, and living room. We prepared our own meals.

Malindi was a quiet tourist town with several hotels and lots of tourist shops. It was the rainy season, so there were few tourists, and most of the places were about empty. Being on the coast of the Indian Ocean, the atmosphere was hot and humid.

Already on Tuesday night, as we were on our way, I was feeling some symptoms, like I was getting malaria again. By the time we arrived in Malindi, I was feeling quite miserable, so I bought some malaria medicine from a local pharmacy. I felt better on Friday, then worse on Saturday, so I went to a local hospital. A blood slide confirmed a malaria infestation was the culprit. I got an additional hand-full of pills and an injection. I felt some better though a bit drugged. I pondered the mystery, "Why do I always seem to get my sicknesses scheduled to coincide with my vacations?"

The beach was perfect: gently sloping, fine sand, very little seaweed and other garbage. It was much nicer than the beach at Mombasa. The Indian Ocean was completely warm, and there was a nice breeze most of the time. We visited the marine park where we took a glass-bottomed boat tour and I even tried snorkeling. What a beautiful world down there! I was fighting a fever, so I didn't get the maximum enjoyment out of the trip.

For their June mid-term break, Sheryl went on the senior class trip to Mombasa. We took Kristina and her roommate, Norma, to visit the Meru National Park, a known game preserve. We borrowed a vehicle from MCC in which the girls could ride inside instead of on the back of our green pickup.

The park is located a seven-hour drive to the northeast of Nairobi, on the eastern side of Mt. Kenya, which is the highest snowcapped mountain in Kenya. The Meru National Park is on a downward slope towards the desert lowlands to the east. We found a campsite where we stayed in a little cabin for two nights while the girls stayed in our tent. During the night, we could hear lions calling.

In the morning, after a late breakfast, we drove around in the park. There were not many animals to see as it was already getting hot, and the animals sought the shade. We did see an albino giraffe among the others. We also saw five white rhinoceroses.

I took photos of the girls and Vera petting one of these dangerous white rhinos! They were under the protection of armed guards day and night. Imagine our alarm when, three weeks after our visit, we read in the local newspaper that all five of these rare "protected" rhinos were massacred by poachers. Where were the armed guards?

This was a short vignette of the ongoing struggle between the Ministries of Wildlife and Tourism and the illegal but lucrative trade in rhino horn and ivory. The rhino horn could bring up to $30,000 in those days in China where it was ground into powder and sold as an aphrodisiac. The guards were paid a mere pittance for their work. Should they really lay down their lives to protect these animals? Or should they find a way to cash in?

Vera, Kristina, & Norma petting this "wild"
rhino under the watchful eye of a guard

On our way back, we drove around the north and west side of Mt Kenya. Its peak reaches 17,057 feet above sea level. It takes about two and one-half hours to drive to the other side, even on a good, paved road. We wanted to see the glacier-covered peak, but it was shrouded in a bank of clouds.

We travelled through beautiful countryside known as the "white highlands," where white colonialists used to live. The farms looked like those back home on the prairies—large cattle herds and wheat fields spread out—reminded me of the Carstairs, Alberta area. Some yards even had the farm machinery standing outside, like in Alberta.

On the way, we saw a sign pointing to a youth hostel, so we turned to check it out. It was on a road going up the mountain. The hostel was empty except for one American guy who wanted to climb the mountain the next day. The clouds lifted, and we got a nice view of the mountain top, the rays of the setting sun accentuating its beauty.

At the hostel, the girls wanted to camp, so we put up our tent for them while Vera and I slept in the girls' cabin. The kitchen was available to us for cooking, and we all had a hot bath. It was a bit cool that evening, so we built a fire in the fireplace. After playing some games, we ate popcorn and drank hot chocolate. We returned to Nairobi the next day.

In the middle of April, we held a youth seminar for about thirty young people from the various church districts. It was our first youth retreat and was well received.

While the seminar was going on, we entertained six visitors from Alberta. Brian and Ardith Butler from Vegreville were on an MCC assignment, teaching school in Northeastern Kenya. Brian's uncle and aunt and Ardith's former roommate and friend came to visit them in Kenya. In showing them around, the Butlers brought them out to see us. They camped in our yard for one night, then drove to Maasai Mara National Preserve for the next night, and then returned on Saturday and went out to the Maasai church with us for Easter Sunday. After dinner they went on their way.

CHAPTER 13

Church Growth

Dedication of a Church Plot at Enemasi

I t was the custom in Kenya for schools to be registered under the name of a church that was seen as the sponsor of the school. If that church could rally the community to build the structures, the government would supply and pay the teachers. If the church community did not approve of a certain teacher, it could demand that teacher's replacement.

At Enemasi, upon the wishes of the community, land was demarcated for a primary school and a church building in the name of the Kenya Mennonite Church. Then the community requested us at OSP to help them construct a church building that could also serve as a first school classroom.

Church elders organized and held a dedication service for the plot on Sunday, March 8, 1987. We brought our truck loaded with leaders from the other churches to the meeting place under the tree. Besides us, there were disappointingly few present for the worship and dedication service. The members consisted mostly of women, and they spent all morning cooking food and preparing tea, so when the service was finished, they could provide us with a feast.

I preached in English, Andrew Okech interpreted into Swahili, and John interpreted that into Maasai. I asked a few questions. It went through two translations, and the answer was given, then translated back through the two steps. That was the way communication took place on these occasions. It definitely put a crimp in my oratorical style.

The community elder could not wait for the building to commence. With government assistance, they hired a teacher and started grade one in the open air with the pupils sitting in a row on a log in the shade of a tree at the site where their future church building would be.

Leadership for Growth

The Ogwedhi Sigawa Church District leaders came together for a business meeting. Among the issues they discussed were five requests to start new churches among the Maasai. The question was raised, "Where are we going to get leaders to start all these requested churches?" The leader of one of the older churches volunteered, "No problem. We can send them some. We are training our people to lead." So young weak churches send their stronger members out to help newer weaker churches. That is the way Christianity spreads around the world!

Yes, we were all very weak and small, but there was a good spirit among us. Our churches were led by very simple and humble folk. Some were illiterate or semi-literate. Only two had some high school training. Some were young boys still in their late teens. A few were illiterate women. Yet, the churches grew, and their leaders grew with them.

The next Sunday, we went early with one of the Luo evangelists to start another new church. We found the appropriate holy tree selected by the local people. The brush and undergrowth had all been cleared away, and some rather flimsy branch "benches" were nicely in place. Three little girls were already seated, each holding her infant brother or sister and eagerly awaiting our arrival.

One of the infants, upon seeing us strange pale monsters, broke out screaming in terror and had to be taken home. This was not uncommon with small African children upon first seeing a white person. We do look rather bleached and hideous to them.

Slowly, people gathered while the leader and some Luo friends who came to help went about fixing the benches, so they could be used. Eventually, with us who came to inaugurate the Indoinyo Oretet Mennonite Church, there were about forty-five persons present. This included ten Maasai women and one man plus children from that community. We were all very happy and enthusiastic about the new church. Some of these people had been attending one of our other churches, but it was very far away. They were delighted to have their own church close by.

Church Roofs

Eastern Mennonite Missions had an agreement to help local churches in Tanzania and Kenya by putting on the roofs of their church buildings. If the people would build the walls and the floor using permanent materials like brick or cement block, EMM would match their effort by providing the metal roof. In the Southern Sub-diocese of Kenya, two congregations, Luendo and Osingo, had worked on the walls of their meeting houses and were qualified for the gift of a roof. However, due to delays caused by the Kenya Mennonite Church's conflict, EMM didn't send the money for the roofs. Those walls stood roofless for more than two years.

Finally, moved by compassion for the people of those two congregations, EMM officials relented, and bypassing the church officials, released the funds to me. I was to supervise and pay for the installation of those roofs on the two churches. This meant that I had to take the measurement of the building, calculate the number of materials needed, purchase those materials, have them transported to the respective sites, and pay for the builders to install the roofs.

We took the first steps to implement the plan on January 23, 1987. We went to Migori and loaded a truck with supplies to put the first roof on the church at Luendo, about seventy kilometers west of Ogwedhi. By the beginning of March, the roof at Luendo was completed. The roof on the Osingo church was installed later that same year.

CHAPTER 14

Joseph Sankale Ole Kasae: A Called Man

We had been praying and searching for a solution to the leadership need. About this time, two young Maasai neighbors, Joseph Sankale Ole Kasae and Francis Rekai, came to visit me with a proposition. Joseph and Francis were both farming close to OSP. They were both Christians and were trying to start a Seventh Day Adventist (SDA) church nearby. They had been rebuked by some visiting Maasai Maranatha evangelists who chided them for working alone. "Why don't you unite with the Mennonites and work together in bringing the Gospel to the Maasai?"

Joseph and Francis were moved by this suggestion, and after much prayer and discussion, decided to approach me with their suggestion. Could we discuss the doctrine and practices of the Mennonites? Joseph had a grade ten-level education and Francis, his disciple, had finished high school. Joseph was the older and the leader. After careful study and discussion, they both joined us with the Mennonite work, becoming very active in strengthening the emerging Maasai church in the Ogwedhi Sigawa community.

Let me share the story of Joseph Sankale Ole Kasae's early life as he recounted it to me in different settings.

Nariku-nkera Ole Kasae knew suffering. Her suffering stretched her faith in *Enkai*, God as the Maasai understood him. All human beings disappointed her, but her sufferings just deepened her faith in God who was just and fair, who would remember her sufferings and vindicate her in the end.

In the beginning, both of her parents failed her and left her an orphan. Her older brothers raised her and made her work. They often beat her and abused her. As soon as they could, they married her off in exchange for cows to an older man who squandered his wealth on strong drink. He also squandered her personal cattle in six months.

This was taboo among the Maasai, so her brothers took her back and later gave her to Ole Kasae, an elderly man who already had three wives. She was given her new name, *Nariku-nkera* which means "escorted by children."

Her sufferings were greatly increased by the fact that she was barren. Her husband abused her and sometimes sent her away. He would later call her back when there was much work to do.

The older wives mocked her and beat her as if she were still a child. They humiliated her and gave her the hardest work or the menial tasks of a child. She was taken to the *laibon* or local medicine man, to herbalists, medical doctors, and to hospitals, but there was no cure for her infertility. Her people said she was cursed. She could bear no more and decided to end her life. She overdosed on strong herbs, but as she says, "God did not let me die."

Then she "ate the news" that there was a good medicine man among the Kuria in Tanganyika. She decided that she would go all by herself. It was a long journey that would take several days walking through enemy territory.

On the way as she passed through a deep forest, she met a mother leopard with her four kittens standing on the path before her. She stopped and waited, hoping that the leopard would move away. But the leopard just stood there.

For about twenty minutes she waited. In those minutes she felt the inner assurance of God telling her that she also, like the leopard, would become a mother of babies. She talked to the leopard, "Don't eat me because I am looking for children like you have." It just kept turning its tail from side to side as if to tell her to pass. With renewed courage, she inched her way slowly forward past the leopard.

She went to the famous specialist and returned. Another year passed, and nothing happened. She went to another herbalist and prophetess among the Siria. She gave her some herbs and prophesied, "Go! If God gives you children, bring me a reward!" That was in her ninth year of marriage.

In her tenth year, God heard her cries and vindicated her faith. She started to bear children. In all she bore two sons and four daughters.

When she started bearing, her co-wives all stopped bearing. In the end she had more children than they.

It was during the seventh month of her pregnancy with her second son that she had a severe attack of malaria. A local doctor was called to treat her. The only medicine he had was an injection of chloroquine. He hesitated and said, "If I give you this injection, the child may come out." She was very sick, so insisted that he give her the injection.

Sure enough, the baby was born prematurely. They all thought that it was stillborn, so they threw it out on the manure pile beside the house. An older half-brother, Ole Ngumme, a young warrior, examined the discarded fetus, pushing back the mucus membrane from its face with the tip of his spear. The baby gasped for breath. Ole Ngumme called the women, saying, "This one will live!" They came out and took the baby back inside and took care of him. His nails were not completely formed yet, only on the big toes and thumbs.

This second son was born on a night when there was very heavy rain, and water was seeping into the house. It was also the night that visitors came from Purko country. As was the custom, the visitors were given the honor of naming the infant. They named him, *Sankale,* after a famous Purko chief. That was in 1962, near Ole Reiko on a hill called Ole Karoni.

His father had died before Sankale was born. His mother took care of him and taught him how to care for the goats as other Maasai children did.

While herding the sheep and the goats, he would watch the clouds moving so quickly across the sky. He asked what force is pushing the clouds so fast? A Catholic nurse told him, "God is up there." She sang a song about hundreds of thousands who have defeated the world and will go up to heaven, a place where orphans and widows will get their rights. That was the first Christian song he heard. It touched him deeply because of his family's sufferings.

As he grew older, Sankale was herding goats near a school at Enosaen. He was a very curious child, so he would go to the school to investigate what went on there, eavesdropping outside the window. After a while, he was invited to sit inside. The goats were forgotten. He would be punished when his mother or uncles found out. Finally, his uncles agreed to let him go to school. That was in 1971.

In 1973, Nariku-nkera was expelled from the family by the eldest son of the father. She and her children would get nothing of the inheritance. They moved to Sikawa.

Little Sankale attended the Sikawa Primary School. The Maranatha Mission started a church there. Sankale knew the story of his mother's sufferings and heard her affirm her faith, "God is there!" He wanted to know more. Now in school and in church, they were teaching about God. He scored his highest grades in the compulsory Christian Religious Education class.

Sankale accepted Christ as his personal Savior and Lord in 1975. A white missionary came from the Maranatha Mission to hold a meeting to bless the place where a big church was to be built at Sikawa. He talked about giving tithes and offerings to God. Sankale's mother had given him ten cents for the offering. He refused. He wanted to give his big bull. His mother refused. He cried and cried until his eyes were dry. His mother finally told him if he cooled down, they could give it in the future.

The new Christians were being given "Christian" names. The Sunday School teacher wanted to give Sankale the name "Joseph," but he refused because there were too many "Josephs" already. So, the teacher told him the story of Joseph, the husband of Mary. That convinced him of the value of the name, so he became known as "Joseph Sankale." The next Sunday, seventy new believers were baptized. Like Joseph, they were mostly children. Today Joseph can't remember any besides himself who remains a Christian.

Shortly after that, the war started when the Maasai morans massacred the Luo squatters. Suddenly, all the Luo children and Luo teachers fled to safer territory. There were only three children left in school and no teachers. Joseph's brother-in-law sent him to a Catholic boarding school in Kilgoris from 1976 to 1979. The Catholics chose him to teach catechism to the other students, which he did for one year.

Then, the Africa Inland Church people arranged to bring him to Sikawa every Sunday to help with their church. He continued to help in 1980 when he completed grade seven at Enosaen. He would walk home on weekends to teach or preach in the little church. His peers and adults mocked him, calling him "pastor" or "preacher."

The next year, Joseph was one of two chosen from Kilgoris to go to the Maasai Technical School in Kajiado, which was a day's drive east of his home. He was sponsored by his brother-in-law. He did well in his studies until July 1982, when he received a letter from his mother outlining all her problems and demanding that he come home. His older brother had joined the *Il moran,* or warriors, and was acting irresponsibly. His mother was left alone too much, was sick, and needed help. She wrote, "I have suffered enough, either come home at once, or never come home!" So, Joseph left school intending to return, but he never did.

He went home and took his sick mother to Nakuru to her son-in-law's home where there was a good hospital. While being treated there, they got news that Joseph's sister died. So, his mother insisted on returning to Kilgoris. In September they migrated back to Sikawa.

Joseph gave up ever returning to school, so he decided to put what he had learned into practice. He would become a farmer. He got a plow and some oxen and began to plow the land and planted maize, beans, vegetables, and trees.

In those days it was still taboo for a Maasai to plow the land. The soil is what produces the grass which sustains the cattle which sustains the Maasai. To break the soil is an act of sacrilege and was tantamount to bringing a curse down upon your own head.

Consequently, the young Joseph was seen as an outcast, one whose mind had been disturbed and character ruined by being in the modern school system. He was a rebel to be scorned and despised. He had turned against the traditions of his own people. They let their cattle graze on his crops. When he confronted them, they also uprooted the trees he had planted. He found it difficult to live at peace with his neighbors.

Two of his peers took it upon themselves to drive Joseph out of their community. They wanted to attack him. Joseph went to the elders for protection.

When he returned in the morning, he found one of his enemies there waiting for him. His house had been ransacked, and his enemy demanded that he leave at once or he would attack him. He lifted his *orinka* (knobkerrie, a short stick with a knob at one end, usually carried by men as a weapon for self-defense) to strike Joseph. Two women standing by begged the man not to strike.

Joseph faced his enemy and said, "I don't want to fight; just give me six hours and you won't find me here." He wanted the elders to come and help settle the dispute. However, the angry man was impatient and asked, "Will you migrate right away, or not?"

Joseph replied, "I'm going, but my load is too much. I need time to carry it all away." He had five boxes of books and things to take with him.

The angry man could wait no longer. He swung his *orinka,* but Joseph ducked. He swung again, even harder. Again, Joseph evaded the blow. He picked up Joseph's bow and arrows and tried to shoot him, but Joseph was too close. The women screamed. The arrow scratched Joseph's arm.

Then, Joseph became angry, and said, "Okay, if you want to fight!" He put down his machete and picked up his *orinka* and threw it at the man. It missed. He had another one, which he now swung menacingly at the man. The *orinka* slipped out of Joseph's wet hand and struck the enemy on the head right in front of the ear. The man fell down unconscious with blood running out of his ear. They all thought he was dead. The women covered him with a sheet. Maasai do not like to look at corpses.

Joseph went to report his fault to the chief, Ole Ng'atuny. People carried the fallen man the two and one-half kilometers to his house. By the time Joseph arrived at the man's home, people were busy slaughtering a sheep. It was a Maasai practice to make a substitutionary sacrifice. They believed that, by pouring out blood for the critically ill, they might persuade God to accept the sheep's life instead of the man's life. Joseph felt terrible about what had happened, and he feared what the elders and family members would have to say.

The young man's father came to Joseph to comfort him. He said of his son, "He got what he deserved. I tried to dissuade him from his course of action this morning. But he refused. If he dies, it is not your fault!" Joseph felt tremendous relief and comfort in those words.

The unconscious man was eventually taken to the Catholic Mission Hospital at Tabaka. He had a broken bone where the weapon struck. In one month, he recovered and returned home. He still did not want to make peace with Joseph.

Joseph had moved to Ogwedhi the same day as the fight. For the next three months, both enemies refused to make peace with Joseph. The other man was hunting for an opportunity to attack him.

Joseph reported this to the chief and to the police and got a letter issued authorizing the arrest of this enemy. In the meantime, this man wanted to marry a certain girl. The parents of the girl refused, saying, "Unless you make peace with Joseph Sangale, we won't give our daughter to a man who wants to die!"

The elders invited Joseph to go back to the land from which he was evicted. Joseph refused. He told them that he just wanted to live in peace. To do so, they asked him to pay the hospital bill for his enemy. Joseph sold three cows and paid the 1,700 Ksh bill. Then a neighbor, Kilingoni, killed a sheep, and Joseph and the man ate it together in the same house. Thus, they made peace.

The other enemy, however, was still waiting for a chance to get Joseph. He was a big strong fellow and had a reputation for meanness. One day he found Joseph at Ole Kitiyia's house and wanted to fight right away. Ole Kitiyia, a much respected elder, stood between them and separated them. Ole Kitiyia rebuked the young man severely and ordered him into the house.

Joseph went away in great anger and hid himself along the way with the intent to ambush and kill his bitter enemy. He waited until midnight, but the man never came that way. He said later, "God spared me from murder that night!" For a long time after, Joseph carried with him that letter authorizing the arrest of his enemy. However, that young man went off to school, earned a degree in India, and years later, married Joseph's younger sister and thus became his brother-in-law!

In 1983, Joseph started preaching to his neighbors in Keshuek, just across the stream from the OSP. He gathered a few women and children under a tree and taught them what he knew.

Some Seventh Day Adventists found him, encouraged him, and gave him some teaching materials. He followed their doctrines and started sending offerings to the Ranen Mission. He applied to attend their theological college. The pastor gave him a letter to take to the mission director, but he was not accepted because he was too young, and his parents were not members of an SDA church.

His evangelistic efforts began to pay off when Francis Rekai, a student about ten years younger than Joseph, accepted Jesus as Savior and agreed to follow him as Lord.

The next year, Joseph met Paul Otieno, the Mennonite evangelist.

He moved next to OSP and farmed there raising maize, potatoes, vegetables, and chickens. For a while he lived with Paul Otieno, but his mother could not bear to see Joseph living like a Luo, so he moved back to stay with his mother.

On the night of February 4, 1984, his neighbor, Mapengo's cows were stolen. Joseph heard the cry of alarm. He quickly picked up his weapons—a bow, a quiver of arrows, a spear, and a short sword—and ran to join the other Maasai warriors. They followed the tracks of the cows for about twelve miles across Luoland to Ekirege deep inside Kurialand. There the tracks disappeared into the tall grass.

As was the custom in such cases, the police and the chief were called to witness the end of the trail. The people in this community would be held accountable and would be forced to produce the stolen cattle or an equivalent number to replace them. Leaving the matter in the hands of the police, the chief, and the local elders, the band of Maasai warriors returned home.

Joseph, being the one who could write, Mapengo, the owner of the cattle, and Ole Kosium, a friend, stayed behind to write an official statement for the police. Here they were, three Maasai warriors alone in the heart of enemy territory.

A band of rather drunken Kurias took notice and began to shoot arrows at them. Should they fight back? They were hopelessly outnumbered. Instead, they ran to hide behind the Kuria chief. But the Kurias kept on shooting. The chief could not stop the drunken mob, so he ran with the three Maasai to the shelter of a house nearby and locked them inside until the police could come. They stayed there all night.

Joseph didn't sleep much that night. He thought and thought about the matter of killing. He could so easily have shot someone in that moment of skirmish, in pure self-defense. But what would Jesus think of him had he done so? Did Jesus defend himself when he was being arrested, tried, and crucified? If Jesus didn't defend himself, should he? What about that commandment that says, "Do not kill!"? If a Christian is a follower of Jesus and is dedicated to do the will of God, can he really kill in self-defense? If the answer is "no," then why was he here with these weapons?

The next morning, Joseph and his friends returned to their homes. Joseph went out and began shooting his arrows into the forest until his brother came along, and thinking he must be mad, grabbed Joseph's quiver from him with the remaining arrows. Then, Joseph broke his bow and threw it into the bush. Joseph said that was the point of his real conversion when he decided to trust God for his protection and to follow Christ in the new way of defenseless love.

It was not easy to be a non-resistant Maasai Christian in those times. The culturally appropriate way to honor one's father was to become a great warrior, to collect the largest herd of cattle, by stealing, of course, by protecting those cattle from other would-be thieves, by killing the most enemies in times of theft or war, and by being the bravest and cleverest fighter in helping one's age mates when their cattle were stolen.

It was hard for Joseph. His mother did not understand his faith. At times she ridiculed him, "You ought to wear a skirt. You don't have any weapons in your house. You don't even go and help your age mates in their war against the Siria people. You haven't even stolen one cow from the Luo. Even I am a better man than you!"

Joseph continued to join with his warrior neighbors to follow the tracks of stolen cattle. However, he only carried a long walking stick and his Bible. The neighbors mocked him but let him come with them. He reminded them that he was protected by God.

Joseph's mother wanted him to get married, but he wanted to find a Christian girl, so he refused the one she suggested. In retaliation, his mother refused to milk his cows and cook his food anymore.

So, Joseph milked his own cows, a disgraceful thing for a man to do in Maasai culture. He also cooked his own food, putting beans, potatoes, and maize all in one pot. But most disgraceful of all, he built his own house and smeared it nicely inside and outside with mud. No self-respecting Maasai man would do such "women's work." People laughed at him. His mother even got drunk to annoy him.

This being his situation, Joseph started to think of marriage. He prayed to God to show him a good Christian girl who would help him make a good foundation for his life and support him in his work with the Word of God. He approached two Christian girls from the Maranatha Church but was turned down in both cases because he was not a member of their church. He tried the same with one from an SDA family with the same results.

Then he contacted a Catholic girl he had known in school in

Kilgoris three years earlier. She had dropped out of school in tenth grade due to lack of school fees. She had refused to marry the one her parents chose for her and was staying at home. She was interested in Joseph's proposal, so arrangements were made for marriage.

Joseph was a Christian, and he wanted a Christian wedding and a Christian marriage. This meant that he would not be satisfied with a traditional ceremony alone. He refused to supply alcoholic drinks to the parents and the guests. He insisted that there would be a ceremony in the church in which both he and his bride would covenant before God that they would be faithful to each other and keep themselves from sexual relationships with any others, as long as they both shall live.

This meant they were vowing that polygamy and adultery would not be a part of their future relationship together. This was completely counter to the cultural practices and common view of marriage. Most of the Maasai boycotted his wedding. They disregarded him as though he were a fool, and worse than a fool, a cursed person.

So, on April 29, 1984, the wedding took place in the Ogwedhi Mennonite Church in the midst of Luo Christians. Pastor Nashon Arwa, also a Luo, performed the ceremony and pronounced them husband and wife. Mr. and Mrs. Joseph Sankale Kasae were social outcasts among their own people, a couple cursed.

After being married for some time, Joseph got a job assisting at the Ogwedhi Sigawa Project Dispensary. He had just worked there for one month before his wife, now pregnant, became sick with malaria which made her very anemic. He took her to the Ombo Hospital in Migori and donated his own blood for her.

Two weeks later in July, she became sick again. This time Leon Ressler, the missionary at Ogwedhi, took them to the farm of Joseph's brother-in-law between Lolgorian and Kilgoris and left them there. His wife got worse and started to miscarry. Joseph went out to the road to wait for a *matatu* (taxi) or any vehicle that might come along to take her to the hospital. It was night, and the elephants threatened him, but no vehicle came. The baby came, and the mother started to hemorrhage. It was 11:00 a.m. before they finally found a vehicle to take them to the hospital in Kilgoris.

Joseph went around town and found two friends to donate blood. But it was too late. At 7:30 that evening, she passed away. Joseph went to her parents' home to tell them, and he spent the night there. Her two brothers comforted him and took responsibility for her burial the next day.

Joseph came home alone, very bitter and angry. This was his hour of trial and temptation. His faith in God was stretched to its limits. The elders shook their heads knowingly; this marriage was cursed from the beginning because he defied the traditions of the ancestors. He decided that he would never marry again.

The mission gave him a one-month bereavement leave. In the meantime, the doctor left his post, and the dispensary was temporarily closed. When it reopened, Meshack Omondi, a medical practitioner from Tanzania, was the "doctor," and Francis Mosero was his assistant. Joseph was never called back to work.

Now he had no wife and no job. He wrote a sign and put it on his house wall, "One is a whole number!" His mother stood by him in his grief, sharing his sufferings, and encouraged him to marry again. She quoted a proverb, "A man can fall nine times and still stand the tenth time!" She told him, "The one you got was not yours, yours is just there, look for her!" She even chose a certain girl for him, but he refused. He would remain single!

Time healed the wound in Joseph's heart. He again became active in the ministry of the Word of God, and he continued to work hard at developing his farm. It was at that time, several Maasai evangelists from the Maranatha church convinced him and Francis Rekai to work with the Mennonites in bringing the Gospel to the Maasai.

After some years, Joseph began to see the advantage it would be to his ministry and to his farm operations to have a good wife. He started looking for one again.

There was a striking young girl called Esther that Joseph had known some years back when she was still a child. Now, she was finishing grade seven, was almost seventeen, and was about ready for marriage. She was a Christian and attended the Church of God at Il Pashere.

One night in 1987, she awoke suddenly from her sleep. She found herself sobbing and crying, worrying about who would marry her. Then and there she prayed, asking God to find her a Christian husband.

Shortly after this, Joseph decided to see if Esther would be

97

suitable. He prayed, "If she is the right one, let her say 'yes,' and if not, let her say 'no.'" Then he sent his friend to ask her if she liked Joseph and would be willing to marry him.

Esther recalled only seeing him once in her lifetime, yet she heard some positive things about him, so she replied, "Yes!" They went through all the negotiations with her family and the ceremonies that were required. They planned to marry in April 1988.

In the meantime, Joseph became very ill with chronic stomach ulcers and went to Nakuru to his brother-in-law's for treatment. There, he got worse and was hospitalized for six weeks. That ate up 7,000 Ksh, the money that was to cover the expenses of the wedding. When he recovered, he simply brought Esther to his home in the traditional way in late June. This time the traditional elders were satisfied. This was a real wedding and would be blessed.

Joseph and Esther Sankale with their first two sons

CHAPTER 15

Family Connections

The summer of 1987 brought changes in our lives as a family. In the USA, Karen had completed her second year of college. She was holding down one and one-half summer jobs in Philadelphia, living with Cindy and John Kreider. Karen cleaned houses for well-to-do people during the day and delivered pizzas in the evenings. It was a case of two poor-paying jobs equaling one good-paying job. She was able to make most of the money she was expecting to make. She seemed happy there. She enjoyed driving fast in the big city. She always did love to drive in the city—Edmonton, Los Angeles, and now Philadelphia. She was making bonuses for getting the pizzas delivered quickly.

Cindy was paying the bills with her social service job while John was in graduate school at Eastern College.

That same summer, on Saturday, July 18, Sheryl, with seventy-eight others, graduated from high school. Rift Valley Academy was a good school, and even though she found reasons to complain, Sheryl benefited by spending two formative years there. She had skipped grade ten and still maintained good grades.

After spending two days with her in Nairobi following the ceremony, sadly, the time came to bid our third daughter farewell at the airport. She and Leona, her roommate, flew off, leaving Africa together. She also left a big empty void in our home and in our hearts.

After spending a day together in Amsterdam, they parted ways, Leona flying to Calgary, Canada, and Sheryl to Philadelphia, where she joined her siblings. She stayed with them and worked with the same company that Karen was working with for the rest of the summer until she enrolled as a freshman at EMC in the fall.

Kristina decided to stay home in the fall and take grade ten by correspondence. The mission budgeted funds to enable us to add a room onto our house to accommodate her. There would also be an indoor bathroom with shower and flush toilet.

A further incentive for adding more living space was the prospect that my mother would decide to pay us a visit, perhaps as early as September. Could we have this room completed before her arrival?

Enlarging the House

We began the work by hiring a young man to make cement blocks in our yard. By the end of July, workers had dug a hole in the back yard to serve as a septic tank and put in a drainage system for the new bathroom. Then, they laid the foundation and built the block walls. By the end of August, the walls were up and the rafters on, ready for the roof.

The construction of the house was progressing but too slow. The local builders were not used to such complicated buildings, although it was very simple by North American standards. They needed constant supervision. They did not seem to have an eye for straight lines and were quite happy with inexactitudes. Putting in plumbing before the foundation and cement floor are poured was new for any house in the area.

Unfortunately, it was long after my mother had come and gone that the building was completed. With the finishing of the new part, we had the outside of the original house plastered as well since it was never really finished properly. After plastering, we painted both the inside and the outside of the whole house. When it was all finished, we had a lovely little house!

Lorne and Evangeline Paetkau of MCC near Nairobi were our guests for a few days. Lorne was a building instructor from Saskatoon, Canada. He helped with the house project for a few days. They had two cute, lively, pre-school boys. The boys were quite intrigued when our cat started labor while Kristina was holding her. They watched in awe as the cat gave birth to three kittens right on the study floor.

The enlarged and completed director's house in 1988.

Mother Hansen's Visit

"I will be arriving on the 19ᵗʰ." My mother's message set our hearts pulsing with excitement. Elizabeth Hansen was on her way! She was actually coming to see us. This notification settled the long debate between mother and son as to whether she should come to visit us in far off Africa.

Since immigrating with her family from Russia to Canada at the age of four, she spent her whole life pretty much tied to sedentary rural living. At age sixty-seven, she found the prospect of international travel by herself intimidating. Also, she had to resolve ambivalent feelings of loyalty and obligation to her husband, my father, who was stretching out his last years, helplessly, in the local nursing home. Would it be right to leave him for a whole month? Mother decided, and now, she was on her way. Imagine our excitement!

First, she stopped in Germany, where she spent a week visiting her Dutch-Russian relatives who had recently migrated from Russia. She had never met most of them who had been born following her parents' departure back in 1924. What a reunion!

Her notification reached us at Ogwedhi on Monday, September 13ᵗʰ. Fortunately, we had planned to be in Nairobi on Thursday, so we could easily meet her on Saturday, the 19ᵗʰ. Kristina, her friend Marney Hopkins, Vera, and I met Mom at the airport on time. It was past midnight before we got to bed at the Mennonite Guest House.

The next morning, eager to show Mom as much of Africa as possible, we took her to the Ethiopian church service in the Eastleigh Fellowship Center where I gave a few words of introduction and exhortation. She was impressed with the lively singing and the friendly spirit of these refugee people. Then, we went to the Swahili service in the same building where she met some of the Kenyan leaders.

After lunch at the guest house, we sat around and talked for a while. Late that afternoon, we drove Mom to Kijabe to show her where our girls had been living and studying. She found this one-hour drive fascinating. The road passed through a rather densely populated highland countryside with the most beautiful landscapes and scenery. It was a great introduction to Africa.

We had shopping to do for the project, so we entertained Mom in Nairobi until the following Thursday. She was fascinated by everything and especially enjoyed being at the guest house, admiring the flowers and trees, and meeting the gardeners who could speak English.

She enjoyed meeting the many guests, missionaries, and dignitaries from different missions and other organizations. She expressed her feelings as being so privileged to meet all these important "high and mighty" persons. She always admired missionaries as being true heroes, herself being only an "insignificant uneducated farmer's wife!"

We took her on shopping trips downtown and to an Ethiopian restaurant. She enjoyed the food very much. Like a dry sponge, she absorbed as much as she could possibly soak in. She kept a detailed journal of all she observed and experienced.

We were still driving the old, green, single-cab Toyota Hilux pickup. Vera put some pillows in the space between the two bucket seats in the front, making it possible to seat a third person inside the cab, so she and Mother could squeeze inside. Kristina had to remain outside on the uncomfortable, improvised benches in the rear which offered protection from the elements only when we installed a tarp over the welded pipe frame.

On Thursday, we set out for Ogwedhi. We took our time, making several stops on the way, including the Nakuru Game Park where we saw what Mom described as, "A whole lake full" of flamingos, as well as monkeys, elands, and wild pigs. We stayed overnight in Kericho at the Tea Hotel, a popular, colonial era, tourist hotel, which kept the decor and customs of the British. She was impressed with the tea plantations. The next morning, with a few more stops along the way, we reached Ogwedhi in the early afternoon.

We had hoped to have the addition to our house finished before Mom came, but she was in a hurry to come, and the *fundis* were very slow to complete the work. They had promised to have the house ready for Kristina to move into her new room by the time we came back.

To our disappointment, they were still working on the ceiling, and the painting was not yet done, nor were the cupboards and closets yet installed. Outside, there still were piles of soil and rocks from the excavation of the septic tank. Consequently, Mom had to sleep on the lower bunk with Kristina on the upper bunk of the bed. Kristina did her correspondence lessons in the living room, which made it extra crowded. But we were all so very happy to have our mom and grand mom with us!

On Friday, we took Mom to a local *harambee* organized to raise funds to add a classroom at the God Ngoche Primary School, a school owned by the SDA Luos, where the project manager's children attended. In Kenya, it was common practice that the community built the school buildings, and the Ministry of Education provided the teachers.

In a Kenyan *harambee*, the whole community is invited to come together to raise money for a certain cause. They invite an important person, or official, like a member of parliament (MP) or a district commissioner (DC) or someone in authority to be the guest of honor to lead the meeting. This person is expected to bring a sizeable contribution to the cause. In this case, it was an official in a finance company known to the community. The program is usually a long, drawn-out affair with school choirs, traditional music, cultural dances, acrobatic displays, speeches by important community leaders, and, of course, a speech by the guest of honor.

When it came time to make the collection, the guest of honor would announce his generous gift. Then others would add theirs to it. Every time someone gave a generous gift, his/her name and the amount given was called out. Then the audience would clap, and a fiddle or drum or horn would let out a few notes. There was an element of competition. People might give several times.

When an important person gave, the people would support him/her by adding another gift to it, making his total bigger. The secretaries sat there counting and recording the amounts donated. Every so often, they would announce the total. Since that was "not enough for the classroom" they would encourage the people to start again and add some more. When the people stopped giving, someone would lead in a prayer, and then, there would be a feast.

We went late to avoid some of the long-winded boring speeches of the politicians given in Swahili or in the Luo language. We arrived in time to witness the actual fund-raising process. When we got there, we were given seats of honor in the pavilion they had erected with a shade of branches covered with banana leaves.

Then, there was the meal, starting with the important guests, among which we and our mom were included. The rest would follow. Mom enjoyed the program and the Luo cuisine which included rice, chapatis, two kinds of ugali, cassava and corn meal, two kinds of chicken, one boiled and one roasted, lamb, and meat sauce, all very tasty.

As the meal ended, there was a heavy downpour of rain. Most people ran for shelter. When the rain let up, I drove the truck up to the meeting place. Immediately the vehicle filled up with children who wanted a ride to town. However, they all had to get out when we had to make room for certain officials to go on a secret mission.

With all that cash on hand, the officials needed to spirit it away to an undisclosed location, out of the area, where it would be safe until Monday morning when it could be taken to a bank in Migori. Thieves had been known to break in and make off with the proceeds of a *harambee*. Therefore, we, with the treasurer, the headmaster, two policemen with their guns, and another elder, drove out of the area to a secure house in Rabour, some four kilometers away.

The next day, we took Mom to a dinner appointment in the home of Michael Ogumo's parents near Rabour. Mom was a bit surprised at the custom of not killing the animal until the guests have arrived. If the guests don't arrive, why would you want to waste the precious meat since there is no refrigeration? We made the mistake of not arriving early, as it was already 5:30 p.m.

The family welcomed us into their home, and the men engaged us in conversation for most of an hour before the women brought out and served the customary snack food of chapati and tea. The conversation continued while the slaughter and preparation of the evening meal was going on.

As it got dark, at their request, I entertained the family and some of the neighbors by showing a cinema. I showed some film strips featuring Bible stories and then some on family planning. The old man, Michael's father, didn't like the family planning topic and asked me to change the subject. However, I went ahead and finished (for the next generation). The old man had two wives and oodles of children, all of them as poor as church mice, but he was set in the old ways. Family planning was taboo. Finally, we had the long-awaited dinner. It was after eleven o'clock p.m. when we got home.

Mom was intrigued by a neighbor who joined the dinner party, a man who would not formally greet anyone with a handshake. Had not Jesus commanded, "Greet no one on the way!"? He belonged to one of many indigenous churches. He wore a dirty white uniform with the letters "S" and "T" embroidered in red on the front, symbolizing our "Suffering Savior."

The next morning, there was a joint service of Maasai and Luos at the Ogwedhi meeting house, which included a baby dedication. After the service, which included a long sermon translated in both languages and many choir numbers, Mom was asked to give greetings from her home. She was taken by surprise. It had to be translated into Maasai and Luo, but she did okay and was warmly welcomed. The service was followed by food. In Mom's words:

> Lunch was at the pastor's house. The men eat inside. They are the V.I.P.s, while the women and children eat outside, after the men are served. Hopefully, there is something left for them! Soft drinks are widely served to the guests, men mainly, women and children don't count. They have a hard life.

Having cared for a husband and raised five sons, Mom did have this thing about male domination and the injustice of sexual discrimination. She noticed.

Mom was impressed by the discipline, respect, and obedience shown by the primary school students. One day, coming from Migori, we stopped our vehicle at a school warehouse on the way to pick up cases of milk cartons for our students. This was a kind of repository where milk was stored by the government for distribution to the schools in the area. Our primary school was entitled to a certain number of cartons to be given on a daily basis to our students.

Seeing our truck drive into the yard, curious students, all in white and blue uniforms, gathered around to see what these foreigners looked like close up. A teacher came out, selected about a dozen boys, lined them up in a row, and ordered them to march into the storage room. Just as quickly, they marched back out, single file, each with a case of milk on his shoulder. Just that quick, the milk was all loaded.

Mom was impressed. Back home, in her society, the boys, even high school boys would stand around and watch, while the dads, men, or employees did the work. Here, the idle power of the student was utilized when there was work to be done. For example, if a classroom was to be built, the principal would order each student to bring one rock, a pan of sand, or a bucket of water to school each morning. If 400 students each bring one rock, it does not take long to have a pile of rocks. In the same way, if a fence was to be made, each student was required to bring one branch from a thorn tree each morning. The building supplies quickly piled up so the work could progress quickly with little money outlay.

Before Mom left Kenya, I took her alone to Maasai Mara to see African animals in the wild. It was a nice day, and we saw a lot of animals.

It was getting late and time to head back before dark. We had not yet seen any lions or elephants. She was disappointed, so I prayed, "My mom has come all the way from Canada and wants to see some lions and elephants. Couldn't you please show her some before she has to go back?"

As we were heading towards the park gate, we spied several elephants running towards the road from afar, as if someone was chasing them! So, we drove off the road towards the herd. The elephants temporarily stopped, and we got really close in the questionable safety of our little cab and took some photos. Then, one big bull came towards us and flopped his big ears, a sign of hostility.

Mom, being a little unnerved, said, "Let's get out of here!" I put the truck in reverse and backed to turn around and almost backed into a hole. I got the truck turned around and started going. The elephants kept on coming towards us. Mom was alarmed and commanded, "Faster, faster!" I laughed, and said, "Mom, this is the first time in my life where you told me to drive faster!"

As we neared the park gate, we saw two tourist vehicles a bit off the road with tourists looking at something. There were two female lions resting on a large ant hill close to the road. They were just lying there resting, so I turned and drove up to them and took some pictures. Mom was very happy. After all these years, it was a special day of bonding between mother and son!

On October 7th, Mom recorded some of her experiences with the Maasai in her diary:

> Today was the groundbreaking ceremony (to build the church at Enemasi). Carl took some men from here to help the Maasai get the building started. They left early in the morning. Carl worked for a while and then came for us to take us to visit Magdalena's house. She prepared tea and we visited and took pictures. She told us we were wanted at Rosa's house next door. Magdalena had to cook for her husband (She is one of his four wives.).
>
> So, we went to Rosa's house. She served us lunch, ugali with greens. It was good. More pictures. Then we had to go and round up the cows and take pictures of them with the cows. The Maasai are cattle people and are very proud of them. Finally, we got away.
>
> Carl was to pick up the workers at the church site … Then we had to go to Samson Masake's home for food. We ate outside in the shade of some trees … The women brought food—ugali with chicken and broth and tea with cooked bananas for dessert. Quite a crowd gathered, some very ancient people and some young ones too.... Very friendly people. Had good fellowship around the meal. Everybody shakes hands.
>
> There was a donkey tied, and every once in a while, he would let out his "song." I had never heard a donkey bray so there were humorous comments on

that. I had brought my tape recorder, so said I would record him. He wouldn't oblige for a while.... Then all at once he brayed and I quickly recorded.

Then I had to play it back, and oh what fun! The donkey perked up his ears and got interested and let out a two-song, which I also recorded. When I played that back to the people, they had great fun, and the donkey brayed some more!

Everybody gave affectionate "goodbyes" and greetings for Canada. They think I should come and live here. What a day, visited in two Maasai homes and ate in a third one!

... Another time, a wise old Maasai man, after hearing Andrew Okech preach, said to his people, "What he is saying is the truth. You listen to him! When I was young, some missionaries came but we wouldn't listen, and now we are behind!"

One day, we were sitting in a sister's humble home, in the living room that smelled of cattle urine. Our hostess was in the other room preparing *chai*, tea with milk and sugar. I turned to Mom and said, "Well, what do you think?"

She replied, "It is not as different as you may think. I was born in a similar house in Russia. Our home had a dirt floor, and the walls were also smeared with clay and cow dung, but with whitewash." The Maasai hadn't started that yet.

The next day, we took Mom to Muhuru Bay to visit Pastor Paul Otieno and his family, to see Lake Victoria, and to visit a fishing village. Paul was fishing to earn a living for his family. He gave us two large Nile Perch. Mom recorded her impressions of that special visit with the Luo people in her diary:

We visited there along the lake shore. It's very rocky. I'd never seen such rock piles. It looked like the Almighty had taken huge loads of big rocks and dumped them in odd piles.

We had to have lunch at Paul's house and meet the family. Ugali, chicken and tea. Visits are lengthy and hospitality is generous. Eventually, we left …

Then we stopped at Peter's house (his parent's home at Luendo). He had prepared another feast. Peter Otieno works on the project (OSP) as a milker. He had come with us on the way to spend a few hours with his wife and child and to visit his father, Pastor Samuel Otieno, who had been sick. But none of them were home, so he had to content himself with visiting mother, grandparents, and siblings. We were royally entertained and left. Peter came along. I am sure it was a disappointing day for him. That's the sad part in these situations, families are often separated because of jobs.

On the way we had to stop at a place for a pump and rope (for the well digging). We got the rope, but the pump was not available yet. So, it goes. So many trips for one thing. When we reached Migori, we were to pick up wire mesh and cement. Joshua, the storekeeper, had promised to be there, and of course when we came, he wasn't. He had gone to the disco. It was Fair day in Migori.

The following morning, October 9th, I drove with Mom to Nairobi and had dinner at the Guest House. Vera and Kristina stayed home as I was going to stay a whole week to do research at Daystar University College on strategies other missions were using in working with the Maasai in other settings.

After dinner, I took Mom to the airport, and she left that night for home. Thus ended a very meaningful three-week episode in our life journey and in her's as well. It was fun to show my mother around, giving her a glimpse of what our life was like so far away from her world. We think she enjoyed her stay, but for us it was much too short.

CHAPTER 16

Expanding the Reach

With fresh funds made available from Lutheran World Relief (LWR) in the summer of 1987, we were able to expand the reach of the Ogwedhi Sigawa Community Development Project in the months and years ahead.

We hired two additional extension workers, Andrew Okech from Osingo and Francis Ole Rikei. Although they were to work together, Andrew was to cater to the Luo side of the border while Francis was selected by the Maasai elders to work with the Maasai side.

In Nairobi, at the end of July, I ordered a new Toyota Hilux double cab, four-wheel drive pickup truck to be imported to Gudka Motors in Kisii duty free. Also, while in Nairobi, I looked for two motorcycles for the new extension program. I didn't find them on that trip.

The dairy crew included two milkmen who delivered the milk
to patrons along their routes by bicycle each morning.

The field crew tended the crops, tree nursery, fishpond, and other maintenance tasks which made the project a success.

The tree nursery grew to produce up to 20,000 seedlings per year.

Digging for Water

Since the beginning of time, people and animals alike drank their water from the rivers, streams, springs, and puddles as nature provided. As the human population increased, pollution of these primary sources of water also increased. Nature endowed both humans and animals with a built-in immunity that enabled them to tolerate most of the water-borne diseases and parasites. However, there was always a portion of the population that became infected and suffered the debilitating and sometimes fatal effects of these contaminants.

As Leon Ressler launched OSP, he strategized to introduce exotic breeds of animals, which were less tolerant of the local water-borne parasites and diseases. In the interest of better health for all, he immediately dug a water well to provide clean water for the project's livestock and for his family. He did not allow any of the animals to drink out of the creek that ran through the OSP property.

As we planned for the second phase of the project, we included a budget item to provide a number of sanitary wells for public use.

We found that digging the wells was not a simple thing. The earth was highly compacted, decomposed fractured rock. Diggers had to use hammer and chisel to loosen the fragments bit by bit. Progress took hard work. By the end of October, we had two crews digging for water at two locations. Both struck water, one at nineteen feet, and the other at twenty-eight feet.

As the water began seeping into the holes, digging became more difficult. Dewatering pumps had to be installed and used to clear the space for additional digging. This slowed progress as the digging cycle was interrupted by stopping to pump, then, dig again until too much water interferes, then, stop and pump out the water. Then, dig some more until the water level makes digging impossible again. Then, pump some more, and repeat.

Finally, when too much water came in, the dewatering pumping and the digging stopped. Then, concrete culvert rings, measuring one meter in diameter, were inserted and stacked into the hole, forming the curbing, and a concrete top and apron were put in place. Finally, a hand-operated pump was installed.

The completed well on the Ogwedhi Sigawa
Primary School premises.

The Boarding Facility

From the time the Ogwedhi Sigawa Project was first conceived, the Maasai community leaders felt the primary school must have a boarding component. Still in their semi-nomadic state, they were somewhat familiar with practices in other parts of Kenya of putting children into boarding schools. They assumed it would be the right practice when they would settle and build primary schools in the Ogwedhi Sigawa area, that some of the parents, especially those from a distance, would want to include a boarding facility.

When we arrived, the project was largely built up, and this need for a boarding facility was next on the agenda in the minds of some of the management committee members. I observed that most of the local Maasai children were walking to our primary school, and other primary schools were being started in the various communities in the Maasailand interior. I did not see the urgency for establishing complicated and expensive boarding facilities, so I did not make it a priority in my fund raising.

However, when World Vision offered OSP the above budget "give away" items, the committee members voiced their priority for a boarding component to be added to their school. Accordingly,

World Vision allocated 120,000 Ksh. towards implementation of their vision. This was another example of available money triumphing over common sense, where injection of unexpected money determined the priorities of a project rather than the real need.

The Ogwedhi Sigawa Project was charged with building the facility, which would include a dormitory for boys, a kitchen, a dining hall, and a latrine. The launching and operation of the boarding component was to be in the hands of the school administration. A second dormitory for girls would come later.

However, even with the financial assistance of World Vision, there was not enough money to bring this vision to reality. The community had to be involved.

The management committee decided to hold a *harambee* on November 28th. We expected about 400 people to turn up that day. A lot of enthusiasm was generated, and a lot of energy expended in planning the program, in publicizing the event, in inviting the people, and in preparing food for the expected crowd.

The *harambee* was well organized, well executed, and well attended. However, the people didn't give as we had expected. We had hoped for 200,000 Ksh., but only raised 41,000.

We anticipated opening the boarding facility in January 1988, but with such a shortage of funds, this became an impossibility. A large boys' dormitory building was completed, However, we still needed to make 120 wooden bunk beds, finish the walls, roof, and floors of the dining hall and kitchen, as well as the toilets. We had to postpone the opening of the boarding school until the needed funds could be found.

It was not until January 1989 that the Ogwedhi Sigawa Primary School boarding facility for boys was finally opened with only twenty-five students. It had the capacity to accommodate 120. Many of the parents who clamored for it when the decision to build was first made, now felt they could not afford the fees.

The lesson to be learned from this project was do not take the clamoring of a community about a need too seriously until the people themselves make a significant contribution towards meeting that need. We had started with OSP providing the money up front. The failure of the *harambee* to raise a significant amount of funds locally should have been warning enough that the community, as a whole, was not behind the boarding school project. After operating at half capacity for several years, it was closed.

In retrospect, we should have used that money to assist the Ogwedhi Sigawa Primary School which needed six more classrooms. The kids in some classes were studying under the trees. The two grade one classes each had about ninety students per class. Such overcrowding was hardly conducive to learning. Yet, the previous year our grade eight students, taking the national exams, scored the highest in our area. The school ranked number one out of seventy elementary schools in the region.

Because of its good performance, kids were leaving other schools to try to find a place in our school. Where we had 300 students back in 1984, by 1989, that number had risen to 570 students. Classes were overcrowded. Vera's sewing class, which used to have fourteen students, now had forty-seven. Could she really teach them all to sew on four machines? We really needed more classrooms and more sewing machines.

Guests

Two missionary couples from Somalia came to visit us for four days in December 1987. One was an MCC couple from Guelph, Ontario, and the other couple, Kevin and Sharon Yoder of Elkhart, Indiana, were serving with EMM. We had a nice time with them. Young people have so much energy and enthusiasm. They plowed with our oxen, cut napier grass, and fixed the eve troughs on the house.

On Sunday afternoon, one of the men accompanied me on a journey to Narok. We started out after church, taking seven Maasai men to a weeklong church conference for Maasai arranged by CMF in Narok. After driving for five and one-half hours, arriving at 8:00 p.m., we were disappointed to discover that the meeting had been postponed until next Sunday. Again, a phone would have saved us a lot in terms of time and money!

Two Christian families gave us lodging for the evening and breakfast before we all set out to return home. Narok is beyond Maasai Mara towards Nairobi. We had a nice view of some animals near the park including a pack of wild dogs and a cheetah family, a mother and five almost-grown babies.

A week later, we took the men back to Narok on our way to our annual EMM/MCC Worker's Retreat. The men returned home the following Saturday by public bus.

That fall, Beth Brubaker, a twenty-year-old student from Pennsylvania showed up for a visit. She was with a group of students from Earlham College doing a cross cultural study in different parts of Kenya. She spent one week with us, then joined her group for a final week of study. She decided to stay on after the study and returned to us on December 7th, living with us and working on our project up to February 24th.

Beth was a farm girl who was willing to do any kind of work. So, we drafted her to paint many of the OSP buildings. Beth painted all the wood trim on the barns and office building green. They looked much better.

Beth was a nice big sister to Kristina. After her time with us, she and Kristina took a few days off to visit the coast near Mombasa.

Another Quiet Christmas

We returned home from the retreat two days before Christmas. Kristina and Beth, our volunteer, worked together baking all kinds of good things. It was nice to have young people around. Vera and our house helper, Pilista, worked on a large batch of plum, rhubarb, and strawberry jam. On Christmas Eve, I showed some filmstrips to the interested people at the Ogwedhi Church. We closed the meeting at 9:30 p.m. and went home to open our presents. Some of the church people stayed on for an all-night service which ended at 9:15 a.m. Christmas day. After having a group breakfast, they went home for the big day.

Our celebration continued with a visit and a Christmas meal in Barack and Lois Ogola's home. We came home around 6:30 p.m. and enjoyed a quiet evening with the girls, eating snacks, playing games, and singing Christmas songs like "Silent night, holy night, all is calm ...," and retired for the night. It had been a nice, quiet, peaceful Christmas day.

CARL E. HANSEN

The calmness and silence of this holy night, and our deep peaceful sleep, was suddenly shattered at two a.m. by loud knocking and excited voices outside our door. Half-awake and groggy, I fumbled for a flashlight and stumbled down the hall over to unlock the door. There in the darkness, stood a policeman and several agitated Maasai men. There had been an attempted cattle theft, and one young *moran* got a spear stuck into his abdomen. There were two cuts and intestines were hanging out of both cuts! Could I rush him to the hospital in Kilgoris?

So, I did and got back around 6:00 a.m. The boy was one of the thieves. The others fled into the night. We later learned that the boy had shown signs of getting well, but then died of the infection caused by his wound. If he had survived, he could have faced court and a stiff jail sentence of three to seven years. It was so sad that a promising talented life, full of potential, was wasted, cut short, lost. To the mother, father, siblings, family, friends, community, a great loss. Who gained? "When will these young fellows ever learn?"

Handsome, fashion-conscience moran, so full of potential for good.

The day after we left to go to the retreat, our dog, Toto, died suddenly. We wondered whether she had been poisoned. She was an exceptionally good watchdog who kept a lot of undesirable elements away, and we always felt safer with her around. Now we only had Ngema, a sort of useless, friendly, floppy fellow who would just as soon be petted by a thief as by one of us. It was unfortunate that the policemen had recently been transferred away from their station near our gate.

When the policeman and the Maasai woke us up that night, our two watchmen were both fast asleep, and they never woke up when I drove out. Can you imagine how secure we must have felt in the midst of a community of cattle thieves, drunks, thugs, burglars, men of violence, and sleepy watchmen? Yet, in the naivety of our faith, like the Psalmist, we never lived nor slept in fear because:

My help comes from the Lord, the maker of heaven
and earth.
He will not let your foot slip.
He who watches over you will not slumber ... nor sleep.
The Lord watches over you ...
The Lord will keep you from all harm—he will watch
over your life.
-- Ps. 121:2-7 (NIV)

In retrospect, in our naïve faith, we did not connect the fate
of that murdered missionary in Migori with our situation. In that
oversight, we saved ourselves a lot of needless worry and sleepless
nights! Living daily by faith has many uncounted benefits!

A Mennonite Disaster

Before leaving Canada for Kenya in mid-1985, we had authorized our
close friend, Joe W. Kauffman of Tofield Alberta, to act as our power
of attorney to take care of our business. We had sold our acreage
to a middle-aged couple in August 1984. We naively and trustingly
sold it, requiring no down payment but held the mortgage on which
they were making monthly payments to us. That had worked fine
until early 1987, when their business went bad, and they stopped
making monthly payments. Instead of informing us or our legal
representative, they simply abandoned the place. They had little
equity in it so had nothing to lose.

This meant the property legally returned to us. That was okay; we
could easily sell it to someone else, but there was one big problem.
The foolishly ambitious couple had undertaken a major remodel of
the house, inside and out. They had demolished the three upstairs
bedroom partitions, planning to make a grand bedroom suite in
place of the three small rooms—a plan they left unfinished. They had
removed the staircase and cut a hole in one of the downstairs room
ceilings, planning to install a grand spiral staircase leading to their
grand suite upstairs—staircase incomplete.

Outside, they had removed the front porch, planning to make a
large deck instead—no deck, no porch, and no steps to the front door.

They had done all the demolishing work, which cost them nothing, but had no money to install the new grand ideas they had.

Thus, the property was left with no front porch, no staircase to get upstairs inside, a gaping hole where the staircase had been, another gaping hole in the nearby ceiling where the new staircase was to be. It was a huge mess to repair and clean up before we could rent the house out or put it on the market for sale. And we, the owners, were in far off Africa trying to be missionaries helping others with their development problems.

Our dear Christian brother, Joe, a retired farmer, and frequent Mennonite Disaster Service volunteer, shared our problem with another dear brother, Lloyd King, also an older retired farmer and frequent Mennonite Disaster Service volunteer. Both were members of our Salem congregation. They decided this also looked like a "Mennonite disaster." Therefore, they set to work donating over three months of their time and energy and expertise to restore the house into a livable and sellable condition. They put the stairway back in its old place, patched the hole that was made for a new staircase, and put in partitions upstairs to make two bedrooms and closets.

Because the entire yard, including the raspberry patch, had turned to thistles, Joe cleaned the whole acreage. Then he rented it out on our behalf. They did all this for us. We did not have to do anything, only pay for the replacement materials. True Christian brotherhood!

Later, when we returned to Tofield on furlough in the summer of 1988, while the renters were on vacation, Vera and I slept in our old house for a week and repainted the outside and installed steps to the front entrance where the porch had been.

Maasai Mutual Aid

The above story reminds me of the time I was driving through the bush near Osero. There were no roads where I was going. Suddenly I came upon a most unusual scene. There before me, near a small stream, were a group of about a dozen Maasai men washing a large herd of cattle with buckets of water and scrubbing them clean. Some of the cattle were dead. Some of the cattle were laying in various stages of dying. Others were standing but showing signs of being in great agony while the men were frantically washing others. Their efforts seemed to be futile.

I stopped to greet the men and learn what was happening. One of the men explained that the herd belonged to the one young man sitting there looking very dejected. As was the custom, he had sprayed his cattle with a caricide to control the ticks that brought tick-borne diseases. Instead of buying the regular caricide from our project or a reliable retailer, he had listened to a slick salesman who brought this "effective" caricide contraband from Tanzania for a much cheaper price.

Being illiterate, he could not read the labels, so in good faith, and to save considerable money, the young man bought the chemical and sprayed his cattle, more than one hundred of them. Now the animals were dying. The caricide was actually a deadly chemical, pure poison that was used to control weevils in cotton plantations.

The less than twenty-year-old owner of these cattle was sitting devastated watching his cattle die before his eyes, all his wealth wiped out in one fell swoop. I went over to him wishing I could give some words of comfort and encouragement. But, because of the language barrier, I was tongue tied.

A couple of elders came over to him to comfort him. They begged him to do nothing rash to himself, like suicide. They assured him, "The cattle we will replace, but you we cannot replace. You are more important to us than the cows." I asked my interpreter, "Will they replace the cattle for the young man?" My interpreter, said, "Yes, each one of us will bring one or two animals from our herds, and in the end, he may get even more than he lost!" An unbeatable insurance policy!

This was an illustration of a very deep value we found in Maasai culture. They were nomads, but that did not mean individualistic. They were a very communal people. Within the clan or tribe, they really looked out for each other.

Whenever thieves stole someone's cattle, all the young men of the community went after the thieves. Whenever there was a wedding or a circumcision or any kind of celebration, the whole community was involved. Often a whole truck load of beer and another load of soft drinks would be delivered to the home of the one putting on the celebration. Several bulls would be slaughtered and roasted over an open fire. And everyone in the community was welcome to come to the feast and celebrate for two or three days. Each one was encouraged to eat and drink as much as he/she could.

When the feast was over, or whenever a participant felt the need to go home, he would thank the one who put on the feast, compliment him on the good time they had and invite him to "Send one of your youths over to collect an animal from my home." The offered animal may be as small as a sheep or goat or calf, or even as large as a cow. Leon Ressler once commented to me, "Besides the Maasai, I have never heard of a society where someone could put on huge parties and get wealthier in the process!"

CHAPTER 17

Church Developments in 1988

Reconciliation in the Church

I n January of 1988, David Shenk, now replacing Harold Reed as EMM director for East Africa, and his delegation came on their annual visit. They met with the pastors and the bishop and tried to work out some of their disagreements. They persuaded Bishop Zedekiah Kisare and Pastor Musa Odongo to meet and talk at Kisii. Musa was the recognized leader of the opposition at Kisumu. Kisare apologized and asked Musa for forgiveness. The talk went on for three hours, and Musa also asked for forgiveness, so they embraced.

The next week, Bishop Kisare went to Nairobi for several days. Pastor Musa and the other two pastors from the Kisumu group came to meet him and to formally ask him for forgiveness and to call off the rebellion. In return, Bishop Kisare agreed to ordain Musa to be the bishop of the Kisumu area churches.

However, the division between the Southern sub-diocese and the Kisumu sub-diocese was not healed. Bishop Kisare decided to have a second bishop ordained in Migori. So, there would still be a divided Kenya Mennonite Church. Being the younger and better educated pastor, Joshua Okello Ouma was the logical choice to fill that office. The date for the two ordinations to take place was set to be in August 1988, a time when we would be on home leave.

Preparations were made, and guests were invited. It was going to be a big event in the history of the church. Bishop Noah Hershey, representing the North American Lancaster Mennonite Conference, was to come as a fraternal guest.

As the time approached, Bishop Kisare and seven other people were travelling in their Land Rover on their way to Kisumu when their vehicle collided head on with a big lorry near Kisii. Four of the eight were flown to Nairobi with broken bones. The other four were driven back to Shirati the next day. The bishop was the only one with no broken bones but sustained a bad cut on his head. His wife had a broken bone in her neck. Each one recuperated in his or her own way, but they all missed attending the ordinations. Bishop Kisare authorized Bishop Noah Hershey to do the honors of ordaining the two men in his stead.

Extending the Expatriate Presence

The mission board delegation visited Migori and us at Ogwedhi on February 4-5. In response to our request, they agreed to try to recruit and send another missionary couple to work with us, exclusively in Maasai church planting. We anticipated that this other couple should live somewhere in the interior of Maasai land away from the OSP compound and its Swahili culture. They should learn the Maasai language and culture. They would oversee the evangelistic and church development aspects of the OSP work and would be accountable to the Kenya Mennonite Church. We would have to build a house for them.

We also requested the mission to send a nurse, but they did not promise. About fifty percent of the Maasai babies died before reaching school age. Magdalene's twin babies, Aaron and Anna, both died before reaching their first birthday. We tried to hire a Christian Maasai nurse to do a community-based health program. He promised to come but never arrived.

Since the third year of our contract would be completed that spring, the EMM representative informed us that we were invited to return to the present assignment for another term, after a three-month furlough in the summer.

A House for Pilista

Our house help, Pilista, being an outcast widow, felt the need to have her own home. She saved her pennies and began talking of the need to buy a plot of land in her home area. This became an obsession for her.

Finally, in the spring of 1988, we gave Pilista a sum of money to make a down payment on a plot of one acre of land at Luendo, about forty kilometers west of Migori. She planted a crop on it, while we were on home leave that summer. Later, we made another contribution and she built, or had someone build, a simple house on it for her. At the time, we didn't know what her plans were, if she would continue with us or become a farmer at her own home.

According to Luo tradition, when a person dies, he/she must be buried somewhere close to the door of his/her own home. Thereafter, no one will live in the house. It may be used as shelter for farm animals until it falls into disrepair and is removed and forgotten. Then the land returns to be cultivated, and the grave is eventually forgotten. The spirits of the dead are believed to hover around the vicinity until lost to the memory of succeeding generations.

Consequently, even in modern times, every Luo who moves to and lives in the city must have some kind of "house" in his rural homeland, and his body must be transported back home for burial at all costs, which are sometimes exorbitant. This tradition seemed to be the motivation for Pilista, rejected by her deceased husband's family, to provide a home for herself, a retirement home, and a place for burial.

A House for Domtilla

One Sunday afternoon back in the spring of 1987, some of the men from the Ogwedhi church met with me. They wanted to discuss how to build a new house for Domtilla, a poor elderly widow whose termite-eaten mud and thatched hut was about to collapse. She was living on church land behind our house. Her late husband had been the leader when the congregation was first founded. The elders wanted to build a one-roomed, stick and mud house with a tin roof but weren't sure how to raise the money, about 2,000 Ksh ($200).

The matter was put on the agenda for the next church district leaders meeting. On July 4, 1987, twelve leaders representing nine congregations met, and after much discussion, decided that the churches would build a house for the poor widow, Domtilla. They would have to organize a *harambee* to raise the funds.

Now, in the spring of 1988, the church elders started to build a simple $200 one-room hut for our neighbor, Domtilla. By March, they had completed the installation of the tin roof and mudded walls.

Before the door and one window were installed, her old grass-roofed hut succumbed to age and termites and collapsed. Domtilla moved into the new one, though it was not finished. She was very happy but was now demanding a cement floor. In all the great achievements of humankind, there is always room for improvement. My hardened conscience was slightly troubled as I recalled how much money we had spent to add a bedroom and bathroom to our large comfortable house the previous summer. What does the injunction, "love your neighbor as yourself," mean in this context?

Pilista and Domtilla with neighbor children

Baby Dedication

One Sunday, we attended a worship service and baby dedication at Osero. About seventy people were present. Twenty-two babies were dedicated. Some of them were not actually babies but older children. Baby dedications had become an important ritual in Kenya because upon completion of the process, a dedication card was issued by a recognized church with the child's name, parent's names, and date of birth. This became an important document for later when the person would apply for a national identity card or need any other form of identification.

Baby dedication at the Osero church, note the pews.

Church Growth

About thirty Maasai women gathered at a home on a Friday near the end of March 1988. The woman of the home was sick—all except one of her children had died. Her husband decided that, since they had tried all the local medicine men and she was still unwell, they better try the church. Therefore, he called this meeting of Christian women in his neighborhood. We also were invited to come and pray for her. The husband who invited us was an influential man in the community, but he himself was not present. The men did not like to meet when a group of women were involved.

When we arrived, we found that two Pentecostal Maasai evangelists were also present. After a time of worship and preaching, one evangelist gave an invitation to accept Christ as savior and lord. Many of the women responded, committing themselves to follow him. It was a very meaningful time. Many of those who responded had been coming to our churches off and on. Then we had prayer for the sick woman. I cannot recall the outcome of that prayer, but the whole experience changed the lives of those women. The little churches were carrying on. As is often the case, the interest of individuals waxed and waned. There is so much truth in Jesus' parable of the sower, the seed, and the soil.

Magdalena came to visit one day to pour out her soul. Language was still a problem. I could hear her but could not express all I wanted to say. Her second twin died in January. She took it very hard. "Why didn't God hear her prayers?"

A few weeks later, she came again. She was her usual strong self, very confident that the men would soon come to faith in Christ too. Because many of the women who had been coming to her church were now blocked by their husbands, her group was small, but they were listening to tapes at home and were teaching their children. "In the fullness of time ..." there will be a strong Christian Maasai community. Her church at Osero started a nursery school out under their tree. They had thirty pupils.

We wanted to get started with the construction of the church building at Enemasi. The congregation had held a dedication service for the plot back in March of 1987. Then, in July, we staked out the site and started the heavy work of leveling the land on the hillside by hand. Then, there arose a dispute over the boundary. In the interest of peace, the leaders moved to a new site about one hundred meters to the south of the original and leveled a hillside plot there. Construction started in April 1988. At the same time, we started digging a well nearby.

Later, after the boundary dispute was settled, the former leveled site was chosen as the right place to build a house for the coming missionary family.

In early March, we held another leadership seminar for the diocese. This time we invited guest teachers from World Vision (Kenyans). They didn't stay as long as we planned, so I filled their slot with lectures for a day and a half. I realized I really enjoyed teaching, even if I needed to use a translator. About fifty church leaders from our churches and surrounding churches of other denominations were present. We fed and bedded them for four nights.

Small Steady Steps of Progress

The road from Awendo to Ogwedhi was being rebuilt, at least in part—graded "for the first time since 1974," neighbors said. For the next few months, using it was much smoother and faster. However, the crew did not finish it properly; there was no provision for drainage and no gravel. The same old water holes were reborn as soon as the heavy rains appeared. It soon became the same old dirt road.

Our first order for ten tons of barbed wire and nails from the factory in Nairobi arrived in March 1988. These items became staples in our agricultural supply shop and earned OSP a fair profit in the following years.

During the April rains, we planted about 2,500 eucalyptus trees in the creek area at the far end of OSP property. The banana plantation was growing nicely. We planted a half-acre of potatoes.

On another trip to Nairobi in April we took possession of two Suzuki 125 motorcycles we had purchased for the extension program.

Adding a Driver in Time

As was amply portrayed in this account, a large portion of my time and energy was taken up in driving. After two-and one-half years of wearing myself out, not to mention the vehicle, I finally got enough sense to hire a driver. I do not know why it took me so long. Several people, whom I did not know, had applied for the job from time to time. My automatic answer had always been, "OSP does not need a driver!"

But then, Caleb Omondi, son of our doctor, Meshack Omondi, graduated from high school in Tanzania and came home to live with his father and siblings. When he applied for a job, it suddenly dawned on me that I really needed a relief driver. He had just gotten his license and asked me to let him practice. After I saw him perform, he was hired.

That was one of the best decisions I made. Caleb was smart,

mechanically inclined, and enjoyed his work. His driving took a huge load off my shoulders. Also, he came at the right time. OSP would need a dependable driver if the vehicle was to be used during our absence over our upcoming three-month home leave.

CHAPTER 18

Kristina, a Cross-Cultural Bridge

Kristina adapted well to her year at home, setting up a routine. She did her grade ten correspondence lessons in the mornings and devoted her afternoons to more practical cross-cultural studies. Making contacts with the women in the churches on Sundays, she would visit in their homes on the weekday afternoons. The young women and mothers were delighted to have her come and visit them in their homes.

She learned to communicate with them in the Swahili language. These new friends taught her how to dress in their cultural clothing and decorate herself with their jewelry. She hardened her feet to walk the many kilometers through the Maasai bush barefoot. She tried to learn as much as she could about their culture. As the friendships deepened, Kristina took to extending her visits in some of the homes, even sleeping with their families on some weekends.

The people loved her. The men were forever inquiring about marrying her. Even the women were inquiring about her marrying either their own husbands or their sons. It was an interesting culture.

Kristina shared something of the relationship that led to the receiving of a cow from her friend, in an article published in the October 1988 issue of the *Missionary Messenger* (a publication of EMM).

Noonkipa: Rafiki yangu (my friend)

Kristina 'Noonkokua' Hansen

Noonkipa Enole Sikawa lives near Ogwedhi, Kenya. She is a member of the Kenya Mennonite Church. Noonkipa is a Maasai and my best friend.

Noonkipa is in her late twenties and is the mother of four children, "Noonkipa", which means "prosperous woman", shares her husband with three other women. Her husband, Ole Sikawa, who is about twice her age, has a herd of 1,030 cattle and is one of the richest and most respected men in the community.

Although Noonkipa is probably twelve years older than I, she and I are very close. She teaches me about the Maasai culture, and I try to tell her about my culture. One day I brought popcorn for her family and showed her how to prepare it. They all loved it, (even more than chocolate cake!). Ole Sikawa told me that when I leave, he will be stuck with eating beans again.

Noonkipa and I have a unique relationship. She doesn't speak English, and I don't speak Kimaassai, so we visit in Kiswahili—which I don't know very well. I enjoy going to Noonkipa's home and spending weekends with her. Her home is a simple mud hut with a thatched roof. The front room is a sitting room by day, and barn for the calves at night. The bedroom, which is also a kitchen, is very simple, with stick beds and a fire on the ground. Noonkipa spends many hours there preparing the family meals and cleaning her "kibuyu" (gourds) where she puts the family milk supply.

Noonkipa's daily routine goes something like this: She awakens at 4:30 a.m. and rekindles her fire. Then she prepares tea for her husband and children and cleans her gourds, which are made of dried and hollowed calabash. She puts a burning stick into her kibuyu and rubs the coals against the sides to sterilize the gourd from bacteria. This cleansing not only cleans the kibuyu but gives the milk a pleasant, smoked taste. The gourd she later washes out with water to get rid of the dust.

At about 7:00 a.m. she goes out to milk her cows. Milk is the main food for the Maasai, so her family drinks a lot of it; the extra, she sells for a bit of spending money. At about 9:00 a.m. she finishes the milking and then cleans away the manure from her yard. After that she makes breakfast, which is usually rice and potatoes, for her family.

The rest of the day may be relaxing, or it may be very busy for Noonkipa. She may spend it sitting under a tree making beautiful jewelry and decorating kibuyu with beads, or she may go to a "harusi" or celebration. It may be a day of a marriage or circumcision.

Or it may be time to take corn off cobs and grind it into flour. That requires an hour's walk to town where the nearest mill is located. While in town, Noonkipa will buy her groceries and sell some milk. Or it may be time to mud her house, a hard and tiresome job.

At about 6:00 o'clock in the evening the process of milking all those cows starts again. After that, she must put all those animals to bed and make supper, probably rice and potatoes again.

In the evening the whole family sits and listens to God's word on their cassette player. Even Ole Sikawa listens quietly as the gospel sinks into his consciousness. Noonkipa says he loves God and is very close to making a commitment. Ole Sikawa used to love *pombe* (local beer) but now he has put it away. "It's not good for my head: pombe is bad," he told me.

Kitamooek, the church in which Noonkipa is involved, is simply a few benches under a tree near her house. The church, which was started three years ago at Ole Sikawa's request, now has about ten women and many children as faithful attenders. There are no men as yet, but hopefully that will change.

Noonkipa says that before she became a Christian, she was very jealous when her husband slept at another wife's house. She would pout for a week and refuse him food or tea when he asked for it. But now, she says, when he comes home, she immediately prepares a pot of tea out of love.

"You 'wasungu' (European/foreigners) are lucky not to have polygamy," Noonkipa says, "but now that I am a Christian, I must face it with a good attitude and show my love for my husband."

Noonkipa not only accepts those aspects of her culture that cannot be easily changed, but she knows it is God's will for her to set a Christlike example by having a loving attitude despite situations that are contrary to her Christian faith that she must live in.

In Maasai culture, when a person gives another person a cow as a gift, it is a sign to everyone that those two are very close and special friends. The day before our family left Ogwedhi for our furlough, Noonkipa gave me a cow.

*Kristina and her friend, Noonkipa, with
the friendship gift of a cow*

CHAPTER 19

Intermission: A 1988 Furlough

Retreating as Part of the Missionary Strategy

E very year in early December, about 150 EMM missionaries and MCC volunteers, including their families, abandoned their posts in Sudan, Ethiopia, Uganda, Somalia, or Tanzania, and converged on the campus of the Brakenhurst Baptist Conference Center near Limuru, Kenya. There they participated in the annual East African Regional Retreat for most of a week.

Besides attending such annual retreats, each worker was encouraged to "get away" from his or her place of work for three weeks of vacation each year. Further, they were expected to go on furlough or home leave for a few months every two to four years. The sending agencies obviously believed that retreating is an important part of their missionary strategy.

Jesus included retreating in his strategy for advancing. In Mark 6:7 we find Jesus sent his disciples out on a ministry assignment. After some time, they reported back to headquarters. While the disciples were trying to debrief, the crowds pressed in on Jesus with their needs so urgently that there was no opportunity to "grab a bite to eat" let alone to hear their reports. Finally, when Jesus saw that "enough is enough" he maneuvered them into a boat saying: "Come with me by yourselves to a quiet place and get some rest." v.31. It turned out that the only rest they got was in rowing the boat, for when they reached the "solitary place" they found a crowd of needy humanity expectantly awaiting them. Their planned retreat turned out to be another "ministry opportunity."

From this story we learn that even the disciples had needs. They needed to report back to their leader their successes and their failures.

They needed his feedback, his words of approval and encouragement and his suggestions for improving their ministry skills. They needed adequate food and rest. They needed to become physically detached from their field of ministry, a time for solitude, a time to be alone with Jesus.

We expatriate missionaries, pastors, volunteers, Christian workers all have needs that only retreating can satisfy. We may be recent recruits, almost overwhelmed by homesickness for friends and loved ones, or for anything that sounds, smells, tastes, or looks familiar. We may be in deep culture shock finding everything strange ugly and distasteful, feeling that we don't belong, and wondering why we ever came in the first place.

We may be overwhelmed by the trauma of living and serving in crisis situations such as war zones, refugee camps, famine areas, or city slums. The hopelessness and a thousand injustices that go with it wear us down, and we just "got to get away before we lose our minds!"

We may be older "seasoned" workers that are spiritually, emotionally and physically "burned out." We may be disillusioned wondering, "Why are we here?" What have we really accomplished of lasting value?

We may feel that we are being "used" by the local officials who hope to exploit our presence for their own advantage. We may be disillusioned with the local church leaders who seem to have no vision, who call us "brothers" and "sisters" yet treat us like aliens from outer space and value us only in terms of what material gains we might bring.

We may be disillusioned with our sponsoring agency. They may appear to us to be insensitive or bungling bureaucrats of diverse visions who have lost direction, who mostly react instead of lead, who send us on vague assignments that aren't thought through or that conflict with our gifting and sense of call. Or we are given assignments that we are not trained nor gifted to do, while we see others assigned to do the things that we have expertise in.

We may be disillusioned with ourselves. We spend so much of our time, energy, and resources on self-maintenance. We want to do so much, yet we are hampered and restricted by cultural and language barriers or by our own human limitations. We feel so useless and under-productive. Then, other unforeseen obstacles turn up in our path that destroy any effectiveness we might have had. We see our lives as wasted, as failures. Is this what we were called to?

Then there are those personal flaws of character, our failures and our sins. They trip us up and prevent us from ever being the kind of people that we wished to be or from having the kind of relationships that we hoped to have. God seems so far away and spiritual disciplines so unreal. Maybe we should just quit and go home? How we need a retreat, some refreshment, to come away and rest awhile before we fall apart.

Jesus saw the need and planned a retreat with his disciples. But it was aborted due to the pressing needs of the masses. Then we saw Jesus call upon those tired disciples to minister to the physical need of food for more than five thousand hungry men. They were tired, their spiritual energy was gone. All they could do was to calculate how they could limit the need to meet the resources. They would invite to supper only as many as their budget of two fish and five buns would allow. Too often that is the way most of us missionaries and missionary organizations operate. We cut out programs when the offerings are down. But Jesus had another approach. He invited them all to the banquet, then blessed the resources to meet the need!

Again, we see the difference between the disciples and our Lord. They went off after supper for a boat ride, each with his basket of leftovers. All night they worked up a storm on that lake to get away from the crowd. Jesus retreated to the mountain to pray. Sometime after 3:00 a.m. the disciples were still sweating at their do-it-yourself oars when Jesus finished his retreat and came advancing across the waters, stepping over the troublesome waves and through the storm!

It is so important for us to maintain immediacy with Jesus, to surrender our personal needs to him, the need to be liked or admired, the need to be successful, the need to be rewarded, the need to be recognized or given credit, the need to be right, the need to be in control. With Jesus close, we must renounce ownership of the work. It is his. We must give it back to him! We have been unable to feed the crowd. It is better that we surrender our few sandwiches, our own goodness, our few talents and abilities, each act of service to him, and let him bless them and multiply them to feed the masses!

We need to "come apart" before we fall apart. We need that quiet time on the mountainside alone with Jesus where we can get some rest. There he will hear our reporting in, will sooth our wounds, will forgive our failures, will reinforce us with constructive feedback, will renew our vision, restore our courage, and empower us to walk with him over the troublesome waves and through the storms and the superhuman demands of the crowds that await us where we will advance.

Preparations for Home Leave

After serving a three-year term, following the mission board policy, we were granted a three-month furlough or home leave. It was a time to leave our work and worries behind and go home, visit our children, families, and supporting friends. We ordered our tickets to fly on May 15th, 1988.

As expected, preparation for our upcoming home leave was hectic. To make it even more so, of all weeks, it was during our final week that we all got sick. Vera's case was confirmed as malaria. Kristina and I suffered the negative effects of being inhabited by some kind of flu bug of an undesirable type. The doctor's prescription removed the malaria symptoms in Vera. However, the side effects of the Fancidar cure made her almost as sick as the disease did. In misery, she forced herself to make the preparations to leave.

Getting things in order in preparation for our departure involved several trips. One trip was to Kisumu to purchase medicines to keep the health services in business. On the way, we discovered the need for the aging Toyota to get a broken brake fixed. With the brake fixed, we took another trip to Sotik to purchase and bring home a truck load of eight Holstein/Sahiwal pregnant heifers for resale to interested farmers.

Another two days were spent going to Migori to purchase building supplies and deliver them to Enemasi so that construction on the new church building could commence. I wanted to have some things in place, so work could go on while I was away.

Then Vera, sick as she was, and I were invited with Barack to visit Osingo Mennonite Church. It had rained all night and the roads were at their worst. The people at Osingo wanted to honor us, thank us for putting a roof on their church, and give us a proper farewell, so they had a service at which I preached. Then, we were served a delicious meal in Wilson Ogwada's home.

On the day before leaving, Caleb took the old truck to Kisii to have a squeaking bearing and a noisy clutch repaired. After spending the whole day in the garage, he was able to bring it home late that night.

We arose extra early the next morning, loaded the truck with the building supplies for Enemasi, and sent Caleb to deliver them while we prepared ourselves for leaving. When he returned around nine o'clock, we set out for Nairobi. By that time Vera was feeling a lot better, but Kristina had a sore throat.

We spent the next day shopping for supplies for OSP which Caleb took back to Ogwedhi with the truck. The last day was spent shopping for a few gifts to take along to North America.

Intermission, a Pause that Refreshes

Three months is not a lot of time when one's schedule includes meaningful engagements with family, friends, supporters, and employing agencies spread out in two different countries and several destinations in each country separated by thousands of miles.

Our first stop was in Ontario where we visited my brother Paul and sister-in-law, Irene, their family, my uncle Chris Hansen, and other relatives and friends for three days.

On May 19th, we were welcomed in Philadelphia by our daughter, Cindy and John, Vera's mother and brother and his wife, Sanford and Mildred King, and family. We were able to attend John's graduation from Eastern University where he was awarded an MBA in International Economic Development.

During this time, we visited our supporting agency, Eastern Mennonite Missions for debriefing. We also got our recommended medical checkups. Kristina's skin test showed positive for exposure to TB, though her chest x-ray was negative. She was given a six-month preventative prescription.

On June 29th, we flew to Calgary, Alberta, where my brother Peter, his wife Margaret, and my mom met us. My brother Charles loaned us his old Chrysler as he had just purchased a new one. This gave us wheels to travel around, visiting relatives and friends in various places.

While spending a few weeks in the Brooks area visiting my parents and siblings and their families, we also got to spend some time with our daughters, Karen and Sheryl. They had come home to Alberta for work that summer. Karen was staying with her uncle and aunt, Peter and Margaret, and Sheryl was staying at her cousins, Wanda and John Evans' home. They both had summer jobs in a restaurant in Brooks. Cindy and John also came from Pennsylvania to join in the family festivities.

Kristina's friend and former roommate, Iryne Kamau, flew from Kenya to Alberta and joined us for a few weeks. She was happy to be introduced as "Our Kenyan daughter." She enjoyed traveling with us as a part of our family, even to a family reunion. Her dad was a successful merchant and didn't mind supplying her with all the spending money she needed, even to the point of paying for Kristina's travel to accompany her to California.

We attended the annual meeting of the Northwest Conference, which was hosted by Salem Mennonite Church in Tofield. We lingered and visited friends in the area. Vera and I spent several days painting the exterior of our house while the renters were on vacation. Driving to Eaglesham, we visited my sister, Freda, her husband, Tom King, and their five sons, and my uncle and aunt, Ed and Faye Friesen and family at Fairview, all in Northern Alberta.

We attended a Friesen Family Reunion at Olds Agricultural College in August. As was the tradition, the family held an auction sale to raise funds to pay certain expenses. They sold family heirlooms, donated items, handicrafts, etc. They made about $1,600. Of this, they paid the expenses and gave $700 of the surplus to us for our work in Kenya.

Too soon, the time came to say once again, "Goodbye" to all our children, family members, and friends; to sadly turn away from our loved ones and resolutely turn our faces towards far away Africa for another three-year term of service. We left for Nairobi, arriving on August 19, 1988.

Going home

Upon completing the events of our home leave over the past three months, I wrote some reflections around the question, "Where is home?"

We stow our carry-on luggage into the compartment above our heads. We settle into our seats, fasten our seat belts, and breathe a sigh of relief. The busyness of the final weeks of intense preparations fades away and a fresh excitement rises in us. Our thoughts turn towards home. We are really going home! Now!

But for near middle-aged missionaries, what and where is home? Did we not just leave our home in Ogwedhi, the community where we lived and shared and belonged for the past three years?

Our plane touches down in Toronto, Ontario. My brother Paul is there to whisk us off to spend a few delightful days with his family. Ontario is so familiar. The sights, the sounds, the weather, and even people's accents remind me of the home I knew for seven of my most impressionable years. This is still home, the place where I made the transition from childhood to youth. It is good to be home!

A few days later, we are celebrating our daughter Kristina's birthday in our eldest daughter Cindy's apartment in Philadelphia with all our children present. We have never been here before, never slept one night in this "City of brotherly love." Yet, this precious time of reunion with our children makes this little apartment home.

We are driving into the village of Parkview in Virginia. There is that cozy little apartment by the "E-building" where, for three years, we enjoyed our honeymoon nest. Across the road lies the whole EMC campus dressed in its familiar summer splendor. Yes, this too was our home for five years. Somehow, we belong.

Later, we are fellowshipping around a picnic table generously spread with the finest Pennsylvania Dutch cuisine in the little town of Belleville in Pennsylvania. Around the table are our close family including ninety-five-year-old Grandmother Sadie Hartzler and Mother Elizabeth Yoder. It is really great to be home!

A few weeks later, we arrive in Duchess, a small village in a fertile, irrigated district on the prairies of Alberta. Here is where I was born, where I started school, where I graduated from High school, where I first learned about God and later dedicated my life to his service. Here is where my father and mother, brothers and sisters and nephews and nieces live, and where my grandparents are buried.

This is the place I left behind so many years ago; the place that filled my thoughts, longings, and dreams those first years of separation and homesickness when I went off to college in the East; the place I have always given as my "permanent" address whether I have been living in Virginia, Ethiopia, Indiana, Tofield, California, or Kenya. It feels so good, so right to be home again!

Later, we turn into the short lane to our house near Tofield, Alberta. This at last is our house. We even hold a clear title deed to this little place. For nine wonderful years we raised our four children and entertained our many friends here. Friendly people in the church and in the community welcome us home. Community children have grown, adults are about the same, although a few of the older ones have "gone home." There is so much to hear and say, so many questions to ask and to answer. It is wonderful to catch up, to be home!

And then, so soon, our furlough is over. We stow our carry-on luggage into the compartment above our heads. We settle into our seats, fasten our seatbelts, and look out the little round window searching for the familiar face of a loved one to wave goodbye to. But they are out of sight, gone. A lump tries to rise in my throat. Three months pass all too quickly when one is home!

Again, the question comes: "What and where is home?" A refrain from a catchy song learned long ago comes to mind. "This world is not my home, I'm just a passing through. If heaven's not my home, then Lord, what will I do?"

Yes, I recognize there is yet another deeper dimension to home than we have yet experienced. But I leave that to the future and to God. I appreciate all the many homes I have here below. Jesus' promise comes to mind: "There is no one who has left house or brothers or sisters or mother or father or children or lands, for my sake and for the gospel, who will not receive a hundredfold now in this time ..." Mark 10:29-30 (RSV).

I like that and am satisfied. Our thoughts turn to Ogwedhi. Anticipation mounts: How are things at home?

CHAPTER 20

Re-engagement

U pon our arrival back in Kenya, we spent a week in Nairobi doing business and waiting for Kristina. She and Iryne arrived the following Saturday night. The two young girls had had a good time in California, saw Disneyland in Anaheim, and visited some of Kristina's acquaintances in Pasadena.

Our welcome back to Kenya included getting my pocket picked on a bus in Nairobi. We had been to the bank, took out 5,000 Ksh., put 2,000 into Vera's purse, and put the rest as a wad in my pocket. We went on a bus to save taxi fare. It was crowded, and we had to stand in the aisle. When the bus stopped, some young people from the back made a mad rush to get off. There was much pushing, and immediately I felt my pocket. The wad was gone, 2,800 Ksh. of it! Only 200 remained. So much for earthly treasures. I knew I was back in the fray.

On Monday, we drove to Ogwedhi. As we passed Kisii, we checked in at Gudka Motors. Our new truck still had not arrived.

Rumors of War

Rumors circulated of a fresh outbreak of warfare between the Wuasinkishu and the Siria clans, in which "many people were killed on both sides." However, upon reaching our community, we found, from local sources, that one man was killed, and two others were wounded. I was still not sure what the whole story was. At the moment, the clans were tense but not fighting. Each blamed the other for starting it. The Enemasi church was on the Siria side. The Osero church was on disputed land on the Wuasinkishu side. Work on the church building at Enemasi was interrupted. People had to hide in the bush for several nights out of fear of raids on their houses. Their thatched roofs were very vulnerable to attack by fire if the occupants were asleep inside.

Church Growing Pains

The ongoing construction of the Enemasi Church building had not gone ahead as planned. The walls, made of stone and mortar, had reached up to the windowsills. The rest of the tasks—completing the walls, purchasing and cutting eucalyptus trees for the rafters, installing the rafters, nailing on the corrugated iron sheets, installing doors and windows, plastering and painting the walls, and cementing the floor—remained yet to be done.

Most discouraging of all, the money supply was depleted. The community would have to organize another *harambee* to raise more. The outcome of the last *harambee* was so disappointing that we were not particularly optimistic this time.

The community elders let us down completely while we were away. They had promised to contribute by raising money, gathering stones, digging the foundation, and carrying water. They had done absolutely none of these.

Only the elder, Samson, and his wives had been gathering all the stones and carrying the water, hosting the *fundis*, and contributing food and money for the *harambee*. He had tried so hard; we felt we couldn't let him down, or else we might have pulled out of that community. We saw him as the only light in a very dark community. We, the church people, must stand with and encourage him so that he may succeed.

Our re-entry into church life began with an invitation to visit the church at Osero. Some of the women from Kitamooek Church joined us. After the service, about nineteen people climbed into or on the truck, and we drove back into the bush to bring condolences to a young woman who had just lost her baby.

We crowded into her hut, had prayer, sang several songs, gave some "words of God," prayed some more, then visited as she and her co-wives made tea and served us rice, tea, and sodas. Then we gave her a small gift of money and said, "Goodbye!" The Christian women enjoyed doing things like this together.

Another group wanted to start a church and requested us to help them with a teacher. Another challenge. Good evangelists don't just drop out of the sky!

In late September 1988, we visited the church at Oloonkoijoo. A group of about forty people attended the grass-covered *kanisa* or church they had built. We persuaded the students there to plant about 3,000 cypress seedlings, supplied by OSP, to establish a living fence around the plot allocated for a church and school.

On October 9th, all the district congregations held a joint baptism and communion service at the Ogwedhi church. Ten new believers were baptized, four of them Maasai women, and five others were taken into membership on confession of faith. After the service, all were served a snack with tea.

Under Investigation

I was unable to attend this service because our Chairman, Ole Sikawa, was taken by the police the previous night. Two of his wives came early in the morning begging me to help them with the vehicle to find him.

Apparently, a certain Luo man disappeared in the Maasai bush and was presumed murdered. The police had been interrogating people through beatings and torture to gain information. The day before, they came to Ole Sikawa's house, beat him, his wife, Noonkipa, and his children. Then they took him, one wife, and one child to Kilgoris for questioning. So Noonkipa and another wife were rather distraught and came for our assistance.

I took them to Kilgoris and found Ole Sikawa at the police station. He was okay. The police on duty assured us they would release him to go home with us. However, there was a big celebration in town, and the police inspector, the only one who could sign the release paper, was attending there.

We waited five hours and watched the celebration but gave up hope he would be released that day because the "big boys" were going to have a feast after the program. Therefore, we returned home without Ole Sikawa with the promise, "He will come tomorrow."

Like Vera often said, most of my trips "are in vain." At least the wives slept better that night. We never heard the outcome of the police investigation. Did they ever "Get their man"?

In my absence, Pastor Paul took care of the baptisms and communion, so nobody was disappointed that I was not present.

Developments in the Fall of 1988

One Sunday evening, Kristina and Vera got a sudden notion to bake a cake for Kristina to take to school. They moved the only pressure lantern to the kitchen and began their marvelous creative work. I had to move my chair to the doorway to share the light so I could read.

Early the next morning, September 5th, I took Kristina, with the cake, to Migori where she caught a ride with Joe Bontragers who were driving from Shirati, Tanzania, taking their daughters to RVA. I only hoped that her cake would arrive in some semblance of its original artistic beauty.

Kristina had decided to return to complete her high school at Rift Valley Academy. Our baby was beginning 11th grade. Her experience of home study was good, but she felt she needed the interaction of peers and the discipline of a structured setting. Once again, her absence brought back those familiar feelings of loneliness. Somehow, the house seemed so empty. How we missed our children!

The weather was dry in September. The pasture grass was not growing, and the cows were getting skinny. Milk production was very low, despite the fact that the cows had given birth to twenty new calves in the previous four months. We had to reduce the herd, so we sold some of the cows. Barack also sold all our sheep and goats. They were unprofitable and the people were not much interested in them.

We planted 700 pineapple plants and several hundred more banana and mango plants, hoping to create a substantial fruit orchard that would help sustain OSP once funds were cut off.

Official Honor to the "Dear Leader"

The Honorable Daniel Arap Moi had been ruling as President of Kenya for ten years. It was high time his loyal subjects celebrated their good fortune. Therefore, Friday, October 14th, was declared a national holiday in his honor. His loyal supporters arranged for all the *wananchi* (citizens) to have an opportunity to celebrate. They held celebrations all week in the different government administrative areas such as the towns, the higher district headquarters, and of course, the provincial and national levels.

A celebration at our school ground was held the previous Monday for the local community. Different school choirs came and sang the praises of our president. Then, they had sports competitions. Migori had their big celebration on Friday at the fairgrounds.

An International Wedding

For us, there was a conflict. We had been invited to attend the wedding of Jannette Mummaw, an EMM missionary, and Joseph Nyakema, a Tanzanian church leader at Shirati, Tanzania. Friday, October 14th was the day we had scheduled to drive there, and we had committed ourselves to bring the new bishop, Joshua Okello along.

Now, Bishop Joshua Okello was on the program to offer the opening prayer for the festivities at the Migori Fairgrounds, so on our way to Shirati, we had to stop in and wait awhile until he performed his official duty there. These civic affairs in Kenya never got started on time. There was always a long wait until the appropriate official would arrive to officially open the activity. The more important the official, the longer it seemed to take him to arrive at the venue. Of course, we got off to a late start.

When we finally came to cross the border into Tanzania, the officials informed us that there was an entrance fee of sixty dollars (USA) to take our vehicle in. We were prepared for that. Unexpectedly, the officials also demanded that we exchange fifty dollars (USA) into Tanzania shillings before they would let us in.

We were caught off guard. We only had eighty dollars with us. Finally, we persuaded them to let us just exchange twenty dollars instead of fifty dollars. We wondered, given the fact that they could negotiate the fifty dollars exchange requirement down to twenty dollars, how many of these regulations originate with the government, and how many were created by the officials for their own benefit? How accountable were they? I think we knew the answer!

We went to Shirati without any other problem. We stayed at Dr. Tom Ruth's house for the weekend. We witnessed the uniting of Joseph and Jannette into the bonds of holy matrimony as scheduled. The couple were both in their forties and had known each other for a long time. They had a nice wedding, a mixture of American and African customs. More than 300 people were in the church but not quite so many at the reception.

A Conflict of Conscience

As frequently happened, I had a conflict of conscience versus management policy. While OSP had ample budget to purchase a new vehicle plus three new motorcycles plus supplying adequate operating costs, Pastor Paul Otieno had to go on foot to tend his pastoral duties and use the public bus to reach his home in Muhuru Bay. To provide transportation for him was really the Kenya Mennonite Church's responsibility, but they had no funds to cover this budget item, and they made little attempt to find such.

We felt accountable to the donors for keeping these two items separate, especially after he borrowed one of OSP's new motorcycles to go home to Muhuru Bay and kept it there for a week. Then upon his return, he had an accident with it and broke his collar bone.

Fortunately, someone in the EMM hierarchy agreed to supply a good used motorcycle for the pastor to use. We brought it home from Nairobi for him. He had to learn how to check the oil and how to maintain it. Pastor Paul was a very happy man!

Hurry, Hurry Has No Blessing!

A Swahili proverb says, *"Haraka, haraka, haina baraka!"* or "Hurry, hurry has no blessing!" or like our positive statement, "Haste makes waste." In our experience, there was abundant room for *baraka* because "hurry" was a very rare commodity. After returning from our furlough, nothing seemed to move according to schedule. Progress could be counted in very small increments. I was frustrated.

Groundbreaking for the Enemasi Church occurred in October 1987. Thirteen months later, in November 1988, the stone and cement walls of this very small one-roomed building were up. The carpenters were promising to put the roof on "this coming week" (November 12). Then, there were the doors and windows to install and the final plastering and painting to be done. Could it be finished by Christmas, as they promised? Hopefully not Christmas 1989!

Constructing the building progressed very slowly because we refused to do it *for* the members. We insisted that they must raise some of the money and do some of the work, and then we would work *with* them as we were able.

A major cause for the delay in constructing the Enemasi Church, while we were away on furlough, was the flawed character of the builder we hired. He was an Anglican, "Praise the Lord!" type deacon we thought we could trust. However, the open opportunities of the moment allowed his lusts of the flesh to overpower his holier instincts. He took pay for work uncompleted, sold some of the boards, and used some of the lumber to make furniture which he sold to the community folks. Finally, he ran off with the church elder's wife and five children and could not be located anywhere. By his conduct, the name "Christian" in that pagan Maasai community was not enhanced very much. It seems Satan has plenty of willing collaborators, even among the "people of the cloth."

At Ogwedhi, the primary boarding school was to open in January 1989, the beginning of the Kenyan school year. The dining hall and kitchen were almost ready, but construction of the 120 beds, started in February 1988, was only two-thirds completed.

Also, the carpenters who took the contract to finish the beds in May stole one-third of the boards, said they were out of supplies, quit, and ran away while we were on furlough. This required that we had to purchase more boards and hire a new carpenter. Would he do better?

One small Maasai church group stopped meeting because the leader moved away. However, a bigger and stronger group emerged at the place to which she moved. These mostly women's churches were basically stable and growing. We were seeing growth in depth of knowledge and commitment rather than in numbers. The long hoped-for breakthrough among the men had not materialized.

Another disappointment concerned the failure of our mission agency to find and send a second missionary couple to work with us specifically and exclusively as a pastor/church planter. They had begun the process of recruiting an experienced missionary couple from Germany who were eager to join us for Maasai church work. However, this seasoned couple decided to submit to the negative reaction of their sending agency in Germany, and so declined our invitation to join us.

Additionally, there was the matter of the much-needed vehicle we had ordered back in July 1987. In November 1988, we were still waiting to take possession of it.

On Being Worried to Death

During those several months, I was having an uncomfortable feeling in my stomach area. It didn't go away, so I went to a German specialist in Nairobi who gave me an endoscopic examination to see if there was an ulcer or something else.

The doctor found that there was no ulcer, but an acute inflammation which he called a "pre-ulcer" in the lower stomach in the duodenum region. He took some biopsies which showed no abnormalities or malignancy. He informed me that this condition was caused by too much stress and that I must "stop worrying." He said, "Let me give you some advice. You will never change Africa, but Africa will kill you. Stop worrying!"

So, I stopped worrying. No, it was not that simple, but I did deliberately take a more *laisse faire* attitude, relaxed more and let things go, at least I tried to. After some months, the uncomfortable feeling disappeared. I could not change Africa, and up to now, Africa hasn't killed me either! *"Haraka, haraka, haina baraka!"*

I did not think of myself as a worrier, but I found it hard to detach myself emotionally from my work. I was not an "eight to five" man. I did think a lot about our work and all the things that needed to be done. It seemed my sphincter muscles were weak, giving me sensitive bowel syndrome. I had to learn to relax more so they could tighten up properly; then I was okay.

Progress

By the end of 1988, a few positive developments were encouraging. The Enemasi church roof was installed in December. Installing the doors, windows, and plastering the walls was in progress. A few more men were coming to that church.

Progress in water development was moving ahead very slowly. By December, two wells were completed with pumps and were being used. Three more had cement curbing installed and were ready for covers, cement superstructure, and pumps. For curbing we were using one-meter diameter reinforced concrete culvert type rings, stacked upon each other from the bottom of the well. Three more wells were waiting for the curbing to be installed.

Also, in November 1988, we met Fred Darling, a sixty-year-old retired electrical engineer, scientist, and "Jack of all trades." We were introduced to him by Paul and Erma Lehman at the Mennonite Guest House, where he was staying. Fred was a member of their congregation in Newport News, Virginia. He was visiting Kenya for a two-month helping assignment with another mission. His assignment fell through, so he had little to do. He was hanging around the guest house, disappointed and waiting for his flight home.

We invited him to come and help us at Ogwedhi for a few weeks. He was very happy about the opportunity to help. We went shopping for a solar electrical system for our house, and then I took him home to Ogwedhi where he installed the system and wired the house. I let Caleb assist him and learn from him. Fred was very happy to be useful, and we were very happy about his usefulness and for the lights we now had in every room. It was a basic 12-volt DC system with only one panel and could not power large appliances. But we were thankful for the lights and enough power to run our tape player.

CHAPTER 21

Launching a New Year: 1989

A Christmas Surprise

At the beginning of her December vacation, Kristina brought her new roommate, Berit Erickson to Ogwedhi for a week.

Our vacation plans took a sudden change when we got an unexpected telegram from Sheryl. The surprising news was that she would be arriving at the airport in Nairobi on December 9.

Our plans were that we would make a trip to Nairobi in mid-December to attend the Annual Missionary Retreat at Brackenhurst. Adjusting to this new situation, we went a few days early and picked Sheryl up at the airport and spent a few days with her at the Methodist Guest House, then at the Catholic Flora Hostel.

This was quite a pleasant surprise for us. However, we were concerned to learn that she decided to quit college. She had lost motivation. Why go into enormous debt to go to college when you don't know what you want to do with your life? She decided it would be best to work for a while until she knew what she wanted to become. She felt she needed her parents and came for one month.

Sheryl and Kristina went to Mombasa for five days to visit Berit's home and tour the coast while Vera and I took in the Annual Missionary Retreat at Brackenhurst. After the retreat, we did business in Nairobi until the 23rd when we all went home to Ogwedhi.

We celebrated Christmas together. Sheryl got to dress in Maasai clothes and follow her sister to all her friends' houses. She was struggling. She enjoyed being with us and enjoyed being back home in Kenya. She knew she needed to prepare herself, but just wished she could live and work in Kenya.

Kristina went back to school on January 4th by MAF plane from

Migori. Then we followed a few days later with Sheryl. We stayed the weekend at RVA where Sheryl could visit friends and the staff she remembered. On Monday, we took her to do some final shopping. After a last supper in an Ethiopian restaurant, we took her to the airport. After enduring a two and one-half hour check in, we were informed that the plane would not leave that night. So, we all went back to the guest house for the night. Sheryl took a mid-afternoon flight the next day.

It was very healing for Sheryl and for us to be together. She was having adjustment problems and identity issues. She still needed her parents, especially her mom. She also needed to find work to support herself and pay her school debts.

In Kijabe, Kristina adjusted back to her old life at RVA. As before, she was not happy. She was doing well, grade wise, just like her sister. However, she did not like the pushy, pious spiritual attitudes of many of the staff. She felt they were so pharisaical, so censorious and judgmental and hence, hurt a lot of kids by drawing premature conclusions, without really knowing the kids concerned. She felt they treated her, as well as some of her friends, with suspicion as an outsider, like you were guilty until proven innocent.

Truck Troubles

After Sheryl's departure, we spent several days doing business in Nairobi. Our old vehicle was put in the garage to replace three u-joint bearings. That took two days.

Vera decided to stay for a one-week course on "Teaching Adult Learners to Read and Write." This course was taught at a CMF missionary's house at Melili out in the Maasai wilderness near Narok, about four hours from Nairobi. I left for Ogwedhi on Friday at 6:00 a.m. by my lonesome self, with our vehicle loaded with supplies.

Around 7:30, as I started down the big escarpment past Kijabe, descending into the Rift Valley towards Naivasha, there was a sudden rumbling sound and vibration under the vehicle. I stopped to find a new U-joint bearing had fallen out. What could I do but crawl under and take off the drive shaft? I needed to take it back to the city to get it repaired.

But what do I do with the vehicle loaded with valuables that could easily get lost? With no mobile phone and no AAA to call, could I trust someone, a stranger, to watch it while I went for repairs?

I stood there for a while, beside the road with my disabled Toyota, contemplating my dilemma and watching the many cars hurtling past down the hill. I felt very alone, but not for long. Shortly, one of God's angels, a passerby, stopped to see if he could help. He suggested that, since there was a slope downhill, I could let the vehicle coast down around the bend, out of sight, to where there was a small hotel. Perhaps the people there could keep an eye on it for me. So that is what I did.

Then, carrying the offending drive shaft, I caught a *matatu* back to Nairobi, had the bearing replaced again, and this time welded into place. They had neglected to weld it the first time. Then, I hired a taxi to take me back, installed the shaft, and continued my journey at around 2:00 p.m. I arrived home around 8:00 p.m., tired, hungry, and lonely, but thankful.

Busy, Busy

The next morning, we had a seminar at Enemasi for Maasai Christians. The building was now complete except for cement on the floor and some trim and paint.

On Tuesday, I went back to Migori and then to Kisii to finish paying for the new truck. Wednesday, Barack and I went to Kilgoris to see the chief and DC about some applications and school affairs. Thursday, I spent the only day at home in two weeks catching up on OSP business. I spent Friday and Saturday in Migori, attending a church leaders conference.

The closing of the meeting on Saturday night marked the end of my long, lonely, busy week. I was immensely relieved when Vera disembarked from the bus, and I brought her home. She had a very good experience with eleven other missionaries from CMF at the literacy course. Now she could supervise literacy work.

The following Sunday, we took three Maasai to a similar course at Kajiado, south of Nairobi for one week. We expected them to hold literacy classes for adults who wished to learn to read.

A cultural development of note was a dance held in Ogwedhi one night. Somebody rigged up a loudspeaker to a portable battery system. We could hear the music as if it were just over by the barn. I went to bed, "No dancing for me tonight!"

Saga of the Duty-Free Truck

Back in July 1987, we had ordered a new Toyota Hilux, double-cab, four-wheel drive pickup truck through the Toyota dealer in Nairobi, in connection with Gudka Motors in Kisii. We were assured it would come with the next shipment from Japan, probably in January 1988. I was also told that if we applied as a non-government charitable organization, we could get it duty free. Since we could save 190,000 Ksh. or about $19,000, we decided to apply for it duty free.

An essential part of the process included presenting a letter from the DC in Homa Bay, verifying OSP's tax exempt status. Accordingly, we submitted a request to the DC asking for such a letter of exemption.

Four months later, we still had not received the requested letter from the DC, so I went in to see him at the end of November. The DC had not even put the matter before his committee. Since December was a vacation month, I doubted whether we could have the letter before the end of January.

It was mid-March 1988 before we were informed that our new truck would arrive "next week." However, it would be a single-cab model like the one we had, and we would have to pay the full tax. That was not what we had ordered. I gave up on duty free and re-ordered a duty paid double-cab, one like we originally ordered.

Upon our return from our summer furlough in August 1988, the truck still had not arrived. Then, we were informed our new truck was supposed to be in Kisii, although it had not yet arrived when we went to see it. There, we were told that it was being brought in "tax-free," but we would need to present the proper papers showing our tax-free status. The only way to get it duty free was to get that duty-free status paper from the DC, which I had requested thirteen months ago with no action resulting. I needed help.

On September 26th, I went to Migori to appeal to the member of parliament (MP), Mr. Okwanyo, to ask him to help us get the new truck duty free. The MP was also Minister for Regional Development in Moi's Federal Government, so he was important in the hierarchy, far above that of a DC. So, if this MP was my friend, as he said he was, I thought he would put some pressure on him to wake him up.

Mr. Okwanyo promised to do what he could and was to have the answer by the weekend. When I returned to Migori for his answer, the Honorable MP had not returned home that weekend.

In October, we got word from the dealer that the truck was not tax free. However, if we paid the full amount at delivery, and if we could get tax-free status later, we could get the tax portion reimbursed. Could we trust the government to return the tax paid? Could we even get the tax-free status letter later? We did not understand the different messages. Was the dealer passing our ordered vehicle on to others waiting further down the line? We decided to wait and see when it arrived what the real truth was.

In November 1988, while in Nairobi, I stopped in to see if our tax exemption application had been processed. We had started the process sixteen months before. Now they said the truck was coming duty free. Therefore, we had to reactivate the duty-free application. This time that reluctant DC, under pressure and realizing no "gift" would be forthcoming, granted us his signature, so we could proceed with our request to the ministry level. Then, we were told that the vehicle was here but needed the duty paid. Our hopes were high that we could save all that tax, so we decided that we would wait for the next shipment, maybe in late December, to get it duty-free. Even in our most optimistic moments, could we really see this as "progress"?

Finally, in January 1989, while in Nairobi, I got to see our new vehicle at the Toyota dealers before they drove it to Kisii where Gudka Motors was to install the tape deck we had brought from the USA and to register it and have the OSP name and address painted on the driver's door as required by law.

On the first Monday after returning home, Barack and I went to Migori to see the education officer about securing more teachers and then on to Kisii to collect our new vehicle.

Yes, we actually took possession of our long-awaited, white, Toyota Hilux, double-cab pickup. To say it modestly, we were quite happy. It was only three years that month since I drew up the application to fund this vehicle, one and one-half years since the money came, and eleven months since I made the down payment. Of course, we appreciated driving this new treasure, a truck like no other.

We spent the first half of February in Nairobi getting a capsule built on the back of the new truck. It was done at a body shop. Being a Hilux double-cab, the pickup had a rather short box. Therefore, the capsule had to be short as well. The capsule was a metal box on the back with a door at the rear, windows all around, and folding seats for six. Also, there was a roof rack over the cab so we could haul longer things like lumber laid across the capsule and the cab. Not bad. The white color of the truck reflected the heat of the sun a lot better than the dark green of the old one. We loved our new truck. It was worth all we went through to get it.

We had long since promised to sell the old truck to Ole Santian, the father of Francis, our bookkeeper, whenever the new vehicle arrived. Ole Santian troubled us about our promise for more than a year while we waited for the ordered and ever delayed pickup to arrive. Neither he nor his son had any experience nor training nor license to drive or maintain such a vehicle. However, Ole Santian was the owner of over 800 head of cattle and could afford it.

As soon as the new Toyota came, we released the old one to them. Francis soon learned to drive it, and they used it to transport people for hire.

On the way near Kisii some months later, a cow, beside the road, foolishly stuck its face out in front of our truck, as we were hurtling by at about sixty mph. The two connected. The impact knocked one horn off the cow, and I can imagine gave it a severe headache. The poor thing stood there bewildered, shaking its head. The front of our new vehicle was badly disfigured. The owner ran away and left the cow in its misery. It could have been a lot worse. Repairs to the vehicle cost over 6,000 Ksh.

Encouragement from Ethiopia: Kalifa Ali

On one of my business trips to Nairobi, I had the privilege to meet and spend some time with Kalifa Ali, an old friend and colleague from our Ethiopian days. He had come to Kenya seeking medical treatment for cancer in his lymph glands.

Kalifa Ali had been one of my students for three years of high school at the Nazareth Bible Academy, a Muslim boy from Bedeno who became a Christian. I attended his baptism in the Awash River with about nine others. He was always at the top of his class. Later, he joined our team at Bedeno as a teacher and then principal of the Bedeno Mission Primary School. Before we left Ethiopia, he transferred to teaching in St. Joseph's, a prestigious Catholic school in Addis, for a few years. There, he could take university by night school, which he did and completed.

Kalifa was called by the Meserete Kristos Church to be its full-time executive secretary. In 1982, he was among those church leaders imprisoned for four and one-half years by the Marxist government. He referred to that experience as "my long vacation."

While in prison, he was put in charge of work details, like the biblical Joseph. He was active in witnessing and won many to Christ. He and the others also carried out a teaching program. He learned Italian, French, and German while in prison.

Later, after being released, he began looking for a job. He wanted to work for the church. The elders told him now was not the time, so he was praying about what to do. His wife, Yakuta Abdo, had a hospital job and was supporting their three children while he was away. As he prayed, he heard God say to him, "Go outside." He thought that was strange, so he phoned his wife at work and said, "God seems to be telling me to go outside. What do you think?" She answered matter of factly, "Well, go outside then!"

Kalifa went outside for a walk to see what would happen. Soon, he met a man on the street who greeted him, so he talked to him. The man was the director of World Hunger, a relief organization. Kalifa told him a bit of his story and that he was looking for a job. The man said, "Come to my office tomorrow." Kalifa was given a job and was soon promoted to deputy director for the whole Ethiopia program, next to the man in charge. He travelled to places like London and Geneva where he could practice his German.

Kalifa worked at that job for two and one-half years and was being groomed for the lead position when the church elders approached him and said, "Now is the time." He resigned from his post and resumed his work as executive secretary of the church. Yes, Kalifa was that precocious Muslim student from Bedeno, but now, at age forty, he had attained the stature of a spiritual giant. I was reminded of Jesus injunction, to not despise any of "these little ones." God has packed them with potential that no one can predict!

Another of the mysteries of how God runs his universe, that I could never understand, was how and why, in his prime, Kalifa's life was cut short by cancer. Believing he would be healed, he travelled to the USA for treatment, but after another year, succumbed to the disease.

Development Education Leadership Training Activity

In March 1989, with the encouragement of LWR, Barack Ogola, Andrew Okech, and I joined a one-week "Development Education Leadership Training Activity" (D.E.L.T.A.) workshop at Kitui. It was sponsored by a Catholic organization, so we attended mass every day. It was an interesting and learning experience. The course would meet for three more weeks at three more times at three more places during the next two years.

We were among forty participants, three Caucasian and the rest from various African nationalities, mostly Kenyan. Most of the participants were from Catholic organizations.

I found the D.E.L.T.A. teaching very helpful. I was introduced to a lot of new and interesting people. In the final workshop, there were still thirty-six of us, all Kenyans except one Irish sister. Andrew and Barack had dropped out of the program early on. The Catholic presence in Kenya was well established. We drew on the vast resources of this worldwide church. They were well educated, well organized and had done a lot in development and leadership training.

Literacy Classes

While I was at the first D.E.L.T.A. workshop in March, Vera attended another one-week conference on Adult Literacy Training and Evangelism. Upon her return, we sent three Maasai to Kajiado for another week of training in how to teach adults to read.

Following that, Vera started teaching Pilista how to read. Francis

Ole Rikei and Esther Sankale both started literacy classes in the area. Sadly, when these busy mothers and wives discovered that learning to read took a lot of concentration and time, they tended to stop coming. The literacy program gradually fizzled out.

CHAPTER 22

Church Planting and Rumors of War

The Maasai clans were at war again in March 1989, still fighting over land. This time it was between the Siria and the Moitanik. Rumors circulated that a few more had been killed about fourteen kilometers southeast of Ogwedhi at Masurura. Government officials were trying to settle it peacefully. Enemasi was just over the boundary in Siria land.

About two months earlier, we had organized a seminar there for Maasai church leaders. Many of the Wuasinkishu Maasai attended. Later, some of the husbands scolded their wives for going over there. "Are you women really going over there to make peace with the Siria before us men?" It was a testimony that in Christ the enmity has disappeared.

Trouble flared up again in late April. Again, rumors came our way that a few had been killed. I went to Enemasi with a group of Maasai evangelists to try to talk with the elders, but they were not to be found. The men sleep and live in the bush during war because it is dangerous to be trapped in one's house.

Therefore, we went on to visit our newest church at Olmisigiyioi inside Siria land, about four kilometers beyond Enemasi. We were welcomed by Ole Miberre, an older traditional Maasai who wanted to be a Christian. His son, James Kashe, was leading that church. They had ten people waiting to be baptized. James killed a goat to welcome us, and we enjoyed visiting while the goat was being prepared.

Before we left, the men informed us that some of the Moitanik had threatened Ole Miberre, saying, "We are going to kill you!" This called for a special prayer for protection for him and his family.

The following Friday, we heard rumors that a Luo man was killed at Ole Miberre's place. According to the story, on Wednesday at the break of dawn, a group of warriors came to Ole Miberre's home. The Luo man stepped outside the door while it was still dark and was speared. Ole Miberre escaped. Later, the rumor said the man who died was his son, James.

Then, we heard that the victim was not James, but a Kisii neighbor. This later rumor was that Ole Miberre was outside and was attacked by the warriors. Somehow, he managed to flee and escaped into his house. The Kisii man was out in the yard and was slaughtered. Rumors. One could not believe all the conflicting rumors!

The very next Sunday morning, we heard rumors that Ole Miberre's son, James, the church teacher, was killed in a pre-dawn attack on Ole Miberre's home.

Again, we heard that it was not James, but a certain Luo man who had come to stay with them, who had gotten up in the dark to harness the oxen for plowing. The attackers came in the dark and riddled his body with arrows and spears and knives, thinking he was the son of Ole Miberre. They said that Ole Miberre was in his house and managed to escape, passing about twenty feet from the attackers, and hid in the bushes until they left. James had also been sleeping in the house but had gotten up a few hours earlier to sleep in the bush because of the danger.

People heard the attackers running off boasting, "We have killed the son of Ole Miberre!" We were puzzled. What was the truth behind all the rumors circulating? And why would they want Ole Miberre dead?

It was very comforting to see James in church a few weeks later. He confirmed that he and a friend had been sleeping in the house but woke up at four o'clock, and feeling uneasy, went out to spend the rest of the night in the bush. Upon hearing a great disturbing noise coming from the direction of the house around six o'clock, they returned home to find the yard full of people. The Moitanik warriors had attacked and killed the Luo man who had arisen in the dark to get the oxen ready for plowing at the crack of dawn. Then the warriors went away, still in the dark, boasting, "We have killed the son of Ole Miberre!" That seemed to be the final version of the story.

Some days later in May, I was invited to meet the elders of Olmisigiyioi Church at Ole Miberre's home. Nine men were waiting for me. They wanted to discuss their vision for the church with me.

Ole Miberre and James, as a response of gratitude for being spared, wanted to make a special thanksgiving celebration. They also wanted to dedicate themselves afresh to greater commitment to the church and to sharing the word of God in the nearby community.

First, they informed me they wanted to construct a permanent building for their church, "not like these temporary ones that meet under a tree for a while, then soon disappear." Ole Miberre assured us he was donating six acres of land for the church. They showed us the plot on a hilltop that offers one of the most gorgeous panoramic views on all sides. I listened to their plans and asked questions that helped them think through the implications of building. They agreed they would make bricks, cut boards from local timber, and have a *harambee* on July 1. They wanted to build a structure the same size as the one at Enemasi.

Secondly, they asked if we could assist them to improve their way of life through advising and teaching in various ways. They said they, as Christians, should be good examples in the community.

Thirdly, they all wanted to be baptized. Most of them were polygamists. Some of them realized that the Kenya Mennonite Church didn't baptize practicing polygamists unless they divorced their extra wives first. How should we respond? I hesitated, saying that this was a bigger issue that needed to be examined afresh by the larger church before a ruling could be made.

Also, Ole Miberre wanted to start a business that would serve their community. He wanted to buy and set up a *posho* (corn meal) mill to grind the people's maize and other grains. The women were carrying their maize eleven kilometers to Ogwedhi to get ground and then carrying the flour back home. The mill would serve the whole surrounding community. He needed help to find the right machine and set up the business. It was something new for a Maasai to become a businessman. He said he could sell twenty steers to buy the mill.

Further interaction with this group over the next two years revealed that they were better at dreaming than at implementing.

Ole Miberre

CHAPTER 23

Of Neighbors, Colleagues, and Cops

Our *maskini*

The Luo widow, Domtilla, enjoyed being our *maskini,* a poor person. Whenever she came to beg for something, she would come in, say a prayer in which she told God how good we were, how bad the Luos were, and how great her needs were. Then we would give her the requested handout. Then she would say another long prayer in which she again thanked God and told him how good we were, how bad the Luos were, and reminded him to bless us and protect us and our *gari* (truck) since we travelled so much. We almost enjoyed her.

As we learned the language better, she made more sense. We decided she was our "grandmother" over here since we did not have any others nearby. Since children must support their ageing parents in this culture, it became a lot easier to tolerate her constant begging. We just gave as to our own needy grandmother. Her demands were not large, just simple daily sustenance like flour or sugar or tea. The church folks had built her that new metal-roofed house two years earlier. Now she was begging for a cement floor. She had lived nearly "ninety years" without a cement floor, but now it was becoming an overwhelming obsession. Could she not wait a little longer for the "mansion over yonder" with a floor of gold?

My Father

I also had a "father" to take care of. Since I couldn't do much to help my own father, I accepted this role also. His name was Augustino

Ole Macho, a Maasai. He was an interesting old gentleman born in 1901, baptized as a Catholic in 1924, went to school for three years, then worked for the British district commissioner as a translator for many years. He picked up a few English words. "How are you my young boy? Me old man me. Me born 1901." His mind and ears were still sharp, but his eyes were bad. He walked with a cane and lived near the church at Olmisigiyioi. He attended church and slept on his chair. Sometimes he contributed to the discussion for he had a basic foundation in Christian (Catholic) doctrine. He called me his son, *Saruni Ole Macho* (Saruni son of Macho). *Saruni* means "one who helps out or rescues others," in other words, "savior." I took it as a generous compliment.

A Sometime Pastor

Pastor Paul moved back into the community in the spring of 1989. His life seemed to run in cycles. For a while he was a fisherman and lived at Muhuru, making nets, and catching fish, and came out to visit his churches every now and then. Then he would decide to be a pastor first and support himself by farming. He would move his family to Ogwedhi, dig a small *shamba* and plant maize and tomatoes. His tomatoes would do well, and he'd start making a bit of money. Then he would lose interest and decide that he must be a fisherman and would abandon his *shamba* and move his family back to Muhuru. Now, he was back on the tomato farmer part of the cycle, only he had not moved his family this time. Since the mission gave him the used motorcycle, he was giving more time to his churches and going home to his family more frequently.

Generational Conflicts

The young employee, Michael Ogumo, was chronically sick with stomach and back problems. He was off work for a couple of months, so we gave him easier work in the tree nursery. He had taken a wife and lived with her until she gave birth. Sadly, the baby died at birth. They were still living in his parents' home.

Michael's father, who was supposedly a good Christian member, did not like the girl anymore. He said she was weak, lazy, and a bad worker. What does one expect from a sixteen-year-old girl with a difficult pregnancy? For the dowry, Michael had prepared some money for his father to give to the father of his bride. However, his father had used the dowry money for his own interests.

Michael loved the girl and wanted her, but his father sent her away. Without receiving a dowry, the girl's father gave her to another man. This was really a hard blow to Michael. He was having a hard time forgiving or respecting his father. The old man was also at odds with another daughter-in-law, who was living in their home while her husband worked in Nairobi. Andrew Okech and I tried to give the father some pastoral advice, but he had no ears for that.

After the fishponds were dug and stocked with tilapia, we assigned Michael to take care of them. This meant we built a hut for him to sleep in nearby, to prevent theft of the fish, and to feed and care for them during the day. We found him trustworthy and very meticulous about his duties.

Peter Otieno, the son of Pastor Samuel Otieno, came from Luendo. He was married at a young age to a girl who bore him a son. When Peter was given a job as an OSP worker, he tried to persuade her to come and live with him at Ogwedhi. She wrote him a very insulting letter in reply, then took their son to her home in Homa Bay, and refused to return to Peter.

After repeated entreaties for her to return to him, and hearing that she was being unfaithful to him, he sought counsel with his father and local pastors while we were on furlough. He finally divorced her. At Ogwedhi, he met a fine local Christian girl, Miriam, and married her. They were living together very nicely.

Then, for some reason which we could not understand, Peter's father turned against the new wife. He wrote insulting and untrue accusations against her and ordered Peter to put her away. He called the former wife back to his home. She came to Peter's home in Luendo and stayed for several months. Peter was living with his Miriam in Ogwedhi.

Marriage in the local tradition was never just between two individuals. It was a family affair and required the consent and support of the family, thus the interference of the father. When a dowry had been paid, the girl belonged to the family of the one who paid it. In a polygamous society, it was okay to take a second wife, especially if the first one was a disappointment. Peter had adopted the new principle of monogamous marriage as his standard. Thus, the conflict with his father, although the father was a pastor.

Peter quarreled with his father and refused to see the former wife. He said he will never be a polygamist, and he will never chase away the wife he now has and loves. The other one apparently was involved with other men. After some months, Peter went home with his new wife, found the other had finally given up and went to her home again. Peter's father apologized, and they reconciled.

Although Peter had been working in the dairy, he was not satisfied. He wanted to further his education with training in secretarial science. He found a school in Kisii which took him in. OSP agreed to assist with his fees and living costs for six months. He moved his wife to his parents' home while he undertook this training.

Welcoming the New Bishop

Since Joshua Okello Ouma had been ordained to be our bishop the preceding August, it was only appropriate to have an official welcoming reception for him. A practical opportunity presented itself when we invited the new bishop to officiate at a baptism and communion service to be held at Ogwedhi on April 30, 1989.

Preparations were made. A goat was purchased and ready to be slaughtered. Rice was bought and cleaned. Baptismal candidates were interviewed. Eleven congregations of the Ogwedhi Sigawa District were informed.

Bishop Joshua arrived from Migori with Pastor Hellon Amollo in good time on Saturday afternoon. There was time for a late afternoon meeting with church leaders, followed by an evening of food and fellowship.

The big day arrived with people up at daybreak rushing about preparing. Around 9:00 a.m., the "bell" was rung by vigorously beating an old car wheel with an iron bar. By 10:30, people began arriving, and shortly after 11:00, the program was underway with spirited singing in Luo, Swahili, and Maasai.

Bishop Joshua Okello Ouma entered in ecclesiastical splendor. Already endowed by nature with a ramrod straight, imposing six-foot-three frame, the bishop's dignity was further enhanced by his scarlet shirt and white clerical collar, which contrasted nicely with his light brown suit. When he and the pastors had been properly seated at the front facing the congregation, the program continued with introductions, prayers, and more songs.

The little Ogwedhi meetinghouse was packed with about 200 men, women, and children. All seats were taken. Children crowded up front under the very feet of the leaders. Some women sat on the concrete floor in the aisle.

In this sea of radiant, expectant faces, one could distinguish the Luo women with their long dresses and heads tightly wrapped in colorful head scarves, and the Maasai women, not only bareheaded but shiny clean-shaven heads, dressed in their favorite red, orange, blue, and white traditional dresses, lavishly decorated with beautiful beadwork.

Next, the order of the service was to receive fourteen persons as new members upon their confession of solidarity with us in faith. Among the accepted was Daniel, a former leader in an indigenous sect, who renounced the sect because it never led him to Jesus. Also, Joseph Sankale and Francis Rikei, who had been leading SDA churches, confessed their oneness in faith and desire to join hands with us in sharing the good news with their Maasai people.

Then it was time for baptism. In all, the bishop baptized twenty-six people ... Eighteen were Maasai. Among them was Wilson Ole Rana, a youth whom God called in a dream to start a church. He gave up the life of a *moran* (warrior), and although illiterate, called some children and mothers together and started a church in his home.

There was also James Kiloing'oni, a man in his early thirties who, up to six months before, was known in the community as one ruined by drink. His wife, King'asunye, who took the "Christian name," "Jane," had been a strong Christian for several years. Her prayers were answered one day when her husband surrendered his life to Christ. Jesus healed him instantly of his alcoholism. His non-Christian neighbors were watching him closely. They said, "If the church can help Kiloing'oni, then it really is a good thing to have in our community." Then, there was the eldest daughter of Kiloing'oni, named Deli one of the very few Maasai girls who was learning what it is like to live in a truly Christian family.

Each of the twenty-six had a story of God calling them from darkness into light, from ignorance into knowledge, from a position of being "not my people" to being "a people of the living God."

Baptism was followed by a communion service, after which the bishop preached a sermon. After more singing and taking an offering, the service ended. Following fellowship around food, the people slowly dispersed. It was truly a memorable day, not soon to be forgotten in the history of the Ogwedhi Sigawa community, the day we welcomed the bishop!

A week later, I baptized an additional five people at Olenkare, a new church, and served communion. It was encouraging to see new Christians growing but sobering to think of the responsibility of discipleship-making that lay in the days ahead!

Dashed Hopes

Around the end of June, our neighbor's daughter died. She had graduated from Migori Teachers College a year earlier and began teaching at Rapogi. Soon she became pregnant and got very sick. She spent time in several different hospitals but did not get better. Finally, she gave birth to a daughter in March, yet she did not get better. She was terribly weak, emaciated, and anemic, and kept having terrible headaches. Finally, she died, and was buried in the banana grove near the church.

The baby was put in an orphanage, at least temporarily. It was a heavy blow to all of us, especially her father. She was such a pretty, intelligent, young woman. Her father had spent a lot of money to educate her and was hoping to get some help from her to educate her younger siblings. Now she was gone, and his plans failed. Such is the uncertainty of life. Somewhere some boy or man went scot-free while the girl paid the ultimate price for his pleasure. It was not fair.

This was in the early stages of the HIV/AIDS epidemic in the area, and we did not realize what the young woman's ailment likely was. Her baby also perished some months later. Before our community became aware, the AIDS epidemic was upon us. In subsequent years, many of our workers and neighbors died in the same mysterious way.

Rumors spread of the deathbed confession of a male college student apologizing to a list of sixty female students he had sexually contacted. With no medical cures in sight, the epidemic took a terrible toll on the lives of that generation.

Encounters with Traffic Cops

In the arena of public opinion, the reputation of the Kenyan traffic police was very low indeed. I felt they were competent enough but were generally viewed as very corrupt. They set up check points on all the main roads at frequent intervals with heavily spiked barriers sure to ruin any tire that attempted to speed across. Motorists were compelled to stop for the inspections. In most cases, looking for unregistered vehicles, unlicensed drivers, contraband, illegal weapons, smuggled goods, or illicit drugs were the justifications. However, any hint of irregularity became just cause to extract a bribe from the busy motorist.

Sometimes, even if nothing irregular could be found, the cop would brazenly ask for "something little for tea" as if it were his right. Timid souls often paid. It was considered like an extra tax, like a road toll, a part of the costs of travel.

For me, my major driving "sin" was speeding. In those days, in Kenya, one's maximum speed limit was posted on a metal plate affixed to the back of one's vehicle. There were different speeds for different vehicles. For our pickup truck, the maximum speed limit was sixty-five kilometers (forty miles) per hour, even if one was on an empty four lane divided highway where the sedans could go at one hundred.

I, being of a slightly rebellious nature, tended to ignore the speed limits on an open, smooth road. Consequently, I was occasionally caught in an unexpected radar trap and stopped by an alert traffic cop doing his job. Because I was a middle-aged white foreigner, the young Kenyan cop would approach my stopped vehicle very politely with the utmost respect.

On one occasion, a young cop came up to my open window and kindly asked me, "Father, are you ready to go to heaven?"

I replied just as politely, "Yes, but not right now!"

He continued, "If you don't slow down, you will get there sooner than you expect!" He let me go with a warning.

Another time, another young cop approached my open window, almost apologetically, "Sir, you have broken the law. What can I do? You are my father. How can I charge you?"

I replied, "Yes, I was going faster than I should. You are the policeman, do your duty!" He could not bring himself to write out a ticket and politely warned me to slow down.

Another time, a more brash older policeman asked me, "Are you a missionary?" When I affirmed my identity, he let me off with a warning. I learned that they were easier on missionaries who were reputed to never pay bribes unlike other foreigners, such as East Indian businesspeople whom they knew were willing to get off the hook with a nice bribe.

Another time, I was teaching my daughter to drive on our way to Nairobi. At Nakuru, she was caught going sixty in a thirty-kilometer zone. Since she was learning, she did not have a license. As a father, I got out and discussed the situation with the cop. He took me behind the vehicle where mother and daughter could not see and quietly informed me that my daughter was in serious trouble. Maybe arrest, or jail overnight. Then he quietly whispered to me, "Could we have a secret between us?"

I said, "No. She has broken the law. You are the policeman and know what you are supposed to do." When he learned that I was a missionary, he gave me a warning and let us go. Our daughter became a good driver.

CHAPTER 24

The Work Goes On: Spring of 1989

Project Developments

S eeding was done by the middle of March. It was the middle of the rainy season, and the first weeding was underway. Our trees were growing nicely. Our yard, with shrubs and flowers, was maturing beautifully. We had about 20,000 seedlings in our tree nursery ready for sale. People from the community came to buy the tree seedlings as fast as we could produce them. We had about 150 banana plants left to plant before reaching our goal of 300. We planted over 2,000 pineapples.

Near the end of April, we began building a fence around a twenty-acre plot of land at Kiikat, allocated to OSP to be used as pasture and later for a church and a school. It was about three kilometers away from OSP. Fence-building involved clearing the trees and bushes in a strip all around the circumference of the plot, digging holes by hand for each fence post, putting in the posts, and stringing five strands of barbed wire all around.

We also hired people to dig fishponds at the back of the project farm next to the creek. The first one was 50' x 80' x 3' deep, all dug by hand. To fill the ponds, we dammed the spring to raise the water level up so it could run into the ponds. We eventually dug two more fishponds, one of a similar size and another 56' x 108' x 3'. The ponds together had capacity to hold 7,000 tilapia.

We also started building a zero-grazing unit, a place to feed thirty cows so they wouldn't have to go out to pasture but would be fed there. It involved making a cement pad 55' x 55' with feed bunks, water troughs, and a partial roof for shade.

As summer unfolded, uncompleted tasks continued to challenge and occupy the staff at the Ogwedhi Sigawa Project. These included completing several wells, building a water tower to provide water pressure to the director's house, and helping a model farmer dig a well, build a house, a poultry house, and a fence, plus all the regular things that keep one occupied such as running the farm, helping with churches, and going to seminars. There was plenty to occupy one's mind and body!

Church Developments

In mid-March, we visited another of the new churches, this one at Olenkare, about eighteen kilometers to the northeast of us. There, besides many children, we found fifteen mothers present but no men. Along with the morning worship, we had a special child dedication service. Following that, we were invited to one of the homes where we were fed the usual rice, potatoes, and tea. Surplus hospitality required us to visit another home where we were fed again, this time, cooked bananas and tea.

That evening, as soon as it became dark, we showed some film strips—Bible stories. A large crowd gathered, so we got a chance to talk to the men. We stopped the show at 9:30 p.m., had some more food, and drove home, arriving around 11:00 p.m. It was a good day. The happy people sent with us four bunches of bananas, one hen, and some roasting ears of maize. I really liked these young Christians. I felt bad that I had not spent more time learning their language and culture.

One Sunday in April, about 150 people from all the churches in the district met at Ogwedhi to welcome the David Shenk family. David was our supervisor, working as the EMM East Africa Regional Director. On this annual visit, his grown family was travelling with him. David, the son of pioneer missionaries Clyde and Alta Shenk, grew up in Tanzania. As adults, David and Grace served as missionaries and raised their children in Somalia and Kenya. Now, they came back as a grown family to re-visit their roots.

The Shenk family was accompanied by Lawrence and Lourida Chiles. Lawrence was a pastor, a good preacher and teacher, and a member of the Eastern Mennonite Mission Board. He and his wife were our guests overnight. The next day, I took a group of twelve church leaders to Migori for a one-day seminar for diocese leaders with Pastor Chiles teaching. Then the following day, we hosted about twenty-five leaders at Ogwedhi for a consultation on Maasai church development.

Our mission board was processing sending us a young couple, Clair and Beth Good from Pennsylvania, with three small children, to be missionaries assigned exclusively to Maasai church work. To me, that was good news and an answer to prayer. If they got a work permit and visas, they could arrive in late August or September.

A Maasai Wedding - Challenging Marriage Traditions

Francis Ole Rikei was chosen by the Maasai community elders to work as OSP's extension agent. This meant he had the confidence of his people. He was also serving in the church as teacher/preacher.

The time had come for him to take a wife. He secured the agreement of Esther, a young Christian Maasai girl. They arranged to have a "Christian" wedding ceremony held in the local Ogwedhi Mennonite Church. This wedding was the second Christian wedding held among the Maasai in this area.

June 6, 1989, conveniently coincided with our daughter's mid-term break. This made it possible for Kristina and two of her friends to spend a weekend at home helping Vera bake and decorate a big wedding cake. They used six cake recipes and lots of powdered sugar to make it. Vera had made the wedding dress several weeks earlier. On Friday and Saturday, the staff had the inside of the church freshly whitewashed, and the blackboard repainted. They put up a few decorations at the front.

Because of limited transport options, the bride and her escorts were brought on Saturday and kept with us overnight. Then on Sunday morning, I drove ten kilometers to fetch her mother and other family members.

The church building was packed with community people, and many stood waiting outside. The service got started about 11:00 a.m. with Bishop Joshua Okello and Pastor Paul Otieno leading the wedding procession. Following them, we close associates escorted the bride and groom from our house down the lane and into the church building where the crowd of well-wishers joyfully welcomed them. The ceremony lasted until after 2:00 p.m. This included cutting and serving the cake and giving the couples their wedding presents.

Francis, having courage to break tradition in favor of the new, inspired his friend Joseph Sankale to join him in solemnizing a Christian covenant relationship with the wife he had married in the traditional way one year earlier. The focus of the rest of the ceremony was on the newly wedded happy couple.

After the ceremony was finished, the invited guests went to the groom's house across the creek for a feast, while the crowd remaining at the church were served there. It was already 4:30 by the time we ate. After everyone was well fed, I drove the mother of the bride and family members back to their homes.

This wedding ceremony was pivotal in that it set a new standard in this community as a prototype of what a Christian marriage ceremony could or should look like. Future marriages of believers would follow that pattern.

The one thing that baffled the traditionalist Maasai the most was the emphasis of the oneness of the marriage union and the "forsaking of all others." This meant renouncing polygamy and adultery, along with the high commitment of the husband to love his wife and treat her as an equal worthy of respect and dignity. Getting married is no longer a man acquiring a woman as chattel to work for him, satisfy his every need, and produce children for him. Now, it was to be regarded as a "one-flesh union" of two, bonded in self-giving love, each to serve the best interests of the other in mutual love—a revolutionary change!

Francis & Esther Rikei's Wedding

Our Children's Progress

We had not heard a word from our girls back in the USA in several weeks. I was worried about Sheryl being there without a job and no money living off Karen. When I was in the city, I phoned her.

She had just gotten a job with a telemarketing company the week before and was excited about it. She was working with about one hundred employees, phoning all over the USA promoting sales, soliciting funds for organizations, etc. That week she was soliciting funds for the Republican Party. Although she struggled with her conscience and personal ideals in supporting that organization as well as the National Rifles Association, it was a job, and she enjoyed the work. She hoped to get promoted.

Karen was doing student teaching. In another six to eight weeks, she would graduate with a degree in elementary education. We wished we could be there to celebrate with her. It was a big event in her life since, because of transferring from grade eleven in Alberta, Canada, to Virginia, she had skipped grade twelve and never graduated from anything before.

Cindy and John were moving ahead with plans to accept a missionary assignment in Peru. They planned to leave for language school in Costa Rica in August for one year before proceeding to Peru.

A Malindi Vacation

Back in April, our East Africa Director, David Shenk, ordered Vera and I to take a vacation. Therefore, in humble obedience, we decided we had better take a vacation, whether we needed it or not, could afford it or not, had time or not, or we would never get one.

First, we decided to visit the coastal town of Lamu, 150 kilometers north of Mombasa and just south of Somalia on the Indian Ocean. Lamu, designated by the UN as a World Heritage Site, is said to be the best-preserved old Arab/Swahili town on the east coast of Africa, an interesting option for a vacation. However, due to the presence and danger of *shiftas* (bandits), the road was closed to the public. We would have to fly.

When we went to pick up our tickets, we discovered it was going to cost 10,000 Ksh. for the two of us to fly there and back. Seeing how our total vacation allowance was only 8,000 Ksh., we had to face reality in a hurry and make other plans.

Finally, on July 13th, we went by train to Mombasa and took a bus to Malindi. There, we found the Silver Sands Campsite and rented a *banda,* a cabin, just big enough for us two, right on the beach. We were satisfied with it. Hotels were completely out of reach. There were no meals and no cooking facilities, so we scavenged the eating places and marketplace for edible morsels that sustained our good health and spirits.

We calculated so that we could have this one-week vacation for under 5,000 Ksh. including travel, lodging, and meals. Then there was enough remaining in our budget to spend the second week in Nairobi at the Guest House.

While Vera and I were not the ones to complain about missionary support allowances, we did feel there was a lack of fairness in the policy on vacations. For one thing, missionaries who lived in isolation in the bush or countryside had to take their vacations "in the bush" too. That might mean going camping by some lake or park. They could not afford to take their vacations in nice comfortable centers like tourist hotels or even travel to see the distant sights that attract tourists within the country.

The policy allotted us three weeks of mandatory vacation per year. Provision of budget was only enough for about three days in a modest hotel with some allowance for transport to get there. Only those missionaries whose allowances were supplemented by personal financial resources, or the support of friends or family, could afford a nice vacation for three full weeks. The rest of us might feel a twinge of jealousy, especially if one's children noticed the disparity.

Money was a perpetual problem. The missionary call made us world travelers, but mission poverty prevented us from enjoying the advantages of travelling. There was never money to see anything on the way, just a quick shuttle from origin to destination.

However, we set out to enjoy what we had and not gripe over what we did not have. We enjoyed our week, being lazy, swimming in the ocean, snorkeling, reading, walking around, visiting the area, and writing letters.

The beach at Malindi was lovely. The sand had a very fine, almost white, coral texture. The ocean waves reflected the deep blue of the sky when the sun shone or turned a dull grey when there was a cover of clouds.

About one quarter of a mile out in the shallow ocean, a long coral reef stretches parallel to the shore, hugging the coast. It serves as a barrier that keeps the sharks who are at home in the deep water from coming into the shallow water, making it safe for swimming. In low tide the big breakers burst against that reef in a mighty spray of white. During high tide, those breakers cross the reef and pound the beach with a constant roar making swimming interesting.

The local people were out there with their sail boats fishing. Women came and sold us fresh fruit, bananas, mangoes, and pineapples.

One day, we took a taxi about fifteen kilometers south to visit the Gede Ruins. Gede used to be a prosperous Arab trading town along the coast in the 13th to 16th centuries. For some unknown reason, it was evacuated about five hundred years ago and fell into disrepair, and the site returned to native forest.

Recent archeological activity uncovered a palace, about ten houses, and several mosques. Artifacts included fine porcelain from China. There were huge wells dug about forty to fifty feet deep. The stone houses had indoor pit latrines and wash facilities. Sometimes the latrines were less than fifteen feet from the wells. I suppose their ideas about pollution in those days were not the same as ours.

Another thing that impressed me was how completely the native forest reclaimed the land. Huge baobab trees, from three to four meters in diameter, had grown right among the walls, streets, houses, and pavements. Other trees, now grown huge, had upset many of the walls. How short lived is the glory of the works of man! I had to think, this is what our cities could look like in 400 years' time or less. How important it is that we concentrate on doing work that has an eternal dimension!

On the shore at Malindi, we found a small prayer chapel originally built by Vaso Da Gama in 1492, and a graveyard where he laid to rest two Portuguese sailors who died on their journey around the Cape of Good Hope, searching for a route to India. It was kept as a historical site.

Evaluation and Re-direction

Upon returning from Malindi to Nairobi, I met with the Lutheran World Relief officers to discuss and evaluate the performance of OSP. We were not satisfied with our effectiveness level and agreed that we must make some basic changes. We agreed our farm and projects consumed too much of our time and resources, keeping us from focusing attention on developing the community. The neighbors tended to look at our project as something that money and expertise can do but not as something from which they could learn.

The outcome of our consultation was that, upon my return to Ogwedhi, I had to relate the donors' challenge to the management committee to evaluate our performance critically, considering our objectives and priorities. Then, I had to coach the committee in preparing a proposal for a major revision of our program.

Based upon that, the committee agreed that we must vigorously strengthen the extension component of our agriculture and animal husbandry program. To do so, our extension agents must be trained, equipped, empowered, and held accountable to work directly with the people in the community. We must strengthen the health component of our services by upgrading our dispensary into a small health center as well as providing more curative facilities such as a few beds for overnight patients. We must implement a community-based health education program supported by a community-wide immunization program and a family planning program.

We realized that these changes called for more skilled personnel such as trained extension agents, a nurse, a clinical health officer or a doctor, and a veterinarian. This would require more money, which requires more fundraising, more administration, and more report writing.

CHAPTER 25

A Summer of Surprises

An Unexpected Wedding

The voice of our daughter on the phone pleaded, "Can you come for my wedding?" Karen was going to marry Dee. With urgency in her plea, she added the schedule, "... in three weeks!" Her sudden disclosure caught us totally by surprise. Shocked, we tried to gather our wits and discuss this revelation. Vera went to pieces and couldn't talk. Karen wondered if we could all come for her wedding "in three weeks"? Really? What was she thinking? Our initial reaction was, "In three weeks? Of course not! We are working people, we have commitments!"

Reality began to sink into my brain. Wait a minute. This is our daughter pleading. She is saying "... my wedding!" She is saying, "... in three weeks!" Questions poured out, "What happened? Why? Why now? Are you pregnant?"

When the answer was "Yes," my next question was, "Pregnancy is a nine-month enterprise. Why three weeks? Why not have your wedding in the fall or winter? That would give your mother and I time to prepare for it?"

She wanted her sister, Cindy, to be one of the attendants, and she and John were to leave for their mission assignment in Costa Rico in a little over three weeks. If that was the case, and the three-week deadline was written in stone, then, of course, it would be impossible for any of us to come. With that final understanding, we concluded the conversation.

Vera and I had stopped overnight at the guest house on our way home from Malindi. Sheryl and Karen made that call early in the morning, less than an hour before we were to leave Nairobi for the long drive home. We had picked up Kristina for her August vacation at home.

Well, we had a very long, quiet, seven-hour trip home to Ogwedhi. None of us could talk, all lost in private thoughts, shocked. After a few hours, I suggested to Vera that she, being the mother, should consider going. Our daughter needs her mother more than her dad in this situation. Her initial reaction was "No way!" and "Impossible!" I suggested she think about it.

Three days later, Vera decided to go, to swallow her pride, and her hurt, and go out of her love for her girls. It was Karen's wedding, and she needed a mother for this momentous occasion, more than a father. Kristina and I felt much better that we were at least being represented. We agreed to tighten our belts to make the trip possible. Our financial state was tight enough without that added expense.

That decided, we went to Migori, phoned Sheryl to make sure the wedding plans were still on, then phoned the Nairobi office to book a ticket for Vera. She left Ogwedhi on Tuesday, August 1st, on the night bus and flew out of Nairobi on Thursday evening, August 3rd, arriving in Harrisburg, Pennsylvania, on the evening of August 4th.

Vera was met by her mother and nephew, Stanley King, who took her to Belleville. Cindy and John were returning from a language-learning seminar in Michigan and stopped at their grandma's that night. Vera's sister, Vernane, and husband, Dick Stutzman, had also come for a high school class reunion that evening, so there was a grand reunion in Mother Yoder's apartment.

Then on Sunday, Cindy and John took Vera down to Virginia in time to go with the girls to see the church where the wedding was to be held.

We had known a little about Karen's romance. Dietrich Bundick, from Roanoke, Virginia, was also a student at EMC where Karen met him. They had been dating for about two years. We had met him in Harrisonburg the previous summer while on our home leave. He was a pleasant fellow, and we liked him.

Karen graduated with her B.Ed. degree in May. Her plan was to get a teaching job in some elementary school and work so Dee could go back to complete his college degree. She was looking, but the job did not materialize for her. Then she found out near the end of June that she was pregnant. With no one to counsel her, but her wise sister, Sheryl, she decided she ought to get married as fast as possible.

Since she wanted to have a wedding before Cindy and John left on August 15th and before Dee went back to college in late August, the 12th of August was the only logical date. We wondered what they would have done, or when we would have been informed, if Grandma had not told them we would be in Nairobi that day? We had no phone at Ogwedhi.

In Virginia, Vera got busy all week sewing the two bridesmaid's dresses. Sheryl wore one that Vera made for her in Kenya for a Jr-Sr banquet. Sheryl made Karen's dress and veil. Vera cut out the flower girl's dresses, but their mother sewed them.

Everything was a bit hectic to say the least, but by 11:00 am on Saturday, August 12, 1989, all was ready, and the ceremony went well. The venue for the wedding was the Oak Grove Baptist Church, about one-half hour south of Harrisonburg near Waynesboro. Bishop Theodore E. Payne was the presiding preacher who tied the knot.

Before and after the wedding, Vera had time to visit her family in Belleville, Pennsylvania. She spent a few days with Cindy and John in Lancaster and was able to see them off on their journey to Costa Rica. She attended an Ethiopian get-together where she met many old friends we had known in our Ethiopian years. She spent time with her daughters in Harrisonburg, Virginia, then returned to Kenya, arriving on the 6th of September.

All in all, we felt it was good that Vera went and was able to be a mother to three of her daughters over those hectic five weeks. It was time and money well spent!

Of Expected Guests and Unexpected Thieves

Vera found it hard to leave Kristina and myself because we had a busy month planned. We were expecting a team of volunteers to be with us for ten days, and then a week later, the Good family was planning to stay with us for one full week. However, sixteen-years-old Kristina rallied to the cause and took over as hostess, and things went just fine.

The STAT team, seven young volunteers sent by EMM, were

supposed to help us build something. We wanted to build a school classroom, but the local committee did not meet in time, so we scrapped that idea. We took them on a camping trip overnight to Maasai Mara the day after Vera left. Everyone was excited about this safari in the wilds of Africa and the chance to see exotic animals. Then, they finished painting the trim on Enemasi church and later white-washed the inside. They also made a few church benches and worked in our tree nursery.

On Monday morning, we were surprised and upset when we discovered that our shop had been burglarized. Thieves broke in the window and made off with 1,250 Ksh., plus about 4,000 Ksh. worth of cattle drugs.

That night, in discussing it with the STAT team, I boasted that we felt safe, and that theft was not a serious problem. This was the "first in ten years." The very next morning, imagine our amazement when we discovered that all three of our motorcycles had been stolen! They were parked on Pastor Paul's porch, just across the lane from our house.

After a month of dry and dusty weather, the Lord had sent heavy rain earlier that evening, so the motorcycle tracks were easy to follow. We got two policemen and set out in hot pursuit. One cycle was found one-half mile away abandoned in the bushes. It had a broken magneto, so it wouldn't start. We followed the other two tracks winding across country paths until they reached the pavement. Then, following the policemen's advice, we drove past Migori and on towards Tanzania.

Sure enough, we found the tracks again on a dirt road, and followed them until they diverged. We followed one track across the border right up to a village. The trail ended at a certain house. Of course, the owner was absent.

Finally, the police called the father of the owner and made him open it. There we found one of the motorcycles. But where was the other?

We knew it must be in one of the adjacent houses. However, the policeman insisted it was getting late. It was time to leave for home, and we must come again tomorrow to finish our search for the second one. I was baffled by this strange decision. Why not stay a little longer and complete the search?

The policeman insisted. What could we do? I was too weak and compliant with this officer of the law. We loaded the recovered motorcycle into the back of the pickup and took it back across the border. Up to that time, we had not even eaten our breakfast, so we ate in Migori and got home around 10:00 p.m.

The next morning, we took the police back to that trail, followed the other trail and, sure enough, it led to the same village. But the father had also disappeared. On Friday, we took the police again to report the matter to their Tanzania police headquarters at Tarime. Then on Saturday, since the theft occurred in the Rift Valley Province, I had to report the matter to the Rift Valley police at Kilgoris. Consequently, I didn't have many days that week to host the STAT team.

We still had not gotten the one motorcycle back. I felt like giving up. However, the police reassured us saying that they were sure we would get it back or at least get the money back when the thieves were caught. To do so, we would have to go back to Tanzania again. It turned out to be several more trips.

The road was rough. It took most of a day just to make the trip. Our efforts were time-consuming, costly, tiring, wasted, and unproductive. The police said they caught five suspects and beat them. They claimed to have tortured them thoroughly but got no useful information. It was the Kenyan system of justice. We highly suspected the Kenyan police may have been paid off by the thieves to divert the case.

On the third week of August, I went to Nairobi and brought the Clair and Beth Good family to Ogwedhi. They were young. Clair was twenty-nine, and Beth was twenty-six. They had three cute little girls: Rebecca, aged five, Esther, aged three and one-half, and Hannah was less than a year old.

Clair and Beth had been in Zaire for one and a half years building churches. Clair was a mechanic, a builder, a pastor, an evangelist, and a farmer by experience. He was a man after my own heart, someone I could work with.

We arranged for them to study the Maasai language and culture at Narok for approximately one year, then come to help us with the Maasai church work. While they studied there, we would build them a house at Enemasi near the church.

Clair and Beth Good and family

After seven days, we brought the family back to Nairobi on Saturday, August 26th, when I took Kristina back to RVA to start grade twelve. She was on the high honors list. She was a real help in Vera's absence and an encouragement to us in our missionary work. She displayed a very good attitude which made parenting a pleasure. She wrote a report entitled *"Summer in Maasai Country"* that was printed in the March 1990 issue of Missionary Messenger,

The summer started for me at the end of July; that is when our school closed. I went home with my parents from my boarding school, Rift Valley Academy in Kijabe, Kenya. It was a long seven-hour drive, but one that I was happy to make …

The first week was relaxing, just enjoying my friends, and having no worries about term papers. I was baptized in a stream with all my Maasai friends around me. It was a very meaningful experience for me. After the first two weeks, my father and I took my mom to the bus stop in a neighboring town so she could fly to the U.S. for my sister's wedding. After my mom left, my vacation became very busy.

My father and I were in charge of seven STATers (Summer Training Action Team volunteers), ages seventeen to twenty-four. They were at our house for a week and a half. We took them to Maasai Mara, a national game park about two hours from where we live. We saw lots of animals and then camped for the night.

One evening after we had bragged about the security at our place, three of our project's motorcycles were stolen. And then, after a long dry spell, the Lord blessed us and sent rain that very night. The next day we were then able to track two of the bikes. The third one has still not been found. That added some excitement to our holidays.

Another evening, we all went to my Maasai "father's" place for a Maasai meal. Three of the STATers and myself stayed the night as they wanted to experience a night in a mud-and-thatched roofed hut. This house could be called my second home, and it was fun introducing the STATers to it.

When the STAT team left, the house was not empty, as my friend's children came and stayed for a while. Then the Clair Good family came; they are going to be working near us with the Maasai after they learn the language. We had a nice time with them, and their three young girls entertained us. While they were with us, I went to my friend's house, and we went to a circumcision ceremony. We saw many dances. In Maasai ceremonies the different age groups have different dancing styles and all are fun to watch.

A few days later, I had to return to school and that ended my summer.

Resuming the Search for the Missing Motorcycle

Having left Kristina back in school at RVA, I enrolled in a two-week course on "Management for Development" at Daystar University. I was the only "*mzungu*" (white foreigner) in the class.

After Vera returned from the USA and I returned from Daystar, the Kenya police encouraged me to resume the attempt to recover the missing motorcycle. I had strong misgivings by this time. The motorcycle would have been sold and the money spent or hidden. Also, this police chase was costing us a lot in time, energy, and travel expenses. Of course, the police expected us to provide the vehicle and all related costs. For them, it was an adventure of travelling with this foreigner at his expense. Also, there might be some gift at the end if they were successful. I also had the haunting feeling that they may be receiving some payment from the thieves' families to divert the success of the search.

However, at the suggestion of the Kenya police, we chose a day to go into Tanzania. I objected, saying that I had left my passport in Nairobi to be renewed. Crossing the border without it would be impossible. The police assured me that, with them as police officers on a police case, the Tanzanian border officials would give me no problem.

When we reached the border, we discovered that they were wrong. The Tanzania Immigration would not allow me to enter, so we had to turn back, disappointed. Several days later, the police persuaded me to try again. This time they led me to a different border crossing, where the police had friends who allowed us in.

We drove back to the village to arrest the man in whose home we had found the first cycle, but he pleaded innocence, saying it was his son who rode the stolen cycle. His son was sick in the hospital at Tarime, two hours' drive from there, so we took the old man with us to Tarime and found the son being treated for TB. He said he contracted the disease by getting wet and cold on the night he stole the cycle. Although his explanation of the cause of his affliction could be questioned scientifically, could it not also be attributed theologically as Divine punishment?

The sick man named his accomplices, two others being Tanzanians and one a Kenyan whom they paid to bring the cycles to them. It was too late to go and get the other men that night. The police were aware that the village, being close to the Kenyan border, was doing a booming trade in stolen goods. They said it wasn't safe to go there at night, so we came home from Tarime. I arrived home at 12:00 midnight. Having started out at 6:00 a.m., I was very tired from driving all day on rough Tanzanian roads. That was on a Tuesday.

Friday morning, this time at 4:00 a.m., I left home and picked up the police to arrest the Kenyan accomplice in Migori, but he was not at his home. His father directed us to find him in another house sleeping with a mistress. The police promptly took him to jail and started to beat him to make him confess. He said he was guilty and gave the names of the others in Tanzania. Someone told us the cycle was taken to Mwanza, several hours' drive, further south of the Kenya border and sold.

The next morning, at 2:00 a.m., I returned to Migori, picked up the police, and started out again for Tanzania. This time, we took the arrested man along to show us the place where the other thieves lived. The police hoped to spring a surprise nighttime raid to arrest them. However, they were unsuccessful. The thieves, who had been warned, were not at home. Which insider warned them?

The police decided to wait a few weeks and then make another surprise night raid on the thieves' home. Although the motorcycle had been sold, the police said they needed to get these men, so they could tell us who bought it. The one wife thought it went to Musoma which is closer than Mwanza. I got home at 7:30 a.m. the next morning, being gone for almost thirty hours.

I was tired when I got home that morning, took a bath, and went to bed. However, morning is not a time to go to sleep. People kept coming and disturbing. There was a meeting of Maasai elders with the chief planned for the day, and some of them came early and wanted me to show them around OSP before they started their meeting.

The reason I was driving the police around was because they claimed they did not have any police vehicles available and since it was our cycle that was stolen, I had to help them find it for our benefit.

I spent many days with the police. I was trying to help them help us. However, I was suspicious that they really were trying to help me so I could help them. I do not pay bribes, so the police were amazingly inept. They knew who the thieves were but kept changing the information they shared with me. They reported to me that the thief in the hospital with TB had died, and the Kenyan one was sentenced to a year in jail. I wasn't sure I could believe them.

Without any evidence, I suspected they were receiving payments from the thieves, so were using me and my vehicle for appearances sake. They kept on planning more moves to capture the remaining two thieves but never produced results. Slowly, I began to realize that as long as I took them in our vehicle and paid for their meals and other expenses, they would keep up the charade of seeming to work at recovering our lost property. I finally gave up and stopped the pursuit. Anyway, we were thankful for the two recovered motorcycles.

About two years later, the OSP received a check of 28,000 Ksh. from the insurance company in compensation for the permanent loss of the one motorcycle. The original price of the motorcycle was around 80,000 Ksh. I did not bother to calculate the sum of expenses we incurred plus the value of the time expended in our lengthy attempts to retrieve the stolen property. I know it was a costly tuition for a lesson poorly learned.

CHAPTER 26

Challenges in the Fall of 1989

Morality and the Ownership of Fruit

According to the biblical account, the first human experience with temptation occurred when two people stood and admired some fruit dangling temptingly on a tree that they did not plant nor own. Is it really wrong to reach out and take just a taste?

One Saturday afternoon when the workers were not on duty, we noticed from our window a few boarding students looking longingly at the orange trees we had planted in our garden. We were starting to get fruit from our own trees but not enough to supply the boarding school. There were about fifty students, and they were not getting very much fruit in their diet.

In Africa, although fruit can grow so easily, it was still a luxury item for many. This is partly because it was not thought of as "food" to eat at mealtimes, but something to snack on when passing a fruit tree and not necessarily one's own tree either. If fruit on a tree belongs to everybody, it also belongs to nobody, so nobody bothers to plant and care for it. That is why fruit was scarce. Is it morally wrong to cross someone's fence to pluck a few juicy pieces of fruit that should belong to everybody? Is it morally right for someone to put a fence around a tree to keep all the fruit just for him/herself?

Church Challenges

It took a period of two years and four months to complete the little church chapel at Enemasi. From the prayer of dedication of the plot in March 1987, to leveling the plot in July, to a groundbreaking ceremony in October, it took a full year to get started with construction in April 1988. It took another sixteen months to complete construction, including applying whitewash and paint in August 1989, although it still needed desks to furnish it.

A service of dedication was held that fall. The local congregations were invited for the festive occasion. Leaders and pastors from neighboring churches came. Maasai and Kuria choirs joined in the worship. Bishop Joshua Okello officiated, and officials from the diocese participated. Prominent community leaders also came to offer their congratulations.

It was reported to us that Mary, the sister who had started the church at Olenkare and was leading it, had withdrawn and returned to drinking. Being concerned, we left early one Sunday in October, taking a few young men with us, and stopped in at her home to make sure she knew we were there. She and her two co-wives served us tea and welcomed us. Then they got ready, and the family filled our vehicle to overflowing, and we took them to their church tree. It was a good service. Francis Ole Rikei was a good teacher-preacher. He was twenty-one years old and showed a lot of potential.

I had last visited that church in May when I had baptized five people and served communion. Young Francis had been traveling eighteen kilometers every Sunday to preach and teach them until the motorcycles were stolen in August. Since then, he had not been going, and the church was without a preacher, so we went together in our vehicle.

After church we visited a home about two kilometers away where the husband Paul Saiyua and his wife were both Christian Maasai of the Africa Inland Church (AIC) tradition. They were both educated, modern thinking people. He had an administrative job in the sugar factory nearby, and she was a trained teacher. They were developing their farm and wanted to talk about water wells. They fed us a nice meal, and then we agreed how we could help them dig a well near their house. We were impressed by their fine Christian spirit and home.

On Sunday, December 10, Vera and I, together with Nelson Ojango, our new veterinarian, and Joseph Sankale walked three kilometers to the church at Kitamooek. There was one lady and a child waiting under the sacred tree at 11:00 a.m. when we arrived. By

11:30, a few more had arrived, so we started singing. By noon, there were several women present, so Joseph started preaching. By 1:00 p.m., the service was over. About ten women and thirty children were present. Four women decided to follow Jesus. They knelt, and we had prayer for them. A few sick came for special prayer. The women were serious about following Christ. There was much repentance and turning away from prevalent sins.

Of Bribes and the Rule of Law

Ten minutes after arriving home, one late Sunday afternoon, we heard gunshots in the marketplace and people screaming. We went outside to hear better. Soon we saw a stream of Maasai men running on all the paths past our place, running to their homes. Finally, some friends stopped by to tell us that the General Service Unit (GSU) soldiers were beating people and shooting in the air.

This was a market day, so Ogwedhi was full of people. There was still a lot of tension over demarcation issues. The Siria Maasai had been given the right to demarcate a certain disputed section where Wuasinkishu Maasai were living and claiming. While the Siria were dividing all the land and giving it to their own people, the Wuasinkishu squatting on it were angry and tensions were very high. To keep the peace, about fifty General Service Unit (GSU) soldiers were camping at Enemasi.

On this particular Sunday, the police had arrested one of the main Wuasinkishu opposition ring leaders for organizing delegations to take bribes to officials to stop the demarcation. Witnesses said, his son was so angry he drove their truck around in the marketplace like a wild man, so the police arrested him too "for driving without a license and no insurance." The arrested men were taken to Nakuru. Emotions were running high among the Wuasinkishu that day. Apparently, some of them were conspiring as to how they could release those arrested or so the police thought.

As a response, a Land Rover full of GSU brutes came from Enemasi, speeding into the marketplace. As it screeched to a halt, the troops bailed out and scattered into the market, firing into the air and beating people.

Most Maasai men were peacefully drinking in the bars at that hour. They were beaten mercilessly. Old men, respected elders, young men, women, old and young, were beaten, and those who could, fled as fast as their legs could carry them. Many Luos were also beaten and driven from the market. Several other Wuasinkishu were arrested. We heard that the police were searching for about eight more who were in hiding, some for bribery, some for murder or other infractions of the law.

It seemed the GSU tactics were to demonstrate to the whole tribe how weak and helpless they were in front of the government. If the government decides to take their land from under them and give it to the other side, it will be done. Their protests mean nothing. Their bribes mean nothing. The law rules!

In reflecting back on this issue from my current perspective, I recall that on my last visit to Osero twenty-eight years later, our Wuasinkishu friends were still living on their disputed land. Without knowing the details, my question remains: Did law and order prevail on their behalf, or did bribes pay off in the end?

Finding Qualified Quality People

A big crisis came to a head when our bookkeeper quit his job after a large amount of money was found to be missing. We spent two years training him, and then, he left. We had to start over again. Vera was drafted to be interim bookkeeper and cashier until a new bookkeeper could be found.

Nelson Ojango recently graduated from university as a veterinary doctor. He joined our staff in early October 1989. We were happy to have this enthusiastic, dedicated young man join our team. In addition to maintaining our dairy herd health and breeding program, he was to work with our extension agents to introduce improved breeding stock and better animal management practices among the Maasai.

Since Nelson was not from our community, he had no relative nearby nor home in which to live, so we invited him to live with us for a few weeks until he could get a room ready. We allowed him a small room in the dispensary, where he could have an office, which also served as kitchen and bedroom.

Although Nelson adjusted well to the work, as an outsider of a different ethnic group, he did not feel at home with either the Luo nor the Maasai culture and language. He depended a lot upon us and the few educated Kenyans for social and moral support. Further, his salary as a qualified veterinary doctor was high. The promised funding required to keep him on staff was delayed. Some donors were interested, but the bureaucratic red tape took too much time. We couldn't see that we would be able to get the money until sometime in 1991. After seven months, the drain on our budget was too much. We had to let him go in June. I felt this was a major defeat in our livestock program.

Malaria, the Number One Killer

As in most of sub-Saharan Africa, malaria was and still is the number one killer of humans, especially babies and small children. This was obviously true among the Maasai in our area.

In a letter, Vera wrote to Kristina: "There are so many babies dying here. Rosa's baby died last week. It was sick for several months. Otaro's baby died last Saturday ... Paul Sangai's baby is still sick, and Jane's baby is not that healthy, so I don't know how many more will die. Malaria is really bad at this time of year."

The babies often died, and most of the adults suffered from malaria from time to time, and occasionally also succumbed. At the time, I was also battling malaria. Clair Good also got sick and attempted to go to Nairobi but was hospitalized at Kericho. It is hard to estimate what the toll might be on the life span of the human body, affected by a lifetime of combatting repeated infections of this dreaded parasite.

Il Pashire Maasai Women's Group

In the emerging Kenyan nation, the formation of community-based women's development groups was in fashion and highly promoted by the government.

We were invited by a newly formed Il Pashire Maasai Women's

Group to visit and advise them. The group membership consisted of eighty-five women. The land demarcation committee allocated a nice plot of land that they were fencing. They wanted to keep improved cattle, improve a water spring, and start a tree nursery, besides building an office and shop in which to sell agricultural and veterinary supplies.

We were excited about their initial enthusiasm. We took a delegation of their leaders to visit an established Luo women's group to learn from their experience so that they could improve their own plans and set goals as a development group.

Il Pashire Women's group in front of their new building

A House at Enemasi

We had committed ourselves to construct a missionary house for the Good family at Enemasi. The community also wanted us to build two classrooms for the primary school that had been started there under a tree and was now using the church building as a classroom.

At the beginning of October 1989, we gave a contract to a *fundi* to make 10,000 pressed soil bricks. He worked five days, made bad bricks, and left "to get an assistant" but never returned. He said no word, left no clue, simply never returned. Disappeared. How long should we wait before hiring another contractor? These were the kinds of situations that I had to face each step of the way to the final coat of paint, the things that gave my leather stomach ulcers. I wished I could just do the work myself, but I had to delegate.

It was not until early December that a different *fundi* took a contract to make the pressed soil blocks to make the walls and partitions. Another contractor started to lay the foundation.

Model Farmer Program

We launched a "Model Farmer" program. We started by identifying two farmers, one on the Luo side, and the other on the Maasai side of the boundary. Our model farmers agreed to try some of the innovations we suggested, at OSP expense, partly as research, but mostly to model improved techniques that we thought would be beneficial to the neighbor farmers, if they were imitated.

Unfortunately, the model farmer on the Luo side died suddenly. He left eleven children. His eldest son was twenty. We decided to keep his son on in the model farmer program.

Joseph Sankale was a known innovator on the Maasai side, so we chose him to be one of our model farmers. He kept a very nice Ayrshire bull and did cross breeding. He planted a lot of trees around his farm. We helped him set up the first Maasai poultry house in the area and installed one hundred pullets. They were doing fine.

However, instead of viewing his work as a model to learn from and imitate, his Maasai neighbors thought he was a fool. How could anyone in their right mind build a house with a tin roof for his chickens, while he and his own family were still living in a hut covered with grass? Even the more progressive Luo neighbors were not building poultry houses yet. Changes sometimes come slowly.

The Year In Review

At the close of 1989, we looked back on our work with some regret. The pressure had been intense. We always seemed to be three or four steps behind where we wished to be. Too many of our daily actions were driven by events and circumstances, rather than by careful planning. In other words, instead of being in charge and leading the way, too often our activities were determined by forces outside of ourselves, like sick people needing transportation, police requiring our assistance in pursuing our thieves, or demands of church authorities.

In church development, there were signs of hope. Forty-five new people were baptized in the past year. Included in that number, eight were Maasai men, two of whom exhibited leadership potential. We noted a spiritual awakening among the women, and many new ones were coming to the church fellowships. There were now nine such groups. This revival had to do with person-to-person evangelism, deepening understanding and commitment, demonstrated by forsaking adultery and other sins common to the culture. It was not another program. It was just happening as God's spirit led.

During her December break, Kristina enjoyed a wonderful class trip in Zanzibar. She highly recommended it to any tourist!

In Nairobi, I had another accident. Our new vehicle got hit broadside by a huge tanker rig as I was trying to enter the busy divided Haile Selassie I Avenue from a cross street. After a long wait, there was a small opening in the heavy traffic, so I foolishly attempted to dart across the oncoming traffic to enter the stream of cars going the way I wanted to go.

Just then a little red car suddenly appeared and cut in front of me and stopped, blocking my way and forcing me to stop in front of a behemoth tanker trailer loaded with alcohol. There was nothing I could do. Its horn and its brakes could not save me. At least I saved the little red car. Our vehicle spent some time at the rehabilitation center in Kisii undergoing a restructuring process.

CHAPTER 27

Of Welcome Guests and Not So Welcome Thieves

Guests

From time to time, the tedium of our hectic lifestyle was relieved by family activities. For example, on her mid-term break in February 1990, Kristina brought her RVA friends, Iryne, Norma, and Alisha, home on the Thursday night bus, and I met them at the Awendo junction and brought them home in the morning. They went walking in the bush to meet Kristina's Maasai friends, and otherwise stayed in the house and read books.

On Sunday, while Vera and I went to church, the girls got busy and made a birthday dinner for her. When we arrived at home, the lasagna, buns, tossed salad, and chocolate cake were all ready to eat. The celebration was enhanced with homemade ice cream, made in Vera's kerosene refrigerator.

After returning our girls to RVA, Vera and I celebrated Valentine's day, the anniversary of our engagement, at the Minar Restaurant, a popular Indian eating place in Westlands. Dr. Vic and Christina Buckwalter accompanied us.

A Guest from Pennsylvania

At the Guest House, we were introduced to John Yost, a remarkable seventy-seven-year-old retired dairy farmer from Red Hill, Pennsylvania. John was Erma Lehman's cousin. He was one of the larger contributors to support the Eastern Mennonite Mission. He had travelled to a lot of countries of the world with Heifer International

Projects and Mennonite Economic Development Associates (MEDA) to help third world Christians get into dairy farming. He entertained us with very interesting stories about those times.

John was on his way to Tanzania to see some of the projects to which he had contributed. As we were going the same direction, we took him along with us to Ogwedhi for a couple of days. From there, he went on to visit the sites in Tanzania. We also took Gary Miller with us. He was a thirty-one-year-old single truck driver who decided to take an extended vacation to see Kenya.

After many days, John Yost returned to us from his tour in Tanzania. He was a frank, outspoken person who shared his mind. He was disappointed in how the mission and the Tanzania church leaders were interested only in getting money to build church buildings. He would have preferred to see his money used in afforestation projects, soil conservation, or improvement in agricultural practices. He reasoned that the members could finance their church projects by themselves if they would increase their production. He was very impressed with our Ogwedhi Sigawa Project, introducing improved dairy livestock and developing our magnificent tree nursery. We took him to Migori where he caught a bus to Nairobi.

It was some weeks later that we received notice that John was donating funds for OSP to purchase a welder and tools to set up a welding shop and to teach our people that practical skill. Yes, "Guests are a blessing!"

A Guest from Ethiopia

We were honored to have an outside guest visit us during the summer of 1990. Dr. Ketema Belete came all the way from Ethiopia to see us. I had first learned to know him as a student in my class back in Ethiopia, and then he worked with us as an evangelist at Bedeno. Later, he graduated from EMC in Virginia, and after thirteen years in the USA, returned home with his PhD in Agriculture from the University of Oklahoma. He was teaching and doing research at the Alemaya University of Agriculture in Harar Province, Ethiopia.

Ketema shared a lot of news about the situation and people of Ethiopia. After the 1974 revolution, Ethiopia suffered sixteen years of turmoil, cultural upheaval, political struggle and terror, wars, famine, economic chaos, and religious persecution. Now, with the collapse of the international "cold war," religious oppression was easing up a bit in Ethiopia.

There was more religious freedom, but the government refused to return the confiscated buildings and properties to the churches. Government officials said they would grant the believers permission to build new ones, but the persecuted believers could not trust the government. What would prevent them from deciding tomorrow to expropriate or nationalize those buildings as well?

The war was going terribly. The Tigrayan Liberation Front was within one hundred kilometers of Addis Ababa. The Eritrean Liberation Front was closing in on Asmara, the second biggest city. Men, boys, and old men were being rounded up and shipped to the military training camps against their will for a few months and then sent off to the slaughter at the front. Many never returned. Many of those who did return came back missing a limb, mentally disturbed, or with another injury or disability. Farm work and food production fell to the lot of women, resulting in increased hunger. All signs pointed to the pending collapse of the Marxist Dergue Regime. What would take its place?

Other Guests

We also had guests from the USA and Canada. Mary Oyer, an ethnomusicologist and professor, led a tour of nineteen Goshen alumni to Kenya. She included OSP and our community in their itinerary. To welcome them, we made lavish preparations: killed a bull, cooked a lot of food for more than 200 people, organized a tour of our project, and prepared a music program of two Maasai choirs, a Luo choir, students' choirs, and a traditional dance group. The guests were to leave their camp in Maasai Mara early in the morning and arrive at Ogwedhi around noon. After being shown around OSP, they were to sit for the program from 2-4:30 p.m., enjoy the feast, and then go off to a hotel in Migori for the night. That was the plan.

Well, we waited and waited and waited. The local people came, the Maasai men wearing the cleanest Maasai blankets and sheets ever. The women came all decked out in their finest beaded splendor and equally clean. Spirits were high. We waited some more. Finally, around 4:00 p.m., we let the program begin without the guests. The Maasai choirs sang first, so the women could eat and go home before too late for their evening chores. Then the students ate. Finally, we and the elders sat down to eat. Then we saw three vans come in.

By this time, it was 6:00 p.m., and the food was mostly consumed. Some students were still around, so they performed for them for about twenty minutes. Then our guests ate what was left, and by 7:30 p.m., were on their way to the hotel at Migori. The muddy roads from Mara were terrible, and it had taken them all day to get through. They did not see anything of OSP except the dining hall at the school. Our people were disappointed, but then again, I am sure our guests were too!

Some weeks later, on a Saturday night, Mary Oyer returned to visit us with her taxi driver, Justus Kamau. She was very disappointed about the outcome of her botched visit with the tour group. Therefore, she came again, stayed overnight, went to a Maasai church service with us, and really enjoyed herself. They returned to Nairobi on Monday morning just before we packed for our trip to Maasai Mara.

A Thief in the Family

A thief broke into our store. This time he only took our automatic syringe and a bottle of Terramycin worth about fifty dollars. Mwanyakiti, the twenty-two-year-old son of our doctor, Omondi and younger brother to Caleb, was caught with the evidence. I had to take him, the policeman, and witnesses off to Kilgoris to court the next day.

It was annoying to be distracted. Having just arrived home from Nairobi, there were so many things needing our attention. Then, since we had guests for a few days, I took them along. They were impressed mostly with the terrible condition of our roads.

Mwanyakiti had already developed a bad reputation as a thief. He had been involved in several cases and was a prime suspect in our motorcycle drama. The community people were hoping we would press charges and have him imprisoned.

What should we do? In the first place, he was the son of our devout, kind, and respected doctor. Some in the community suggested we expel the whole family from our community. I had problems with the injustice of that course of action. Further, I liked the rascal though I knew he was a thief. I was teaching him to drive our vehicle. He was one of the best gardeners I had known. Now he turned and robbed us! Furthermore, he had a young wife. They were planning to open a restaurant in town. They had most of the equipment ready but lacked 2,000 Ksh. to get started.

In the end, ministers of justice gave Mwanyakiti four months to enjoy the dubious "hospitality" of the Kisii prison for his selfish act. Somehow my heart remained stone cold. Before turning him into the police at Kilgoris, I gave him some very plain and very serious words of advice, which I hoped and prayed he would think about in those four months.

One day in mid-March 1990, Ole Musukeri's cattle were stolen. He came and asked me to help him with the OSP vehicle. I used that opportunity to question him as to why he acted like our "enemy," not paying for past use of the vehicle, and now asking for additional favors. After getting that point across, I sent Caleb with the vehicle taking Ole Musukeri and his neighbors as far as the bridge on the Migori River. They found the cattle and returned them.

That afternoon, Rosa, his wife, came with an invitation to come and eat roasted meat. It was an established custom that, when the neighbors helped to recover stolen cattle, the owner should slaughter one of the animals and share in a feast of gratitude. For me, to be invited was a sign of no hard feelings. We thought we better go to renew the relationship!

Robbed Again

It was mid-May that Ole Miberre and his son, James, accompanied me to Nairobi. We stopped at a dealer to investigate the possible purchase of a posho mill they were hoping to set up near Enemasi as a venture into the world of business. They had many steers ready for the market that would make this venture a real possibility.

While we were inside the venue examining the available machines, someone else was outside breaking into our truck. The enterprising thief took off with an empty gas cylinder and my briefcase which contained crucial legal documents, Kristina's and my passports, my Bible, and about 5,000 shillings.

Not only did that selfish deed thwart our business plans, but it cost us days of valuable time and energy to replace all the missing documents. I only hoped and prayed that somehow, the thief, his associates, or his loved ones (if he had any) would somehow read my stolen Bible (with all my sermon notes) and meet the Lord of the sacred book. After all, it is written: "Everything works together for good for those who love the Lord." It would do my wobbly faith good to see just how this truth works out in this particular case. However, the passage of time proved that it was not for me to know. The matter is still in his hands.

More About Thieves

One day in September, we were having a committee meeting at Ogwedhi with some guests. Vera had locked up our house and joined our committee for noon lunch. When she went back, she found the door unlocked and our desk lock broken and about 5,000 Ksh. missing.

We immediately started investigating and found witnesses that confirmed that the Omondi boy, Mwanyakiti, who was back in the community after serving his four-month prison sentence, was seen approaching and later leaving the vicinity of our house around noon. Another witness said he had come into his home shortly after noon, changed his clothes, and went out toward the town. Another had seen him set off on foot for Oyani about half an hour later.

So, we sent a man with a policeman on our motorcycle. They caught up to him near Oyani, eleven kilometers away. When they put on the brakes and the policeman dismounted, the boy took off full speed for the bush. The policeman was rather heavy and out of shape and stumbled and fell, so the boy got away.

About one week later, we drove to Kisumu to replenish the drug supply for our clinic. We parked the truck outside our pharmacy wholesaler and went in for about forty minutes. When we came out, we found our new vehicle had been broken into and the radio/cassette player was gone—ripped out in broad daylight, high noon on main street, in full view of all passersby. No one raised any alarm. What kind of citizens inhabit our cities?

Sometime later, on one of my business visits in Nairobi, as I was being driven to the bus for my return home, my wristwatch was stolen right off my arm as we sat in stalled traffic on that hot day with the window open. I got out and chased the thieves, but they (four of them) were young and streetwise. I was the ranting, raging, helpless victim, shouting madly, as they scampered for cover into a crowded side street. It was the best watch I had ever owned—a six-year-old quartz electric—kept perfect time. It was a remembrance gift from Hong Kham Nanthavong in appreciation for my part in settling his family as refugees in Tofield, Alberta, back in 1979. Anyway, another involuntary contribution to the welfare of Kenya's "poor".

Near the end of our six years of living and working in Ogwedhi, I counted at least a dozen times we or the project suffered from large or small incidents of theft. The list did not include all the little and not so little pilfering's of tools, milk, vegetables, seeds, and other assets that disappeared unnoticed. One might get the impression that our main development activity was to support the theft industry.

Anyway, thanks to the Lord, we were rich enough to pay this "tax" and still survive.

CHAPTER 28

Confessions: Our Physical, Mental and Spiritual Wellbeing

Like all good mothers, my mother was always concerned about the state of our physical, mental, and spiritual wellbeing. In my letter written on March 24, 1990, I attempted to put her mind at ease. I shared the following:

> Howdy! We're still alive, believe it or not! I'm very healthy or at least I was until this morning when I hurt my back while mixing concrete by hand. So, I'm walking around with a little extra stoop like a seventy-five-year-old. Vera is fine also. Her tests were all clear. Seems she had some minor infections that wouldn't go away and that left some cysts on the cervix. We hope the medical procedures cleared it all out.
>
> Mentally I'm on more shaky ground. I have had enough tensions that, when coupled with malaria (or typhoid or whatever was getting me down from mid-January to mid-March), I was about ready to explode at the least provocation. The veneer of the tolerant, compassionate, kind-hearted super spiritual missionary was wearing holes through which could be seen something far uglier, more cynical, meaner, and sinister. Discouragement was close at hand.
>
> Anyway, I'm okay today. I'm still mad at the pastors and church rulers and at the sub-manager and his dairy crew, at the thieves we sent to prison, at the brick maker and 101 other crooks, con artists,

cheats, and scoundrels that try to get something for nothing from this naïve and gullible missionary!

However, I still love some other people who are poor, honest, hardworking, loyal, self-giving, kindhearted, and patiently suffering hardships while generously helping family members, distant relatives, and needy neighbors with never a word of complaint. Our lives are surrounded with such good people, and it's possible to appreciate them, but it's "loving" our "enemies" or even "sinners" that is giving me a problem ...

Here at Ogwedhi we are extremely busy every day of the week. Sunday is no day of rest. We go to church at 10:00 a.m. and get home at 5:00 p.m. only to find people waiting to ask us for this or that, or to beg us to take a sick loved one to a hospital. Vera and I are always glad when the sun finally sets and the people go home, that is if they do not decide to stay with us overnight, which often happens. Our little, miniscule gift of hospitality gets stretched to the limits. Sometimes it is awful to be liked by so many people.

Sometimes we complain, and then think of what Jesus went through; the crowds pressing on him, some coming out of dire need, some coming out of curiosity, and many coming for the free lunch or for what they could get out of the master. Our crowds are much smaller, a steady stream of ones and twos ...

By the way, I was not mixing concrete by hand out of necessity. We have plenty of willing low paid workers to do that. But I was supervising, and I do need the exercise and why not dig in? Anyway, it seems like the kind of thing I must not do with such vigor anymore.

My back has been really good these past six months or so. It has been a gradual process from spending several days in bed over two years ago, to living with a sensitive back which healed a lot during three months of furlough (thanks to good roads and Charles' Buick).

Back on these roads again, I was wearing a support belt until a few months ago when everything got fine, and I could go down steps and carry loads without thinking of pain. Having the new truck with a good seat has made a huge difference ...

The pastors and bishop are having a big day with communion and feasting at Remu, (five kilometers away) and wanted us to come. I have a bad attitude towards them for several reasons and decided to be ornery and stay at home. So, I helped the boys with cement work this morning, building a yard for our dairy cows (hurt my back as a punishment?). This afternoon I worked on fixing the truck, then took a bath and decided to devote some hours to unloading this stuff on you!

... Well, the fifth shower of today just ended at 5:45 p.m., total was one inch of rain.

The pastors and bishop just arrived back from Remu on foot in the rain, so they got soaked a bit. We'll eat with them tonight at Pastor Paul Otieno's house. Tomorrow, we have a joint service at Kitamooek among the Maasai. Several people expect to be baptized ...

On another Sunday a month later, I wrote another letter to my mother sharing some random reflections on what we were doing and evaluating the long-range results.

I've often thought about our being here. I left pastoring the biggest, best organized, and most stable Mennonite Church in the Northwest Conference in Alberta to come here to try to teach small groups of illiterate ladies and children, sometimes only two or three adults in a group, out under a "holy" tree in some Maasai bush, having to use an interpreter and sometimes two interpreters to try to get a few basic and simple concepts across. And most of my energy is otherwise expended in such earthy and mundane tasks as running a dairy farm, building, or doing taxi service for desperate or not-so-desperate people.

Yet, after four and one-half years we see a Maasai church emerging. We have our "twelve disciples," a core of three or four older men and some bright and not so bright young men who are committed to following Jesus as Lord, and about fifty baptized women who face the opposition or scorn of husbands, brothers, parents, and neighbors because of their enthusiasm for following Jesus.

We have Magdalena who has recently been expelled from her husband's home and chased away from her children because she steadfastly refused to stop following Jesus. She says, "I will never give up following my Lord and Savior no matter what the cost!" She has her suckling baby, and her parents allowed her to come home to live under their shelter for now. Pray for her and her husband!

Then we have another hundred or so women who are greatly attracted to the church who have not yet made the decision to be Christians or who have not yet completed instructions for baptism. But their enthusiasm is contagious. One would think that sooner or later it will sweep over to the men.

When I think of all this, even though I can't see much direct connection between our being here and what is happening in the church, I am gratified and feel good about being here …

Well, now It's 6:15 p.m. Vera served a nice dinner, and our afternoon slipped by with a steady stream of callers as usual. It has been raining a bit off and on. Now it's getting dark soon, so maybe the traffic will stop for the night.

… But wait. Sure enough, another knock on the door. This poor Luo man wanted me to drive him and some policemen to a village about twelve kilometers from here tonight, hopefully to recover goods that were stolen from his house recently.

Having a policy that I don't drive at night, or daytime either, for other errands than to save the lives of sick people, I sympathetically but firmly refused. This also happens to be the same man that I took to Migori hospital twice about two weeks ago and he had not paid fully for his second trip!

He had gone to a local medical expert, a woman, complaining of his sickness. She insisted there was only one cure. She would have to cut out his uvula. He didn't like that idea much, but she insisted he would die if he didn't accept her "help." So, she cut it out and he almost bled to death.

His family came to me for ambulance service. He was so weak from loss of blood (or was it the original sickness?) that he could hardly walk. A few days later, after being discharged, they were back at 11:00 p.m., asking for the vehicle to rush him to the hospital again, for bleeding had resumed and he was weakening fast. So, off the vehicle went on his behalf again with our driver.

Now, tonight? Did I do the right thing? I sympathize with the poor man for wanting his things back. Who enjoys being robbed? But I remind him that the place is within walking distance. He says the police refuse to walk that far. They need a healthy bribe to stimulate them. I calculate that if he can't afford to bribe the police, can he really afford to pay for the vehicle mileage charge?

Anyway, I want to stay indoors and write this letter tonight. I can't help all the people solve all their problems, so I'll just abide by our policy. Besides, I must get up early tomorrow to go to Migori anyway.

Oh yes, we have another visitor. A young man, who works at Enemasi for our contractor, decided to try to go back to school. So, he dropped in at 2:30 pm. knowing that this is a free hotel with fair food and accommodation, and that there would be a free ride out to civilization tomorrow, all without even asking. Not bad, eh?

213

In the midst of this constant stress, I realized how much I needed to keep renewing my relationship with God. I needed help to carry on. I needed more of his love, compassion, patience, and forgiving spirit to control my life on a day-to-day basis. In my turmoil, I prayerfully identified with the song by the Maranatha singers, 1974:

Cause me to come to thy river, o Lord.
Cause me to drink of thy river, o Lord.
Cause me to live by thy river, o Lord.
Cause me to come, cause me to drink, cause me to live!

I sang and thought, some people are like camels. They take one good long drink, then go away and wander far in the desert for thirty or forty days before returning to drink again. Some are like cattle, driven by their master, seeking grass in the highlands, but forced of necessity to return to the water every second or third day to drink desperately and deeply.

Others are like deer that go about the day's activity early before dawn. When the sun reaches its hottest, they retreat to the shade of the trees close to the life-sustaining streams.

Some are more like hippos who spend the whole day submerged in the cool life-giving waters, and only come out at night to forage in the tall grass and bushes close to the water's edge, never wandering far from this source of life.

Still others, like fish, live their whole lives submerged in the living waters. They depend entirely upon the river for their very life, deriving from it their nourishment, their breath, their recreation, their protection, and their destiny. They would not even for a moment think of abandoning its protective coolness to look for "greener pastures." For them, there is no other option. They are satisfied to remain in the river, finding perfect freedom and contentment within its boundaries. I questioned, which kind of animal do I most resemble?

"If anyone remains in me and I in him, he will bear much fruit. Apart from me you can do nothing." – Jesus (John 15;5, NIV)

CHAPTER 29

Anecdotes Along the Way

Taxi Driver

The enterprising owner-operator taxi driver was five minutes early for his pre-dawn pick-up appointment at the Mennonite Guest House gate. We squeezed my oversized suitcase and things into the back seat and myself into the miniature front seat and were soon roaring off into the darkness. The driver carefully, almost lovingly, guided his precious little "fixed-it-myself" mechanical marvel through the labyrinth of pot-holed back roads until it reached the Mombasa Highway.

Slowly, the ancient relic of a simpler era gained momentum as the driver, ever eager to gain favorable standing with his special client by not delivering him late to his appointment, urged it on to keep up with the flow of Pajeros, Mercedes, and Nissan vans rushing to the Jomo Kenyatta International Airport.

I looked at my watch and relaxed a bit. Thanks to his keeping up the speed, we were still in good time. We had already slowed down for the round-about just before the toll booth that guards the airport zone, when something went terribly wrong under the shabby conveyance. It made a strange noise and shook violently. With grave concern, the driver-owner coaxed it to the side of the freeway and stopped just before the toll booth where you pay a twenty-shilling fee "for parking."

I looked at my watch again as my escort got down on the wet asphalt and crawled under his car to investigate. We still had two hours before ET Flight No. 950 was to take off. No immediate problem! How happy I was that this didn't happen twenty kilometers sooner back on some dark, deserted, rain-soaked road!

My friend re-emerged from down under, to announce with grave concern that it was a serious problem indeed. However, he was quick to reassure me that it was fixable, just allow him twenty minutes! He got out an assorted collection of "tools" from the boot and sunk back down under. I looked at his tools and at my watch and had my doubts.

I got out to satisfy my curiosity. He showed me that the tie-rod had become completely detached from the front wheel. The wheel was completely free of any control from the steering mechanism!

I just had to breathe a prayer of gratitude and wonder at the mysterious fact that it didn't become detached while speeding down the freeway. I could only imagine the consequences if it had. We might both be lying, stretched out somewhere in a dark roadside ditch. We would perhaps be dead to the discomfort of the drizzling rain that delayed the approaching light of dawn. Our corpses would likely be quite cooled before they could be rushed to the hospital or morgue by the first "good Samaritan" that chanced to notice the roadside wreck when the darkness and fog finally lifted. What an abbreviated end to an intended journey that would have been!

But thanks to the One who watches, that didn't happen. And the problem we faced was much different than that which could-have-been. I waited outside watching as the driver-mechanic jacked up the car and hurriedly tried to remove bolts where the thread had long since been disfigured and jammed. Dozens of cars, many of them almost empty, slowed down to creep through the toll gate.

I made it a game of guessing how many would pass by before a "good Samaritan" would stop to ask if I needed a lift to catch my plane. I was amazed how many potential candidates for that honor passed me by. Did I really look that dangerous? The criminal type? Too dirty? Perhaps a carrier of a deadly disease? Finally, one man, a Christian Swede, working for a Christian organization, stopped and invited me to transfer my luggage and myself to his car.

I paid my hapless owner-driver, *de facto* mechanic, his much-needed 600 shillings, thanked him for his inconvenience, and leaving him under his much-adored breadwinner, departed with my new-found "Samaritan" friend. We still had plenty of time to catch the flight!

Church Developments

As the year 1990 dawned, I brought seven Maasai on Monday to Ewuaso-Ng'iro to attend a seminar conducted by the Christian Missionary Fellowship (CMF) folks. It was where the Clair Good family was studying the language and culture. I slept in the Good's house and drove to Nairobi the next morning early. Those that came were David Ole Shaai, Samson Masake, Yohanna, Joseph (the skinny one), Maurice Ole Macho, another Joseph from Ntuka, and James Kiloing'oni. James Kashe joined us from Nairobi. His father, Ole Miberre, never came.

Some of the Maasai Christians had a Christmas celebration at Ole Konchella's place. He had become a Christian and had given up all pretense or claim to inherit his father's *laibonship*, a kind of traditional medicine man or seer/prophet. He killed a fat sheep, and we all had a feast. About fifty people attended.

In April 1990, we visited the church at Oloonkoijoo for the first time in over a year. It was gratifying to see that some new people had joined the group. We had started this church about four years earlier. They were still not strong because they had a very weak leader who figured he was quite a strong leader. He was one who aspired to be a great pastor but could not faithfully tend to his little flock. Now he had gone on to greater things at Narok, so Joseph Sankale was appointed to be their leader, and this was his first Sunday.

We held a two-day Maasai church leader's seminar. About twelve young men were present, plus a few women who refused to stay away. I was reminded of another woman who said, "at least let me eat the crumbs that fall from the children's table." It was a good seminar. We were trying to have these seminars once per month for two days. It was a big help to the leaders who had little Bible training as such.

A Meningitis Epidemic

In March, an epidemic of meningitis swept through our area. We heard reports of twenty-eight people having died. We saw several victims that did not die.

For a while our vehicle was going out to the hospital at Migori every day and many nights, sometimes two or three times per day, taking sick people out and bringing a few dead ones back. One of the dead ones was a TB victim. Most of the sick ones got well once they reached medical help. If given in time, a dose of the right antibiotic enabled the victim to recover quickly. We certainly appreciated our driver who made most of the trips.

One day we drove out to Enemasi. We arrived just after they buried one of our church members. She was a thirty-something-year-old mother of five. She was such a beautiful woman: tall, graceful, intelligent, and a Christian. She could speak about ten languages. Her five-month-old baby was also very sick. We took the baby to the hospital in Migori along with another man who also had the disease. What were the baby's chances of survival without a mother?

After several weeks, the epidemic ran its course and moved on out of the area.

Signs of Progress

Although things seemed to move slowly, by mid-1990, there were signs of progress. After starting a year earlier, we finally were able to put our zero-grazing unit into use. We also finished remodeling the barn with slatted floor for the calf pens, a separate feed room, and an office.

The pit silo filled with chopped napier grass or corn
to feed the dairy herd in the zero-grazing unit.

The fish keeper's house was almost ready for inhabitation. The third fishpond was still being dug. We were excited about our first fish experiment. We could wait no longer, so did a trial harvest. We took out about thirty tilapia which were still a bit small. However, the taste was great. We postponed any further harvest until the fall.

The fishponds were stocked with tilapia.

Well-digging developed into another business. Farmers would bring a deposit of money, and we would contract the digging of water wells for them.

We were about ready to move twenty head of cattle over to the recently acquired Kiikat property. It took a full year to fence the twenty acres, dig a well, and build a corral and a guard house.

The county council gave 50,000 Ksh. to build a school at Enemasi. The councilor also promised he would bring another 80,000 Ksh. to build a doctor's house and a few rooms for a dispensary. While promises do not build buildings, they do build hope and courage. The doctor's house never materialized.

We planned that as soon as construction of the Enemasi missionary house was complete, we would start construction of three school classrooms. That would take another year, according to the general movement of such undertakings.

I found my patience constantly tried. I vainly imagined how interesting it could be if contracted workers would hurry for once. They were so slow. Something that should have taken three months took one year. It seemed they never realized that if they hurried and completed their contract, they would get paid sooner, and with the time saved, they could take on the next contract. Horrible capitalists!

Ole Sikawa was starting to build a small mud and grass house for Kristina to live in after she finished school. She had decided that she would delay returning to the USA to pursue her college education for a year. She wanted to have an in-depth living experience to understand Maasai culture. She arranged to live as a "daughter" with Noonkipa, her best Maasai friend.

Near the end of August, representatives from Christian Health Association of Kenya (CHAK) visited OSP. They signed a formal agreement to remodel and enlarge our dispensary and build two new nurses' houses. They would pay all costs and do all the work. OSP's responsibility was to find and hire a qualified nurse and ensure that adequate services were given.

They began construction in September. The cost of enlarging the dispensary and building the two nurses' houses came to a total of 525,000 Ksh. CHAK made an ongoing agreement to pay the salaries as well as stock the medicines. We were very thankful for this help!

We immediately decided to hire a community nurse. Then, we began negotiations to get a couple from Tanzania to help us start a community-based health program. He was a Christian Maasai medical assistant, with qualifications next to a doctor. His wife was a teacher at a teacher's college. They were to be sent as a missionary couple from the Tanzania Mennonite Church to work with the Maasai church and community.

*Thanks to the Christian Health Association of Kenya
(CHAK), the health center was updated and expanded.*

Signs of Regress

On another visit to the church at Olmisigiyioi, we found that three children had died since the last time we were there. Ole Miberre's child and two grandchildren had died of measles. Several others were very ill, and some old people were sick too. That community really needed a dispensary. The people were asking us to help build one, but it takes money to build, staff, and operate dispensaries. In the meantime, so many people, especially children, suffered and died needlessly.

A sixty-four-year-old Maasai elder informed us that he wanted to be baptized. That sounded good. However, he stipulated that first he wanted to marry one more time. Several of his wives had abandoned him and only one remained. He knew that after baptism, the church would not allow a member to enter a polygamous relationship. So, he wanted to marry a young fourteen-year-old girl now before being baptized.

Imagine a sixty-four-year-old man marrying a fourteen-year-old girl, condemning her to a lifetime of widowhood. We warned him, that if he did that, there would be no baptism, period. He solved the problem by marrying the girl anyway, and to my knowledge, was never baptized before he died a few years later. This was a grave injustice for the girl since widows never remarry in Maasai traditional culture.

CHAPTER 30

An Unforgettable Summer

A Daughter's Engagement

On top of all the normal happenings, the big excitement for us in the summer of 1990 was the two-month visit of our daughter Sheryl and her boyfriend Eric Payne. Sheryl and Eric set foot in Kenya at the Jomo Kenyatta International Airport on June 24th. Kristina came from her school to help us welcome them.

We were all so excited. We spent Monday and Tuesday with them, introducing Eric to Africa for the first time and showing him the sights in Nairobi. We spent Tuesday night with Kristina at Kijabe and then brought Sheryl and Eric with us to Ogwedhi on Wednesday.

It was very special to have Sheryl back home again, and an extra treat to have time to get to know her chosen. Eric was a handsome, six-foot-three-inch, muscular African American from Virginia. He had been working his way through college by pumping gas and fixing the odd car since he was a mechanic. This was his first chance to visit Africa, and he really enjoyed it. At first, he found a lot of things to be a bit shocking or strange.

Over the next few days, he tried to be as helpful as possible. He helped me fix a broken spring on the Toyota and maintained the motorcycles. We spent a few days installing doors and windows, cleaning, and painting the missionary house at Enemasi. The Good family hoped to move in by mid-July.

On July 20th, we drove to Kijabe to help Kristina celebrate her graduation from high school. We brought Ole Sikawa and his wife, Noonkipa, along with us. Although it was a bit out of their natural element, I think they enjoyed being there.

Then we took them to Nairobi, a place Noonkipa had never been before. We visited the Yaya Center, a brand-new, upper-class shopping mall, which had Nairobi's first escalator, a glass elevator, and water fountains. We showed them around the city. Sunday morning, we took them to the bus station to return home.

Kristina graduated from high school on July 20, 1990

The next day, we headed east on the Mombasa road. It took us eight hours to cover the 530 kilometers trip to the coast. We saw a lot of new country, vast empty stretches of semi-arid bush, and grass with few people and little agriculture. There were only a few wild animals along the way. My development-oriented mind pondered the possibilities of utilizing this vast underused space in more effective ways. Africa had so much potential!

The beautiful coastline, white sandy beaches, warm salt water, coral reefs and sunshine make Mombasa and the east coast a popular tourist and vacation area. We had reservations at the Diani Beachlet #3. Our cabin was about one hundred feet from the beach and the deep blue-green Indian Ocean. Coconut palms and other trees gave some shade.

A long coral reef runs parallel to the beach about one quarter of a mile out. It caught and modified the big waves of the open sea, protecting the beach itself. Day and night there was a constant roar of the breakers out there crashing against the reef.

One quiet lovely evening, while we were all relaxing in our cottage, Eric formally asked us for the hand of our daughter, Sheryl, in marriage. We were impressed with his speech and this gesture of propriety. He was the only one of our eventual sons-in-law to show such respect as to formally ask us parents for such an awesome gift.

The family spent most of the two weeks at Diani Beach. I had to spend five days of the second week attending a D.E.L.T.A. seminar held in Mombasa. When it was finished, we all drove home together.

We had to rush home to Ogwedhi to get the "red carpet" dusted off for two guests from Heifer Projects International who arrived on Saturday, August 4th. They arrived three hours after we did. One was from the USA, the other from Nairobi. They were considering the possibility of funding our veterinary program and wanted to look over our situation. They stayed overnight, toured OSP on Sunday morning, and returned to Nairobi in the afternoon.

Monday morning, seven STAT team members came to visit us and stayed Monday night. Tuesday morning, I took them to the bus in Migori to head back to Kisumu where they were helping to build a church.

After their departure, we left on a camping trip with Sheryl and Eric to the Maasai Mara game preserve about fifty kilometers southeast of Ogwedhi. Before reaching the park, we diverged off the road on top of the escarpment overlooking the park. After driving through the grass, we found a spot behind a rise, out of sight of the road, where we pitched our tent. After a supper around our campfire, all five of us crowded our tired bodies into our little tent. We slept really well, only vaguely aware of the natural sounds of the nightlife that surrounded us—the distant laugh of hyenas, the nearby roar of a lion calling to its mates, the grunts and sniffs of unidentified animals exploring the remnants of our campfire or our tent and sounds like the hooves of passing wildebeest or maybe cape buffalo.

Later, we learned such camping in undisclosed, unprotected areas was strictly illegal, not to mention dangerous. Not knowing, and not thinking, we foolish ones slept very well. As the saying goes, "Fools rush in where angels fear to tread!"

The next morning, we broke camp and entered the park, looked the animals over, and camped legally at the southeast end at the Sand River campsite. Despite a little rain, we enjoyed being out there again. We saw all the main species of animals except the rhinoceros. There were millions of wildebeest and zebras, though actually we did not count them. Their seasonal migration from the Serengeti in Tanzania up north into Kenya was on, and they were almost everywhere.

Our Twenty-Sixth Anniversary

We had just returned home from our camping trip on the evening of August 15th. As we were cleaning up, the girls mysteriously requested Vera and I to dress up in our Sunday best and sit in the living room. Then they closed the kitchen door and prepared a big 26th wedding anniversary celebration for us.

Sheryl finally came out and posted a "Honeymoon Café" sign on the door. Later, Eric came out, dressed in his finest, and escorted us into the candle-lit dining room. He guided us to the table set for two. The "servers" waited on us as we dined in fine style. Later, they escorted us to our "Honeymoon Hotel" room, which was also candle-lit with soft music playing and bid us a good night. It was sweet of them.

After a few more days spent around our home, the time came when, as they say, "All good things must come to an end!" Sheryl and Eric's visit came to its inevitable close. We accompanied them to Nairobi, and they flew out on Monday, the 20th of August.

A Missionary House at Enemasi

One of the many challenges that kept us occupied was the construction of the house for our new missionaries, Clair and Beth Good. As each day went by, our anxiety increased. It meant one day closer to the day the Good family would complete their language and cultural studies. The proposed time of their arrival in our community was July 16, a deadline against which we measured all progress in the building.

The decision to build this house had been finalized in August, almost a year earlier. A contract to make bricks was given in October. The foundation was laid in December. However, construction moved very slowly. Bricks were laid for the walls, reaching up to the windowsills in March. By April, there was still no roof, floor, plastering, or plumbing. Excavation for a cistern and a septic tank was not yet done.

In the interest of getting the house ready for his family to move into by the July deadline, Clair had been making building trips to Enemasi from time to time. In May, he came and installed the roof and again in mid-June, to cement the floor.

The building was largely designed by Clair, a super house made of pressed earth blocks plastered inside and out with cement. It was a 42' x 26' structure and had the capacity for a half-story upstairs if he desired to develop it later. It was not yet painted and lacked the ceiling. A cistern, latrine pit, and porch had yet to be added. To get it finished, Clair brought his family at the beginning of July, pitched a tent in the yard, camping with his family, while he set to work. His family moved in on the appointed day.

Constructing buildings in Maasailand was very different from building in North America. No electricity meant no power tools. No backhoe meant excavation by pick, shovel, bucket, and rope. No cement mixer meant mixing by hand. Sand was brought from a distance by hiring a tractor and wagon. Sand was loaded and unloaded by hand. Water was brought by women carriers. Stones were picked up in a nearby field and brought by women on contract. Local craftsmen were contracted to do their parts.

To make the pressed earth blocks, marram soil, a gravel and clay mix, was mixed with a bit of cement, dampened, and pressed in a hand press at pressures up to 3,000 lb. per square inch.

This made nice cheap building blocks. They were laid up like bricks with mortar. Floors were cement. Rafters were made of eucalyptus poles. Roofs were tin. If a ceiling was deemed necessary, it was of hardboard or soft board. The walls were plastered with cement inside and outside. No insulation was required. No frost proofing of the cement foundation was necessary either.

Clair equipped this house with indoor plumbing, complete with a solar water heater. Rainwater was collected from the roof and stored in the cistern. He installed a solar electrical system to provide lights and to power his laptop. All in all, the family found the completed house to be quite comfortable.

Clair Good and helpers building the missionary house at Enemasi.

Unplanned Adventure

Once again, a sudden loud beating on our door and excited voices outside broke my deep, midnight sleep. Groggy and half awake, I stumbled out of bed and fumbled around in the dark until I found our flashlight. Then, staggering down the hallway and unlocking the door, I stared into the glare of flashlights, trying to identify the dark faces by the whiteness of their eyes and teeth, blending into the darkness behind them.

Relieved that they were some of our Maasai friends, yet concerned to know what calamity brought them to my door at this unearthly hour, I listened to their story.

They anxiously informed me that twenty of their cows had been stolen and they were demanding that I help them with our vehicle. Could I take some of them and the police around by the road south about ten kilometers away to lay an ambush to catch the thieves? The thieves were Kuria from Tanzania, about thirty-five kilometers to the south. They carried at least one automatic gun.

I usually refuse these kinds of requests because police work is not my work. Besides, I need to rest sometime, and these thefts were almost a nightly occurrence. This time, for friendship sake, I decided to go.

We woke up a few policemen, took the road southeast, and crossed the Migori River and circled around west to intercept the thieves who were chasing the cattle on foot straight south, taking a shortcut. Many Maasai warriors were following the thieves on foot with spears and bows and arrows but feared to get close because of the gun.

We reached where one of the shortcut paths crossed the road, left two policemen to lay an ambush, and drove on to the next path crossing the road and stopped the vehicle. The rest of the policemen and Maasai got out to set another ambush. Before they were all out of the car, one Maasai, the owner of the cattle, ran out in front of the headlights to look for tracks to see if his cattle had passed there yet or not.

Suddenly, four or five warning shots rang out in the darkness, and everybody dashed for cover. The thieves had arrived at the crossing at the very same moment we did. They had the advantage of the cover of darkness and ambushed us instead. We were grateful no one was hurt. I turned off the lights and reversed the car about one hundred meters and then turned it around, and leaving the police in the dark, I drove back to the other ambush site, picked up those two policemen, and returned to the site.

By this time the thieves had turned to the right, crossed a creek, then crossed the road on the other side, and were heading south again. The Maasai found the tracks again and followed south.

We couldn't follow with the vehicle, so we took a few of the police and a few Maasai and drove east, then south, and then back west, a block of about twenty kilometers. We intended to lay a few more ambushes where the thieves were most likely to cross.

We were there about twenty minutes when a group of Maasai caught up with us. They had run across about twelve kilometers distance almost as fast as we drove around by the road. These young warriors could sure move. They informed us that the policemen had fired shots at the thieves. The thieves had lost some of the herd, and the Maasai were able to recover nine cows. They thought the thieves were coming with the remaining cows on another route to the east of us.

We backtracked, leaving a few men at that crossing, just in case. By this time, it was 3:30 a.m. We headed east a bit and met two policemen on an anti-smuggling patrol. They stopped us, so we told them our problem. They suggested we take them south to a road parallel to the Tanzania border, so we took them there. It was a long, rough road. They said they would look out for us, so we should return. We got back and found our men, but the thieves had not reached our ambushes, and we could find no further tracks.

We searched all the way to Isebania in the west and back following the Tanzania border. No tracks. So, we returned, picked up our men, and drove in to where the thieves had split the cattle into two groups, where the Maasai had lost the tracks of the cattle and thieves.

By this time, it was daylight, and we found the place where the thieves had made a ninety degree turn into tall grass, which had confused the Maasai trackers in the dark. Since we had not found any tracks crossing the road further south, we assumed that the thieves were probably still in the large bushy area. They would be somewhere resting and hiding until they could continue their journey to Tanzania the next evening.

We decided we would leave the Maasai and police at this point to track down the cattle as they were able. Michael, our shopkeeper, and I would return to our work. We set out for home.

On the way we stopped at the place where we were first ambushed. We found four empty cartridges from a Chinese semi-automatic rifle about twenty feet from where the young man had been searching for footprints in the full light of our truck's headlights, and about one hundred feet from where our truck was standing. Either God helped us, or the man was only shooting to scare us. We could have all been dead.

Late that evening, just before dark, the rather tired group of trackers came jubilantly into the marketplace. They had recovered all the cattle but three. It was a cause to slaughter one cow and reward all the helpers with a feast. "All is well that ends well!"

That was not exactly a normal day in the life of a missionary. But then, what is normal? Most of our days had little unpredictable twists to them, and we were seldom bored.

Some days later, after this escapade, Caleb approached me voicing grave concern. He told me that someone he does not know met him in the Ogwedhi market and told him to "warn that *mzungu* to stay out of their game, or he will have his truck blown up!"

After thinking about it, I decided it was wise advice. My duty as an outsider, a missionary, was to be accountable for all the assets of the community development project, including its vehicle. I was also responsible for the wellbeing of my own wife and family and even for my own life. I should not be getting involved in police work, including gun fights with cattle thieves. I decided I should not interject myself into the age-old game played between the Maasai and the Kuria in seeing who can steal the most cattle from the other side!

Was this really the right decision? We were here to help the community develop itself. Development can only happen in an atmosphere of peace and cooperation. Cattle theft had been and still was a plague, a scourge in this society. It was a kind of war. How many have lost a loved one or a close relative? How many hundreds had been left destitute as widows and orphans? When was the last time the men and the women, in some homes, slept through a whole night in peace without having to be vigilant of their animals? How many nights and days had been wasted in pursuit of stolen animals, often with only negative results. How many families had their hopes dashed, having saved for years to buy a team of oxen to plow their fields, only to have their savings gone in one night? How many children had to grow up without milk in their diets? How many fields lie idle and unproductive because the farmer had no oxen to plow with and no animals to eat the vegetation that grows on it?

Is trying to stop cattle theft worth our time, cost, and risk? Is it a thing in which a Mennonite missionary should get involved? Is assisting one side in police work really the way to stop this plague? Perhaps there was a better way. We must find that way.

Kenyan Politics

Trouble had been brewing as President Daniel Arap Moi's government got older and more corrupt. The Kanu Party, in recent years, had forced constitutional changes, creating a one-party system that gave it absolute dictatorial power. Any semblance of democracy was now a sham.

In recent weeks, there was an underground swell of public sentiment, indicating it was high time for change. It was time to

230

restore a multi-party democracy. For a few weeks, Moi allowed enough freedom for debate so that his critics exposed themselves. Then, he declared the debate over and cracked down on all opposition. We heard over 1000 prominent people had been arrested and questioned. Some were detained without trial.

Riots broke out in the streets of many towns. Many protesters were shot by the security police. This show of force put a stop to the rioting, and there followed a very tense calm, but no happiness. The government had the blood of innocent citizens on its hands, and it knew it, and so did the citizens.

Such were the declining years of an ancient and increasingly corrupt regime.

At Ogwedhi, our main source of information were rumors, the British Broadcasting Corporation (BBC), and other external radio broadcasts. No one could trust the local official versions quoted in our papers. Locally, at Ogwedhi, things were calm.

CHAPTER 31

Reducing Tensions

The Clair and Beth Good family had moved into their new house in July. By the beginning of September, Beth had already established her reputation as a "doctor." She had taken a first aid course under St. John's Ambulance back home. She acquired some basic medicines and was treating five to ten people per day. Enemasi really needed to have a proper clinic there with properly trained staff.

We had been trying to have two-day training seminars for Maasai leaders every month. Clair joined me as a teacher, but the attendance was very disappointing. It seemed everybody worthy of the label "leader" was too busy. They were busy with home responsibilities in the mornings; they would arrive around 12:30 noon. Then, they would need to leave in mid-afternoon to get home to tend to evening responsibilities. Those having to travel both ways on foot for such a short time of learning got discouraged.

One Sunday morning, we went to church at Olmisigiyioi near Ole Miberre's home. On the way, we picked up Ole Ranna (not his real name). He had murdered his neighbor six years earlier and fled, living in exile in another community for five years. There, he had come under the influence of Christians and became a believer. Then he undertook the traditional process of making restitution, being reconciled, and was enabled to return home. He was now a warm radiant Christian. He and one of his three wives accompanied us to Olmisigiyioi, although it was in Siria country, what his Wuasinkishu clan considered enemy territory.

Ole Renna shared a testimony that he had no fear of coming into enemy territory. He did not need to come with spears because of his assurance of being with Jesus. If he would be killed, well then, he would just go to be with Jesus. You cannot frighten a man like that!

I preached from the story of Asa, king of Judah (II Chron. 14-16). Maurice translated into Maasai. He had spent several days going around from home to home and encouraging people to come for this special service since Kristina and Beth Good were going to have a special talk with the women. As a result of his efforts, there were about forty adults present and thirty children.

After the service, the women served tea and *nyoyo (Luo) or githeri (Swahili)*, a mixture of corn and beans soaked and cooked and cooled. It makes good cheap food, especially if there are a lot of guests.

The women re-grouped after lunch. Kristina and Beth shared their plan and led a discussion. They were hoping to form several women's groups. These groups could have some Bible studies, teaching about nutrition, health, and childcare, some gardening, and some handicrafts like bead work. Perhaps, they could include some literacy classes. After some discussion, the group decided they would like to begin by doing some gardening together, as well as doing beadwork, to try to raise money for the group.

The project work was moving ahead better. Clair's presence took the Enemasi building load off my shoulders, a real source of tension. Also, we found Michael Sieure to be a valuable addition to the project staff. His service in the shop and bookkeeping departments made the project business flow so much smoother. We sent the former dairy manager, Martin Odhiambo, to be trained as an extension agent for one and one-half years, and hired Julius A. Omongo, a young man trained as an animal health assistant, to take his place. He was also a Godsend. The whole dairy operation was much improved, another source of tension reduced for me.

The work of remodeling the dispensary and building the two nurses' houses was moving ahead. To upgrade the medical services, we were required to lay off the elderly Dr. Omondi. We were looking for a more qualified younger person to run that program.

The retired dairy farmer, Mr. John Yost from Pennsylvania, who visited us for a few days the previous January, sent us 138,000 Ksh. to buy a welder and equipment to open a workshop. He wanted us to train a few Kenyans to organize a training/production workshop, a welding business to serve the community of Ogwedhi. As the nearest welder was thirty kilometers away, this was a very much-needed service.

Clair and I went to Nairobi and bought a welder/generator, a grinder, drill, drill stand, jigsaw, and circular saw. We had enough money left over to buy an old Farmal H tractor we found abandoned at the Rosslyn Academy. We had second thoughts after we bought the tractor and never had it delivered to us at Ogwedhi. It did not really fit into our program of promoting "appropriate technology." Perhaps it is still standing out in the rain at Rosslyn?

We were like a couple of excited boys at Christmas, as we unpacked and demonstrated all the features of our new "toys" to the wide-eyed spectators at Ogwedhi.

CHAPTER 32

Cattle Theft and the "Golden Rule"

M r. Godfrey of the Lutheran World Relief, our main funding agency, came to our management committee with a new proposal, "We want you to do something in the community that is practical, that will help the community develop, not just that evangelism business." Obviously, he was not impressed with the sometimes destructive and divisive impact of the missionary's gospel on the local culture and community. He left us with a grant of 50,000 Ksh. to hold a series of "Cultural Development Seminars."

At our first seminar on April 14, 1990, the Management Committee sat with a group made up of two elders from each of the eight clans of the three major tribes that comprise the broader community. These sixteen elders may have seen each other from time to time in the Ogwedhi market where the boundaries of the tribal lands of the Maasai, Luo, and Kuria converge. However, this may have been the first time they all sat in a circle face to face to discuss the common problems and destiny of their community.

Each elder was given an opportunity to introduce himself. Then our facilitator put three questions to the group, "What are the common problems we all face in our community? Which of these is the most distressing problem? Can we all work together to solve this problem that affects us all?"

To answer the first question, many suggestions were given such as better roads, better health services like hospitals and clinics, installing electric and phone services, improved educational services such as high schools and technical schools, and stopping cattle theft.

To name the most distressing problem, these elders unanimously agreed that the problem that was disturbing all of them most was cattle theft. Behind this most disturbing and devastating problem was the lack of peace, love, and unity between the tribes and clans. They further agreed that they all ought to work together to eliminate this disease from their community.

Truly, every last person in this circle had suffered in some way through cattle raiding. Many were orphans, or had widows and orphans among their kin, as a result of the violence that often accompanied this practice. Most had at some time experienced the shock of having been robbed of some, or all, of their precious cattle. They had felt the bitter disappointment and helpless rage that followed, as all attempts to recover them proved futile.

All had lost much sleep at nights, waking at every sound that might indicate a thief in the cattle yard. All had responded countless times to the call for help, by leaving their beds to join their clansmen following the footprints of the stolen animals. A constant nagging fear bound them to their homesteads at night when they would have preferred to travel or participate in social events away from home.

As each one shared his personal pain and loss caused by this historic plague, they came to realize that, as elders and leaders, they had it in their power and responsibility to work together to stop it. After much discussion the group agreed on the necessity of making people aware of our resolve to work together to stop all cattle stealing. At this first meeting, they agreed that they should form a peace movement. They would meet monthly. To begin, they would each choose two more elders from their communities and meet again next month to work on the problem.

This led to holding monthly peace meetings over the next few years. The sharing of views and experiences was interesting and deeply moving. Each elder was made aware that the hurt, pain, and loss he bore at the hands of thieves from the other tribes was the same hurt, pain, and loss those people suffered at the hand of their own thieves.

Most of the elders had to admit that they also were guilty of cattle theft in their youthful days. They also had inflicted pain on the ones who inflicted pain on themselves. How much better if, instead of seeing the other as "evil" or "enemy," they would learn to live together in peace, love, and unity. If this barrier of enmity could be broken down, then they could trade with each other, work together, share in providing better schools and clinics that benefit everyone. They could marry each other's daughters, merge each other's cultures, and become modern Kenyans.

Those monthly meetings continued. Each time, stopping cattle theft was the main topic of discussion. At the August meeting, there were eighty-four people present from Wuasinkishu Maasai, Siria Maasai, Moitanic Maasai, Luo, and Kuria.

The Kuria admitted they had been the worst offenders. This time it was the Kuria who came out in the largest numbers. They reported that they had really been discussing this issue among themselves and decided to stop stealing cattle. To do so, they would each stop their own thieves. They would stop encouraging their young men and stop hiding them.

They placed a formal curse on all their thieves. If their thieves were caught stealing, they would confiscate their goods, burn down their houses, and prevent them from buying in their shops and grinding their grain in their mills. Then, they waited for the Maasai to say what they would do.

However, the Maasai had not done their homework. They had not met to discuss what they would do. They were quite embarrassed.

Following that, the Wuasinkishu Maasai made a list of ten of their bad thieves and had them arrested. One or two were put in jail. They buried another one.

Ole Sire, one of two sons of the owner of over 2,000 cattle, the richest Maasai in our area, was out rustling cattle one night from a Kuria home. He got a poisoned arrow in his arm. He had it removed, and the wound was treated. It was healing okay, and then it got worse again.

One night, they came to me at 4:00 a.m. (I didn't know the story then). They said, "Ole Sire is very sick with meningitis." Could I please take him to the hospital in Kilgoris? So, I got up and took them. Three days later, he died. The nurses said he died of tetanus. Was it really necessary for a son of the man with over two thousand cattle to be out stealing a few animals from a poor man? His two wives and several children paid a heavy price.

After the Saturday peace meeting in August, five of the Kuria elders approached me with the request to come and start a Mennonite church in their Nyaiguthu area. Their leader, Nashon Mukira Mohagachi, said, "We Kuria have been stealing your cattle.

After visiting this Ogwedhi Sigawa Community Development Project, we have decided we want to 'steal' your project!" They offered land and said they wanted to start a similar project to serve their people. They invited us to take them home, and they would show us the land and discuss their plans. Along with Nashon were his sons, Thomas Mwagachi and Pius Mchagoa, and three elders, Nyagorio Kibwabwa, Rioba Robi, and Mosenye Gitoro.

I notified Pastor Paul Otieno, and we drove them home that evening. They showed us their land and the six acres where they wanted to build a church. We paused to pray on that selected land. It was right in the middle of the path used by rustlers to chase stolen cattle to Tanzania. We made an appointment to visit them in their church service the following day.

The next morning, we found about sixty adults waiting to worship. They had built a small nursery school. This community was far from any established church or school. They had either been staying at home or going far in other directions to attend a Catholic, Pentecostal, or other church. Now they all wanted to form one church in the middle. They wanted that church to be Mennonite because, "the Mennonites care about the problems of the community and encourage development!" We responded by promising we would come again the next Sunday and bring a Maasai choir with us.

We did. The next Sunday, we brought sixteen Maasai with us. There were over one hundred Kurias waiting to welcome us. After a lively worship service, they invited us to a feast in one of their homes. There was great fellowship. The Maasai kept marveling, "This is the first time I ever entered a Kuria's home and ate food with Kuria!" The Kuria were just as excited. This was the first time they had Maasai visitors in their home, and to find that there are Maasai Christians who love Jesus was amazing to them.

The next Sunday, Pastor Paul and Maurice went to preach for them. However, that Saturday night, about twenty cattle were stolen from the home of Francis Rikei, the Maasai brother and church leader who had been with the choir the previous Sunday.

Early Sunday morning, the unique Maasai cattle theft cry rang out across the Ogwedhi countryside, summoning half a hundred Maasai warriors with their swords, spears, and bows and arrows to the chase.

They followed the tracks straight through Luo land into Kuria country toward the Tanzania border.

The tracks led right past the Nyaiguthu church where Pastor Paul was preaching. One can only imagine: the worshipers sitting sedately in their peaceful pews, some of them paying rapt attention and others dozing, mothers distracting their fussing children or nursing their hungry infants, when suddenly, they found their church surrounded by this fast-moving band of fifty fully armed Maasai warriors!

When the Kuria elders understood the cause of this unexpected invasion, they said "Our brother, Francis's cattle have been stolen. We must go immediately and help our brother find his cattle!" All the Kuria men and boys left to join the chase, leaving Pastor Paul with the women and children to finish the church service.

The fierce Maasai warriors, dressed in sheets and beads, and armed with their spears and bows and arrows, blended with the more domesticated churchly Kuria. Two enemy peoples joined in a common cause, pursued those cattle another twenty-five kilometers into Tanzania. They surprised the thieves and retrieved the cows. The next day, they returned home with the cattle, all except one, that is. There was great rejoicing. They say this was the first time that Kuria actively helped Maasai retrieve their stolen cattle. Once they cross the Tanzania border, they never come back.

This experience gave us real hope that cattle theft could be stopped. Joseph Sankale was very excited. He said the real way to stop theft is for the Kuria Christians to fellowship with the Maasai Christians. Hostility will end, and cooperation will take its place. Peace, development, and prosperity will follow.

Samson Ole Masake was at the Anti-Stock Theft Unit (ASTU) camp that morning when Joseph Sankale came riding in with his Bible on his bicycle. The policemen asked him where his weapons were since he was pursuing cattle thieves. Joseph pointed to his Bible and said, "This is my sword and spear!" As he left, the policemen mocked him and said to Samson, "If your God is real, why does he let thieves steal your cattle?" Samson just said, "God will bring them back!" Those policemen were a bit more subdued when they saw the cattle returned the next day all the way from across the Tanzania border.

A new wind was blowing, bringing hope. If ancient enemies can now sit and plan together, and if new Christians can help each other as brothers, there is hope that a cure for this centuries-old disease is close at hand. Someone should inform Godfrey that community development, properly done, does not separate itself from "that evangelism business"!

The peace meetings continued to be held each month. One of the Siria clan representatives, Maurice Ole Maiko, was chosen to become facilitator. As an educated Maasai with Kuria blood in his maternal pedigree and being fluent in seven languages, he had established credibility with the various ethnic groups as a communicator and mediator.

The elders realized that depending upon the federal government's law enforcement was not solving the problem. The key to lasting change lies with a change in the communities involved. The solving of this conflict and the establishment of peace was the shared responsibility of all community members. Outside police and the judicial system, external force, would not bring a sustainable solution. They drew up a Code of Conduct which applied internal pressure within the community.

On March 9, 1991, the peace committee passed the following *Code of Conduct for Handling of Cattle Theft* in the form of ten resolutions:

1. Each community is to elect ten (10) elders who will be responsible for handling cattle theft in their respective areas.
2. Each community is to cooperate with the government authorities to follow the tracks of stolen cattle. In case the footprints cannot be traced, then it will be the responsibility of those ten elders to continue the investigation and hand over the report to the government of their findings.
3. Each community must disclose the names of the thieves from their respective areas to the government secretly.
4. When stolen cattle are returned, they must be returned along with the thief/thieves. If the cattle are found alone, it will be the duty of those ten elected members to carry out the investigation and find the thieves involved.
5. When cattle are stolen from one community by another, the two must unite and follow the tracks together.

6. Elders will be forced to use traditional curses to curse the stealing and the thieves.
7. Because we don't want this evil of cattle theft, when cattle are returned to the owner, they must be the very original stolen cattle. In case they are not recovered, the owner must be given the same number of cattle that were stolen by the thief. His community will also be fined an additional five cattle.
8. If cattle are found alone, the elders of that particular area should investigate where the cattle came from and return them to the owner.
9. If the stolen cattle are found within a herd, the owner of that herd is considered a thief.
10. If cattle are stolen and the owner exaggerates the number that he reports as lost, hoping for extra compensation, that person will also be considered a thief.

Years later, when I visited Ogwedhi, I found that the monthly peace meetings were continuing. Cattle rustling also was continuing, perhaps on a reduced scale, but it still remained a serious problem. At a meeting at Kehancha on March 18, 1994, the ten resolutions were read again, and their effectiveness was evaluated. Elders from each location reported the successes and the failures in their experience. Common problems were voiced:

1. The names of thieves have been turned in to the government officials, but the government releases them on bond. They should be put in jail. When they are released on bond, they use their freedom to steal again to get money to pay their bonds.
2. The fine of five cows should be increased for thieves who are caught.
3. Elders who attend peace meetings should report to their constituents.
4. Chiefs or assistant chiefs who love money (bribes) should be sacked or retired.
5. Elders must practice "peace, love, and unity" (KANU's political slogan) in their homes as well as preach it in their constituencies.

6. Cattle theft is still going on. Some of us are working together, marrying each other's daughters, and living in peace. However, others are still stealing our cattle.

7. All guns should be turned in to government authorities.

8. The traditional curse should be used against all thieves. It is not being done.

9. Thieves caught should be taken to and judged by the elders, not government authorities who release them on bond. On bond, the thieves return and take revenge on those who turned them in.

10. We need to invite the Kuria elders on the Tanzania side of the border to attend our peace meetings and cooperate with us in stopping this cattle rustling.

In summary, one would have thought that this process, begun so well, bringing these community leaders from all the tribes, Maasai, Luo, and Kuria together to work at this disease, would have eliminated cattle theft. It did make some difference. However, the major obstacle remained. The thieves from Tanzania, who carry automatic weapons, were not subject to the local Kenyan Kuria chiefs. They came and stole large herds and forced their way through to Tanzania where they were free. The local people in any of the clans were no match for those with the AK 47s.

Many years later, when I visited in Ogwedhi, I found that the large Maasai herds were no more. They had all been taken by bands of thieves, who came up from Tanzania armed with Kalashnikovs, and systematically reduced the herds. They took them, one herd at a time, south to the markets of Tanzania. Today, the Maasai have become farmers with a few cows and grow crops like their neighboring tribes.

CHAPTER 33

Controversy over Culture and Good News

O ne of the elements of any given culture is its religion or belief system. The Christian gospel transcends culture. It is not a culture. Yet, it is not experienced nor expressed outside of a culture. A culture is the lifeway of any given people group. It is the wrapping, the container into which the gospel is poured and takes form. Originally, the Christians' gospel was given in the context of the Jewish culture under Roman occupation. The gospel changed the culture, but the culture also shaped how the gospel was received, understood, and integrated into the beliefs and practices of the first Christians.

The first Christians were Jewish Christians. After the council recorded in Acts chapter fifteen, there emerged a Gentile Christianity. As it spread westward, it became a Roman/Latin Christianity which emerged into a European Christianity, and then an American Christianity. As the gospel spread south into Egypt and Ethiopia, it became a Coptic Christianity, or north it became a Byzantine Christianity. And, as the gospel continues to be introduced to new cultures, like salt or light, it influences and changes that culture. Also, how the gospel is perceived, received, and put into practice is shaped by that receiving culture.

Consequentially, in every ethnic group the Christian church will manifest slight differences in theological emphases, biblical interpretation, historical understandings, ecclesiastical organization, worship styles, hymnody, art forms, architecture, and expressions of personal piety and discipleship.

In introducing the good news of the Christian's gospel into a culture for the first time, there is bound to arise many issues. Does the missionary inject a pure gospel into the receiving culture, or a gospel already encapsuled and perhaps tainted by his own culture in a package as he perceived it? How much does the Christian gospel shape the culture of a given people, and how much does the culture shape the gospel?

EMM's *Missionary Messenger* carried an article in its January 1988 issue, that I had written, titled, "Maasai, Mennonites, and the Ten-Year Goals."

To this spot in southwestern Kenya, news gradually filters through the postal system about the Mennonites in North America developing some "Ten-Year Goals." I am encouraged and applaud the idea. Maybe even Jesus takes note of the Mennonite mood. Some questions come to mind though.

Can the old Mennonite wineskins really stretch enough to absorb 50,000 people without "Mennonite names", people who are not "our kind", who don't fit into the Mennonite ethnic cultural mold, like, for example, some Maasai Mennonites I know?

Could the brothers and sisters at Plains or Belmont take communion with brother Samson Masake and his two wives who have just recently become Mennonites? Or would the sisters wash the feet of Samson's mother, the 80-year-old Gogo Masake, coming to church in her not-too-lately laundered traditional dress? Would the brothers listen respectfully to the inspired preaching of illiterate sister Magdalena (Noonkipa), one of four women who share the same husband?

Would the refined sisters of First Mennonite greet with a holy kiss, or at least a loving hug, sister Rhoda who prefers to wear her hair done up neatly with an ochre clay and fat mixture which seeps down over beads and dress and gives a definite and contagious reddish color to her whole persona?

Could the big names at Akron worship with Ole Renna, who thrust his spear through his neighbor during a dispute, probably an instinctive act on the part of a man who spent ten years of his youth in

244

Maasai military training in the bush as a leader among a warrior race?

By now you might be raising an eyebrow of inquiry, "Who are these Maasai brothers and sisters?" "How did they get into the Mennonite Church?" "What do they have to do with the Ten-Year Goals?" or "Is it really possible to be Maasai and Mennonite?"

The Maasai are a proud and fiercely independent nomadic tribe of Hamitic Cushites inhabiting the vast plain of the Rift Valley in central Kenya and Tanzania. They are basically cattle people grazing their large herds throughout their territory.

Actually, apart from the "peace position," Maasai have a lot in common with Mennonites. They have steadfastly resisted change throughout the colonial period. They have been very suspicious of outside influences and ideas and have maintained a strong sense of identity and community until recent years.

Also, like traditional Mennonites, Maasai have a great respect for the land and the wildlife among which they live in peace. Apart from warriors proving their manhood by killing lions, Maasai don't kill wild animals for food or sport …

Not unlike the case of the Mennonites, in the past few decades, cracks have appeared in the walls of isolation. Pressures for change from the outside world are forcing their way in through government policies, modern education, land demarcation, commerce, and Christianity. Cultural uniformity, traditional community, and identity are being threatened by spreading diversity and change.

How did some of these folks come to acquire a Maasai Mennonite identity? The story goes back to 1977 when the Wuasinkishu Maasai warriors staged a massacre of "illegal aliens", primarily the Luo who had settled on Maasai land. About fifty to sixty people were killed. The rest fled in terror. Tribal tensions became very high in the Ogwedhi Sigawa border community.

Local leaders were called together from both Luo and Maasai communities to seek ways to reduce the tension and bring about reconciliation. It was finally agreed that Mennonites, a "historic peace church", should be asked to enter the area with a program of reconciliation, peacemaking, and development.

As a result, the Ogwedhi-Sigawa Community Development Project (OSP) was formed in 1979 with an agenda to work in five major areas: primary education, health, agriculture, animal husbandry, and evangelism.

A missionary couple was assigned by Eastern Mennonite Board, first Jerry and Sharon Stutzman, and later Leon and Lou Ann Ressler, to give leadership. An evangelist, Paul Otieno, was supplied by the Kenya Mennonite Church.

Now, eight years later, one can say that a lot of reconciliation has taken place. Maasai and Luos work together on OSP, study and play together in the school, receive treatment together in the dispensary, trade together in the town, and worship together in the churches.

Yes, Maasai are becoming Mennonites. OSP has gained a lot of credibility for the name "Mennonite." Maasai children, when asked at school to fill out forms which include the question of religious denomination, will often write in "Mennonite." Adults entering a hospital will likewise identify themselves as "Mennonite", although they may seldom or never be seen in any of the eight congregations that have sprung up.

Yes, there are Maasai Mennonite congregations. The above-mentioned missionaries and evangelist did a lot of teaching of small groups of mostly women and children and a few men. That was when there still was some nomadic movement. People would attend for a while, then move on. Now we are getting calls from some of these scattered ones: "Come to our area and help us start a church!" We can't respond to all the calls ourselves. We try to find gifted Maasai leaders who need to be encouraged and trained. Some leaders are women, some youths, and some are Luo missionaries who are sent to help with teaching and preaching. Most of these leaders have little or no education. Some are illiterate. But all are called of God and committed to do what they can to bring the gospel to their people.

These Maasai haven't heard of the "Ten-Year Goals" yet. But I am sure they will leave the North American churches in the dust. They don't know a lot about Mennonite identity, about Mennonite names or shoofly pie, or even about Scottdale, Goshen, or Akron, let alone about Menno Simons or Conrad Grebel. But they do know something about Jesus Christ. And they are learning that discipleship means to follow him daily in life. Mama Russie doesn't drink until she is sick anymore, nor abandon her babies to spend the night sleeping in the bush. Instead, she gathers her neighbors and teaches them about the new life to be found in following Jesus.

It is possible to be Maasai and Mennonite. Now there are a few, but in ten years there will be many adding to the glory of God!

The above article was circulated in the rather conservative traditional Mennonite constituency in Pennsylvania and beyond. It raised some serious concerns about how we do mission work in Africa. There were questions about women in leadership roles, illiterate women preaching, women in polygamous marriage relationships, and polygamous men also guilty of murder, giving leadership.

In looking back over this article, I will grant that it was a little colored by exaggerated optimism. However, it was written with the intent of stretching the minds of average, satisfied, narrow thinking, monocultural, North American Christians, to think outside their usual boxes, to be more inclusive and non-judgmental of others that are different than themselves or their associates.

The stance of us North American missionaries was that the Maasai believers themselves must be centrally involved in the "binding and loosing" decisions in obedience to God's word and the enlightenment of the Holy Spirit. The task of the missionary is not to impose changes in the culture from outside, but to introduce the Good News, which includes the invitation to walk with Jesus through the presence and power of the Holy Spirit.

The Good News comes to a culture as it is. However, given time, with teaching and preaching, like yeast in dough, it grows and transforms that culture. The Holy Spirit must bring conviction among the Maasai themselves; then lasting changes will occur. And that was what we were seeing happen before our eyes.

Sister Rhoda with her hair done up neatly
with an ochre clay and fat mixture.

With this understanding, the maturing Maasai leaders called a special meeting to deal with the questions relating to polygamy, church membership, and leadership. About twenty of the leaders, both Maasai men and women, as well as the Luo evangelists, gathered in the church meeting house at Ogwedhi. Clair Good and I, along with David Shenk, representing EMM, were also present.

After the topic was introduced, David drew their attention to the words of our Lord in Matthew 18:15-20 (NIV) that deal with discipline in the church, pointing especially to verse 18 which says, "... *whatever you bind on earth shall be bound in Heaven, and whatever you loose on earth shall be loosed in Heaven.*" He pointed out that God has given his people, the group of Maasai leaders, the authority to make decisions around these controversial issues. What will we "bind," and what will we "loose"?

After much discussion and looking at other biblical passages, the leaders agreed to the following:

1. Polygamous marriage, although it is not equal to Christian marriage, is still culturally accepted as genuine marriage. To divorce or put away is not a biblical solution. Therefore, we must accept new believers who were already in a polygamous relationship just as they are, baptize them, and include them as members in the church.

2. Those first-generation members who came in as persons in a polygamous relationship, cannot take on any additional marriage partners. To do so would result in excommunication.

3. Those who came into church membership with one marriage partner must not take on any additional marriage partners. To do so would result in excommunication.

4. Ordination to the offices of deacon, pastor, or bishop, biblically must be limited to persons in monogamous marriage relationships, or still single.

5. Outside of those office-bearing roles, all members, regardless of their sex, education, or marital status, are encouraged to exercise the gifts God has given them in ways that build up the body of Christ. That would include leadership roles that help the church.

These conclusions expressed the consensus of the Maasai leadership at that time. The missionaries present respected their decision. This "binding and loosing" was done without consulting the leadership of the Kenya Mennonite Church, which was operating on earlier decisions that required the dissolution or divorce of polygamous marriage relationships before baptism, communion, or ordination could be considered.

This led to consternation by some and confusion by others in the broader church. Others secretly agreed with this fresh Maasai approach. A few in South Nyanza took liberty to blame us missionaries, Clair Good and Carl Hansen, for allowing and supporting this deviation from accepted norms, then went ahead, claiming approval by us, following their baser instincts, took second wives themselves. They were promptly excommunicated by their diocese leaders.

CHAPTER 34

Kristina (Noonkokua) an Inter-cultural Emissary

Kristina wrote an article describing her unique relationship with the Maasai which was published in the January 1991 issue of Missionary Messenger.

My Cross-cultural Identification with the Maasai

My first encounter

My first encounter with the Maasai took place one Sunday in August 1985. Our family, Mom, Dad, my sister Sheryl, and I, had been in Kenya for only one week and everything was new ... My sister and I bounced along in the back of the Ogwedhi Sigawa Project's Toyota pickup through the bushes of Maasailand. We were traveling with a missionary couple (Leon and Lou Ann Ressler) and their two children who had worked with these people for five years and were ready to go back to the USA. My parents were to take their place.

We arrived at a tree with a cross engraved on the trunk. There were about a dozen women with their children sitting there, singing strange, but beautiful songs. I remember listening to them and thinking how pretty it sounded. I also thought they seemed very friendly and happy to see us.

During that first week, we visited a few Maasai homes, and I fell in love with the simple mud huts. I thought they were very cozy. I even said I would like to sleep in one, but I was afraid to, as I had heard a lot about the fierce warriors called "morans." I would sometimes lie awake at night; afraid they would come and break into our house.

We leave and return.

After two weeks, Sheryl and I went off to boarding school. Three months later, we came back to Ogwedhi with a bit more understanding of the Maasai. I still remember feeling very uncomfortable when a beautiful lady grabbed my hand to have a church group picture taken. Holding hands was one aspect of the culture that I was not used to yet.

During the holidays from school, I was always eager to go to church or to go out with Dad to spend time with the Maasai. I never quite had the courage or confidence to go out by myself and build any friendships; language was also a problem.

I first came to Kenya as a thirteen-year-old entering grade eight. Well, at the end of grade nine, I was frustrated with my school. I figured if I'm living in Africa, why not experience it rather than spending most of my time in a mini-America (the boarding school). I decided to do 10th grade by correspondence living at home with Mom and Dad.

Tenth grade started out being at home, doing schoolwork, and being bored. I wanted to get out in the community, make some friends, and learn about the Maasai culture. But again, I didn't have the courage or confidence, as language was still a problem.

After studying Swahili for a year at school, I still knew very little. Besides language, cultural differences were also a problem. Finally, I arranged with one lady to go to her house every Saturday to visit. She lived nearby, so it was a good arrangement.

Living with the Maasai

At the end of December, I asked her if I could spend a few days at her place, staying nights as well. She was very happy to hear that, so I went for two nights. I slept on the traditional stick bed with a covering of cow hide. The bed was comfortable at first, but during the night it became less and less comfortable. At that time, I also bought a Maasai outfit which I wore to her place.

The outfit consisted of a maroon piece of cloth to wrap around the waist, a red piece to go under one arm and tie over the opposite shoulder, and a tank top to wear under this. These were all held in place by a leather belt around the waist. Over the shoulders was a white cloth that hung similar to a cape.

After wearing these clothes there for a few days, I realized how comfortable they were and decided I would never wear a skirt while home again. I would just wear "shukas" (sheets).

When my friend started taking off her jewelry and shukas and wearing dresses and a scarf on her head, I was very upset. I didn't want her to change. I felt she should stay traditional and not mix as much with the neighboring tribe, the Luos. But, since she spoke fluent Kijaluo and she wanted to be modern or Luo, as I interpreted it, she began to change her appearance rapidly. Our friendship began to weaken because I wanted her to be what she didn't want to be.

I feel accepted.

One Sunday, at a Maasai church with Mom and Dad, one of the ladies pulled me aside and invited me into her house. She asked me to come and help her prepare food for the group after church. She put me to work cleaning rice, washing dishes, then dishing up the food (rice and beans).

This was the first time I had been invited into the cooking and sleeping room. It was also the first time I was treated as an equal, being put to work. I remember feeling very good, especially when her husband, a good friend of my father, invited me to come and stay there a few days. That started a friendship between us both ... I loved the way they accepted me as one of them. I soon began to greet in the traditional way, by tipping my head towards my elder to receive his/her outstretched hand of blessing. It is a sign of respect and also a kind of blessing.

"This is your home."

I was still studying, so every weekend I would go out and stay with my friend and during the week I would stay at home. I was very flattered one day when her husband told me, "This is your home and you are free to come and go, as you are my child." I felt so happy that these people had accepted me; even this old man had taken notice and called me his daughter.

The women I visited, opened up to me. They talked about their culture, their honest feelings, an experience I would have never had if I hadn't identified with them (By now I was learning to hear and speak Swahili). My best friend took me to ceremonies, and I soon began to know where people lived and who people were. They were no longer just faces.

I began to sleep comfortably on stick beds and to love their food. I drank milk with them, milked their cows, cleaned their gourds, wore their clothes, helped mud a house, walked the long distances barefoot, and crossed the rivers, even when they were up to my waist and had a strong current. For doing these things that I've learned to love and that have become a part of me, I earned their confidence and friendship.

Missionaries have their different ways of reaching people. I found that identifying with the people is the best way for me. When they see you are willing to live like them, eat with them and not condemn them, they will look to you as a friend and listen, as you are now on an equal basis. When outsiders come and comment on my dress, my friends just say, "Oh, she's a Maasai; she's one of us!"

I combine two cultures.

For a while I struggled with the feeling of being two-faced. When I was at home, I was a Maasai; when I was at school, I was an American. That was a problem I had to deal with. I felt I couldn't be both. But with encouragement from my parents, I realized I don't have to be either the one or the other; both can be one. Now I don't feel any guilt about changing my way of dressing or the way I act, because I have combined the two cultures. When I am at school, I dress like an American; I act towards adults or my peers as an American. When I go home, I dress as a Maasai and give the respect to my elders and peers as is cultural, though I myself do not change.

I used to be very upset when the Maasai began to change, but I thought about it, and concluded it is their decision. They are living in a modern country with pressures all around them to change. They were forced to demarcate their land; some put up fences, and some have built permanent houses. If they are forced to settle down, they might as well build block houses and buy vehicles. They have so many cows that will die from lack of pasture if they're not sold off.

The fact is, the Maasai are changing whether we foreigners want them to or not. It saddens my family to see it. But when they ask us to help them build a school or a church, we are willing to help, because it is their desire. I, more than anyone hate to see their beads and shukas come off. But I also know the pressure they get from others to change.

When they go to the towns, they are looked down
on as "backwards" people. I have been confronted by
some people from another tribe telling me that I'll go
to hell for wearing these beads and shukas, so I know
what the Maasai face from their neighbors.

I was very flattered when my best friend gave me
a very special gift, a cow. I know how they love their
cattle and so it was very special for me. Her husband
was just telling me a while ago that my cow can have
ten calves, these ten will each have ten and in a very
short time I could be very rich. The thinking of a
Maasai!

After finishing school in July, I am spending one
year at home, at Ogwedhi. I'm looking forward to
helping in women's groups and possibly teaching
adult literacy courses. But mostly I'm enjoying living
with my friends, learning their language and culture.

As in all construction undertakings in those times and that
place, it took months for Kristina's simple, mud and grass, one-
roomed domicile and a latrine to be completed. Ole Sikawa initiated
construction in late June. In September, the grass roof went on. Then,
her friends got together to do the first mudding.

Mudding was a long-drawn-out process. First, common soil was
dug loose in one place. Straw and water were added and mixed
thoroughly by trampling it with bare feet. The mixture was left
standing to soak and was re-trampled each day for several days.
When it reached the right consistency, a group of neighbor women
came and helped smear the mud onto the dry sticks that had been
tied together forming the wall frames.

This primary coat of mud was then allowed to dry for many
days. As it dried, it shriveled, leaving large deep cracks. The second
mudding would fill those cracks and plaster a fresh layer of mud
over the walls. Again, after drying, a third coat of mud would be
applied. Finally, a last layer of sandy mud would be applied to make
a nice smooth finish. Some of these walls were then decorated with
different colors of mud or by artwork. This process took more than
a month, due to the long drying periods.

Then the door and window were installed. At the same time, a pit latrine was dug, and a brick outhouse was built over it for her and the Sikawa family's use. The round hut was about fourteen feet in diameter and stood close to Noonkipa's house.

Kristina was still living with us while her little hut was in the process of being mudded. She moved into her house in November. She adopted the lifestyle of the Maasai family with which she lived, dressing in their traditional costume, going barefoot, carrying her firewood, water, and food like they did, cooking over an open fire, and milking four cows. She became a part of the family. Her cow had a little brown bull calf.

Kristina enjoyed identifying and learning about Maasai culture and language. She helped start several women's groups where they engaged in a joint activity such as growing gardens, having a health lesson or a Bible study.

Kristina beside her own new house

Kristina milking one of the four cows for which she was responsible.

Kristina cleaning the milk gourd.

Kristina entered wholeheartedly into experiencing Maasai life and culture for several months. However, she started getting boils on various parts of her body. At the clinic, she was treated with antibiotics, and the boils would disappear. However, as soon as she went off the antibiotics, more boils would break out. By early spring, she began having fever with the boils, so the nurses put her on stronger medicine. It affected her attitude and emotional state.

We found that when she came home to be nursed and took showers at home, the boils went away. We finally figured out she had been bathing like all the Maasai in a spring in the bush. In the dry season, the spring water was full of living organisms and covered with green algae. The Maasai had built-in resistance, but Kristina did not. We persuaded her to compromise her total identification principles and come home for her showers. After that, she had no more problem with boils.

Regarding the influence of our daughter locally, during those few years, instead of being addressed as "Mr." or "Mrs." or "Pastor" as the Luos would address us, the Maasai now called us simply, "Baba Kristina" or "Mama Kristina." We were honored. Kristina, by cultural identification had become a bridge.

CHAPTER 35

More Blessings and Thankfulness

Blessing of Guests

I f "guests are a blessing," then, more guests mean more blessings. The year 1991 brought the blessing of more visitors. John and Holly Blosser-Yoder had served with MCC for three years in Zambia as schoolteachers. Now, on their way home to Iowa, they came all the way to Ogwedhi to take advantage of our rather exotic hospitality. We enjoyed getting to know them. Little could we imagine that our paths would cross again more than a decade later, when they accepted an assignment as MCC country representatives in Ethiopia where Vera and I were then working.

Three weeks later, we had more visitors. Marvin and Yvonne Stutzman came to visit us and to attend the ordination of Clair Good. They were administrators in the Nairobi office and served in a pastoral role to the missionaries. They brought with them Wes and Marian Newswanger, who were forced to leave assignments in Somalia because of the civil war there.

January 20th was a historic occasion in that it was the first time that a Mennonite missionary was ordained by an African bishop. Bishop Joshua Okello Ouma led the ceremony and administered the vows and the charge, and Clair became a duly ordained pastor in the Kenya Mennonite Church. In his testimony, Clair said that he had been called to the ministry at thirteen years of age and that he wanted to be willing to follow that call.

The ordination was a festive occasion held at Enemasi outside under a big spreading tree. The crowd of over 350 was much too large to fit into the tiny church building. Most of the attendees walked great distances. There were five choirs, large representations from the three major tribes—Luo, Maasai and Kuria. A cow had been slaughtered, and an abundance of food and tea prepared. Our truck left for Migori at 4:30 a.m. to bring a choir and returned at 10:30 p.m. after taking them back. I was very thankful for Caleb, our driver.

The ordination of Clair Good was held outside because the little church building at Enemasi was much too small.

Blessing of "Angels Unawares"

We introduced Wes and Marian Newswanger to OSP. Since they were free of their Somali assignment, they agreed to come and live in with us for three months. He was a shop instructor by profession, so he agreed to help us set up a training program to launch a welding/production shop. He would train six people in welding and other crafts. After which, we wanted to help the trainees make a business of welding.

Marian was a nurse. She found work to do in our dispensary, helping our new Maasai nurse, Joyce Kipteng. Our dispensary business doubled.

Sharing the small house with another couple for three months turned out to be a lot easier than might have been expected. Wes and Marian were about our age. They were very congenial and adaptable people. In the long evenings, Vera and I would sit in the living room doing our reading or writing. Wes and Marian would sit in their room at the opposite end of the house, probably doing something similar.

It satisfied our North American need for privacy. We usually met in the kitchen and dining room where we had our meals together. From our perspective, living this way in community worked out just fine. We never heard any complaint from their side.

According to our contract with EMM, Vera's and my three-year term of service in Kenya would end in July 1991. We were entitled to a full year of home leave if we should return for another term. The mission was actively but unsuccessfully searching for someone to replace us for that year.

As Wes and Marian became familiar with the workings of OSP, the mission director approached them to ask if they would be open to filling in for that year. The couple had nothing else planned for the immediate future, so they prayed about it and felt they should agree.

This made us all very happy because all the other couples had refused, and we were beginning to wonder if we would really be able to get away for a whole year. They came to us, dropped in unexpectedly like angels sent at the right time for a specific need. Now that the need was settled, we were able to make definite plans for the upcoming year.

To expedite the transition, the Newswangers agreed to work with us until the end of April when Wes would finish his welding classes. Then, they would take a one-week vacation in Mombasa before going to Nairobi for one month of Swahili study. They would then come back and take over our role in June. We wished to leave for home in early July.

Marian was a major help in the clinic. Vera also oriented her to take on the bookkeeping monitor role. She was to monitor the books and the work of the young man, Michael Sieure, who we were training to be our accounts clerk (bookkeeper and paymaster).

*Wes and Marian Newswanger joined the OSP
management and staff team as co-directors 1991-96.*

Blessing of Good Health and Medical Care

Another blessing came to our attention when, at our end-of-term medical examinations, we were both pronounced to be in sound health. I was about thirty-five pounds lighter than three years earlier; however, no parasites nor problems were detected.

Immediately after the exam, however, I came down with a severe case of malaria again. The doctor at Migori did some tests. He found my white blood count was something around 3,000, when it should have been 10,000. He said I couldn't resist much infection that way, "You don't have more resistance than an AIDS patient!" He treated me with the conventional anti-malaria drug, and I was okay for three weeks, gaining strength.

Then, the fever came back. In despair, I returned to the doctor and demanded, "Give me something that cures this problem." He gave me a shot of quinine, and I was cured. Quinine is considered a medication of last resort because it has been known to cause deafness in a few cases. The medical profession was preferring newer, but less effective treatments, and the malaria parasites were building immunity. We thanked God for the blessing of good doctors and effective medications.

Blessing of Youth

A group of thirty-eight Tanzanian youth walked from Shirati on Lake Victoria all the way to Migori, about eighty kilometers. Our vehicles picked them up and brought them to Ogwedhi for a weekend of fellowship with our local youth. They were a large choir and were accompanied by a couple of preacher/evangelists.

We had invited them for a whole week of evangelistic activity. After they arrived, they informed us that they must return to Tanzania on Monday, so the kids could be in school by Tuesday. An all-night youth activity was held in the school.

The next morning, all the congregations in the district came together for a Sunday service which was held in the school's dining hall. A special feature was that a Kuria choir from the Nyagutu church joined with the Maasai and Luo for a unique celebration with the Tanzanian young people. There was a great feeling of oneness and joy among the more than 300 people present.

Blessing of International Partnerships

On April 14, 1991, I went by Saturday night bus to Nairobi. On Monday and Tuesday, I met with the Lutheran World Relief representatives to discuss our future plans. While there, I received a message from Heifer Projects International informing us that they agreed to support our project with a veterinary program for the next three years. They would provide a veterinary salary, equipment, and enough agricultural and veterinary supplies to stock four shops to be built in Maasailand. The shops would enable OSP to run an income-generating service to the communities, thus enabling OSP to continue on a self-sustaining basis after donor funding ceased. Heifer Projects International committed itself to a total of $33,170. We asked LWR to kick in enough to fill the gaps.

Blessing in the Market Place

I returned from Nairobi with Clair. He had left Beth in Nairobi with two children for medical reasons. On the way home, we stopped at Nakuru to buy some milk cans.

Clair saw a cream separator for sale where the price had been reduced from 11,000 to 1,000 Ksh. Clair, a Pennsylvanian Mennonite, farmer-mechanic, ever in search of a bargain, said, "I'll take it!" The seller explained they had sold it to a farmer who returned it because "two parts are missing inside." Clair said it was worth the risk. He took it home, arriving after midnight. He couldn't sleep until he had taken it apart, found one loose setscrew and another small part that had been installed upside down.

We had just looked at another one in Nairobi, and the seller's final price was 12,000 Ksh. We just didn't have the money. Now, we had a much-desired cream separator for only 1,000 shillings. How blessed can we be to have a mechanic on the team.

Thoughts on Thanksgiving Day

When Thursday, November 26th showed up on our calendar, I took a few moments to reflect and philosophize:

> This is a special day. First of all, it is the moment that we have, the now in which we exist. The past is gone, yet not gone but hidden, lying buried beneath a cloud of dim recollections that may or may not coincide with the reality that was. What we remember is a pseudo-reality that is ever modifying slightly, altering but yet not changing in the least the reality that existed and ever remains unchangeably fixed and unrecoverable beneath the thick crust of fading memories, accessible only to the eyes of God.
>
> The future likewise tantalizes, shimmering vaguely, drawing us on; always beckoning, challenging, enticing; yet ever twisting, evading, eluding altering,

shifting, inscrutable; never bringing to fully satisfying realization.

But we do have today. We work and sleep; we eat and drink; we laugh and caress; we desire and love; we think and converse; we dream and hope; we weep and worry; we admire and worship. We live today; therefore, it is special!

Today is a special day. It is the last Thursday in November, the day which Americans have designated as a national day of thanksgiving. It is a day on which hundreds of millions of Americans are not attending their regular places of work or study. They travel hundreds of millions of miles by land and air to spend the day with family and friends. For this special day the lives of scores of millions of turkeys have been sacrificed as roasted (or burnt?) offerings of thanksgiving by the American people.

Today hundreds of millions of prayers are being said in every shade of American English accent and in hundreds of more or less exotic dialects and languages as well. We hope God has a good time deciphering, translating, analyzing, evaluating, categorizing, filing away, or responding to them all in a Godly manner. Will he recognize the voices of those he hasn't heard from since last Thanksgiving? Will he give equal coverage to the less flattering and less thankful prayers and despairing cries of the mothers and children of Somalia or Mozambique?

While God is busy enjoying his Thanksgiving "mail," hundreds of millions of Americans will be busy enjoying his gifts, stuffing their stomachs to the point of discomfort with the bounties of his earth, basking in the pleasures of family togetherness and the comradery of human friendship. Most of them will be enjoying the marvels of technology enabled by his blessing of prosperity, as they spread themselves before their T.V. sets.

There, more than a hundred million pairs of eyes will be focusing on every minute detail of every action of whatever football game is selected for nationwide coverage and of which the final outcome is of absolutely no significant consequence. Will they give equal attention to the latest news bulletin on the spreading disaster enveloping the millions of Somalia?

CHAPTER 36

Farewells

The time approached for us to say "Goodbye" to our friends and leave behind the accomplishments, unfulfilled challenges, and failures of the past six years of our lives. The community responded with an excessive round of invitations and farewell celebrations.

Ole Miberre gave us a goat on Sunday, May 26. Then on May 31 we were invited to the pentecostal Pastor Joram's home in town for supper. On June 1st, we had dinner at Paul Saiyua's near Il Pashire. Sunday, June 2nd was a big day for us at the Luendo church where Peter Otieno and his parents entertained us. The bishop and several pastors from other churches came too, and we had a full church and a big feast. We got home after dark.

On Tuesday the 4th, we were invited to Clair and Beth's home for supper and to Barack's the next evening. On Thursday afternoon and evening, we enjoyed a feast at the home of Bishop Joshua Okello in Migori. On Friday, the management committee put on a little farewell feast for us at noon. That evening, utilizing Ole Miberre's goat, we put on a goat roast feast for compound residents and workers. On Saturday the 8th, we travelled through Migori to a feast at Robert Opanga's home. It was an all-day affair. A big church farewell with several hundred people from all the district churches came for the service on Sunday the 9th. The celebration concluded with a big feast. Then on Monday, the OSP workers and the primary school staff put on an all-day farewell program and feast. It was excellently organized and entertaining.

At these various feasts, the hosts gave us many gifts and made eloquent speeches like Africans love to do, full of praise, and omitting all our short-comings and sins. It made us feel much loved, appreciated, and a bit fatter.

Wes and Marian Newswanger were with us that last week for a final orientation and handing over, which was hectic and incomplete due to the tight schedule of feasting and farewells.

On Tuesday, June 11, 1991, after all the excitement and saying our last "Farewell," we turned our back to the Ogwedhi Sigawa community, and Clair drove us to the peaceful oasis of the Mennonite Guest House in Nairobi. He returned the vehicle back to OSP.

We had reserved some days in Nairobi. We tried to get visas to visit Ethiopia, another home we had left sixteen years earlier. However, June was the very month in which Mengistu's hated government finally collapsed, and a guerilla army, the Tigrean Liberation Front, took control of the whole country. Our plans to visit Ethiopia failed. No visas were being issued. The Embassy officials informed us with a bit of apprehension, "Ethiopia has no government. Everyone is waiting for the talks to begin on July 1st to see what government can be formed."

In the last week of May, as the rebels were approaching, and Mengistu was preparing to flee, the Christians, Evangelical and Coptic, along with the Muslim religious leaders called for a massive prayer vigil, imploring God to spare Ethiopia bloodshed and destruction such as Somalia was experiencing. It was then that the hated and feared dictator, Mengistu Haile Mariam, secretly fled the country, seeking refuge in Zimbabwe.

A week later, the government quietly dissolved. The soldiers simply abandoned the army, government officials fled or went into hiding, and the fighting stopped. The Tigrean rebels took over the capital city with almost no bloodshed. The rebels just quietly moved in and took over "to preserve law and order." In a few days, the whole nation came under their control. Now that the war had stopped, there was a glimmer of hope. God had heard the prayers of his Ethiopian children!

Now they were hoping to have talks in July with the intention of forming a broad-based caretaker government that would prepare the country for a democratic multi-party system with elections in a year or so. This was not the right time to entertain tourists.

On June 24th, 1991, Vera and Kristina and I flew out of the now familiar Jomo Kenyatta International Airport, out of Kenya airspace, and headed towards Jeddah for a brief stop. In Jeddah, it was thirty-seven degrees Celsius, so they asked everyone to shut the window shades to keep it cool in the cabin. We were in Saudi Arabia but were not allowed to see it. Also, we were instructed to hide alcoholic drinks. Muslims can be just as hypocritical as those of us of the so called "Christian" west. We are against drugs but tolerate alcohol and tobacco use. Muslims are against alcohol but tolerate tobacco and khat. What is the difference?

After an overnight in Rome and changing planes, we flew to Toronto and on to Calgary, Alberta, Canada.

CHAPTER 37

A Summary Reflection

F or us as a family, this was another watershed moment. It was a good time for evaluation, to reflect on the successes and failures of OSP and our involvement over the past six years.

It had been twelve years since the Ogwedhi Sigawa Community Development Project was launched. A lot of transformation occurred in the community during that time. While much of the change was bound to come and had nothing to do with OSP, some of this change was a direct result of OSP's activities. What were these successes and failures? How could we summarize what had been accomplished, and what lessons did we learn? What should we have done differently? What foundations that we laid should be built upon, and which should be discarded?

Directly connected to OSP during those first twelve years, the physical site had been developed to include one hundred acres of bushy land cleared and fenced. A project director's house and a pastor's house had been built. A church chapel was serving the needs of a small congregation and doubled as a classroom during the week.

A primary school had been built on both sides of the provincial border and was in operation with a boarding component for boys. Its reputation for quality education attracted over 800 students. Maasai, Luo, and Kuria boys and girls were studying together, playing together, and making friendships across formerly hostile ethnic lines.

The health center was providing basic health care, especially maternal child-care with vaccination services to the community. Other buildings included five staff houses, an office, an agricultural supplies shop, a storage space, a welding shop, a zero-grazing unit, a milking unit, a goat barn, a calf barn, and nine rainwater catchment tanks.

A dairy herd of thirty exotic breed milk cows was producing milk which was delivered to customers in the community via bicycle each morning. Exotic bulls were being sold to progressive farmers who were crossbreeding their local cows. Also, artificial insemination of cattle was serving the same purpose of improving the quality of livestock in the community.

A tree nursery was supplying the community with at least 20,000 tree seedlings and grafted fruit trees each year. Four fishponds had been dug and stocked with tilapia.

In the larger community, the demarcation and privatization of communal land was mostly completed except for a few bitterly disputed areas. Although this developmental change was initiated by the Maasai community and supervised by the appropriate government authority with no input from OSP, the project did have a strong influence in shaping the community's response to its implementation.

The Maasai were now building fences and confining their cattle to their own plots. Nomadism had become a thing of the past. They were beginning to build better houses and dig wells where water was needed. A few of them were keeping improved dairy cows. Others had crossbred theirs.

They had abandoned the tradition of warriorhood, and most were sending their children to schools. Most of them were planting small fields of maize and had learned to eat ugali, collards, potatoes, rice, cooked bananas, tomatoes, and beans in addition to their traditional diet of milk, blood, and meat. They were living at peace with the Luos, many of whom, as sharecroppers, were teaching them the ways of farming.

OSP's impact left its mark on the larger community in many ways. Physically, a second church building, primary school, and missionary house had been built at Enemasi among the Siria Maasai. Also, a twenty-acre plot of land at Kiikat had been fenced in anticipation of constructing a primary and vocational high school at some future date.

The Il Pashire Maasai Women's Group had built a shop and an office north of Sikawa hill. From the shop, they were selling agricultural and school supplies. They were clearing the trees on a couple of acres with the plan to plant sugarcane as an income-generating project.

Further, seventeen hand-dug community water wells had been completed, with concrete casings, covers, and superstructures built in place. Manual-powered water pumps were installed to provide safe drinking water for the people.

Perhaps the greatest long-term impact of OSP was the spiritual changes the introduction of Christianity brought. I emphasize "long term" because the immediate impact was slow and hardly noticeable. Yet, the Kingdom of God comes like a tiny seed that will grow to become a mighty tree. It had profound moral, ethical, intellectual, spiritual, and eternal implications for the individual, the community, and for the whole nation.

An embryonic church was emerging in Maasailand. Small groups were meeting outside every Sunday for worship and instruction. The first small permanent meeting house, built on project land, was used by the Luo and Maasai communities together. Since it was a town church, the language used was primarily Swahili.

Among the community elders who had not yet participated in Christianity, there was a strong sense of identity with the Mennonites. When other denominations asked for land to start churches, the elders refused, saying, "We only want one church here. We will all become Mennonites." Why this loyalty? "The Mennonites taught us that God loves cows!" Somehow, they had come to identify OSP and its interest in dairy cattle with the Mennonite Church.

Growth was very slow at first. By 1990, about seventy had been baptized, mostly women. While the men were open to change and sent their wives and children to be taught, most of them on a personal level were reluctant to "break from the pack" to respond to the call of Christ to become followers. Some opposed their wives in becoming Christians.

According to the culture, it was demeaning for a man to sit with women in a meeting. When things of importance were to be discussed, women were not to be within sight nor sound of men. To come to church to sit with women and children, for men, was difficult. And to have a woman as a leader or teacher was, to "real men," unthinkable.

Clair and Beth Good and their daughters made their home at Enemasi. Since that was in Siria Maasai territory, most of their efforts were directed towards that ethnic group, although several of the nucleus of believers were from the Kisii tribe.

The original purpose of the launching of OSP was to promote

peace and reconciliation and inter-ethnic cooperation and community building. To further that aim, OSP had helped to facilitate the Community Organization and Development Education program, which held peace meetings once per month involving elders from the Luo, Kuria, and Maasai ethnic groups. As a result, the three ethnic communities agreed together on a plan to stop cattle theft. While cattle theft was not eradicated at once, for the first time all three ethnic groups began to cooperate towards this end. The discussions also promoted establishing relationships that led to peaceful co-existence and cooperation between the tribes.

Reconciliation and cooperation was growing. Luos and Maasai worked together on the project. Their children studied and played together in the schools. Their parents traded with each other in the marketplace, and some of them prayed together in the churches. The grip of old animosities and stereotypes was slipping away. A new day of reconciliation was dawning, filled with challenge and hope.

CHAPTER 38

Transition

We had taken our departure in an atmosphere of mutual understanding that we would be gone for one year with the probability that we would return to Ogwedhi for another term of service thereafter. OSP was in the steady hands of Barack Ogola under the guidance of the Management Committee with the qualified oversight of Wes and Marian Newswanger, committed to undertake a caretaker role as director for one year.

After visiting our family and supporters in Alberta and Pennsylvania during the summer, we settled in Harrisonburg, Virginia, to spend the remainder of our furlough year near to our now adult children, Sheryl, Kristina, and Karen with her husband, Dee, and our first grandchild, the one-year-old Jasmine. We rented an apartment in Park View and made that our home for the remainder of the year.

As patriarch, one of my early responsibilities was to assist in the marriage ceremony of our third daughter, Sheryl Justina, and her fiancée, Eric Angelo Payne, on August 9, 1991. The wedding took place in the Community Mennonite Church in Harrisonburg. Eric's uncle, Rev. Theodore Payne performed the tying of the marriage knot.

I had not thought very carefully about what I would do with my time during that year so assumed I should enroll in some form of study or self-improvement. I signed up to audit some courses in the local Eastern Mennonite Seminary. After about a month of attending classes, I realized my heart was not in it. At my age, I should use this time to do some serious reflecting and writing.

Consequently, I dropped the courses, purchased my first laptop computer with a printer, and committed myself to learning to type and to operate the laptop. That was a big stretch for me over the first few weeks. I concentrated on writing some portions of my forebearers' history, namely the story of my grandparents, Jacob and Justina Friesen. That led to recording some of my own experiences in growing up in my family, as well as writing the story of our first eight years as a missionary family in Ethiopia.

At the same time, I found it was not easy to simply detach myself from a project that had absorbed my total attention over my waking and sleeping hours, days, months, and six years of my life, a project that offered tantalizing challenges that could involve us in a bright and exciting future. I found myself dreaming and designing a detailed thirty-five-page "Phase III" proposal in preparation for applying for funding. I researched possible funding partners and equipment resources. The plan got bigger and bigger.

At the same time, I began feeling that perhaps it was time for a change. I was deeply impressed with reports of the long-term outcomes of the teaching we were involved in at the Nazareth Bible Academy back in 1967-70. The teaching our alumni had received from that institution had transformed their lives, and most of them had been making huge impacts for good wherever they had scattered. Perhaps God wanted me to leave the grass roots community development project and concentrate on multiplying visionary, development-minded leaders. That would mean going back to full-time teaching in an appropriate institution.

Two developments moved me in that direction. First, I heard positive reports on how the Newswangers were doing in taking my place at OSP, and they were willing to extend their service there for more years. Second, correspondence from EMM indicated they were a bit apprehensive of my tendency to grow OSP into something huge and complicated, while still dependent upon outside personnel and financial resources. EMM was not interested in big dependent projects in Africa. They were concerned about my "entrepreneurial" tendencies. They didn't really know how to handle this missionary, who tended to think "outside the box."

In the spring of 1991, sensing this change of direction, I offered to EMM that, if they felt it best, I would be open to consider a teaching role rather than the current development role. The outcome was that EMM decided that Wes and Marian Newswanger would continue giving leadership to the Ogwedhi Sigawa Project, and I would transfer to teach at Daystar, a non-denominational evangelical university in

Nairobi. I was given a position in the Daystar Institute of Christian Ministries Training (ICMT) program where I would teach a biblical and theological perspective on development, church growth and development, and leadership and management.

There, we found the next three years, 1992-95, working with the ICMT team quite fulfilling. We organized and taught short courses and workshops for key leaders of various non-government organizations (NGOs), and church programs from all over eastern Africa.

Travel Stresses

At the first light of the summer dawn, we jumped out of bed. Today was the day of our departure, the day that marked the end of our furlough, the day we had to say our sad farewells to our children and loved ones in parting for another three years.

After quickly shaving and showering, I rushed my laptop over to Brian Boettger's place. It was the last chance to have him help install the nine-megabyte Bible program into our hard drive. He was having company, preparing for and taking a final exam, then setting out that day on a vacation trip to Iowa. So, I was conscious that I was impinging upon his valuable time. Yet, this was our flying day, and I knew I didn't know how to install the program myself. I had procrastinated for too long. Yet, he kindly promised the night before, "It won't take more than half an hour!"

Brian soon had the program installed but had problems getting it set up on the menu for easy retrieval. He tried this and that while the clock ticked on and on at an unnerving speed. Something was wrong, it wouldn't work. Soon it was ten o'clock, then quarter past. We hadn't had breakfast yet and still had to pack our last suitcase before we were to leave at one o'clock sharp.

Finally, he hit the right and last key, and the thing was set to work properly conjuring up any Bible word, phrase, or quote that one could ask for. It could show you each use of any Greek or Hebrew word that you desired by the mere punch of the right buttons instantly. And it could take in any notes which you might wish to add to any text, and it could order the printer to print out any portion you choose to ask of it. What an amazing machine!

By now we were desperate to get the final packing done and get it loaded into the van that Eric rented. Amazingly, we were all in the van and ready to go at one o'clock. We were exactly on schedule.

Thanks to the good Lord, the nice van, the safe driver, and a super smooth highway, we arrived at Dulles International Airport exactly on time. All was going like clockwork so far!

The first hint of trouble occurred when we discovered our two luggage boxes were about thirty pounds overweight. We would have to pay $256 extra for the excess baggage. It was too late to unpack, weed out, and repack, so we wrote a bad check (because our bank account was flat empty) and hoped that Kristina would remember to bail us out by covering it with the overflow from her account (It's convenient to have a daughter holding down two jobs!).

When that was taken care of and our luggage checked in, we took the shuttle bus over to terminal C and settled down for the brief wait in the boarding lounge. No sooner had we gotten seated than we were informed that our flight to JFK in New York was cancelled due to bad weather there. The TWA clerk assured us that there was no problem. She simply re-routed us on a United Airlines flight leaving at 6:40 for London where another flight would take us at 8:25 a.m. to Amsterdam where we could catch our Nairobi flight on KLM by 2:00 p.m. local time. Therefore, there was no problem, except we had already checked in our two huge overweight boxes and two enormous suitcases with TWA.

We were informed as to where to retrieve them since the flight was aborted. We took the shuttle service back to the TWA baggage claim, collected ours and took it to the United Airlines desk. There we put it through their security x-ray check and then presented our new tickets which were written by TWA.

But there was no evidence on United's computer that we were booked. They sent us back to TWA. To do so, we had to retrieve our four mammoth pieces of overweight luggage and lug them back to the TWA desk a second time. Again, they confirmed our booking on United, so we lugged the fearsome four luggage pieces back to United and had them X-rayed again. This time United accepted TWA's computer printout and issued us boarding passes.

Then we returned to the shuttle and rode to the departure

island again and waited and waited and waited. That which was to carry us off to London at 6:40 p.m. didn't show up for duty. Due to bad weather, it was diverted to Cleveland. A substitute was being scrounged up from somewhere, maybe taken out of mothballs and dusted off? Around 8:00 p.m. it arrived. Then it had to be serviced and loaded. Finally, after 9:00 p.m. it took off with us and our luggage on board from Washington and headed eastward into the night sky.

We arrived at Heathrow Airport in London in good order around 9:15 the next morning, but of course our connecting flight had already taken off at 8:25 a.m. Now, how were we and our luggage to get to Amsterdam to connect with our Nairobi flight? The United people quickly took us to terminal #4 to the KLM desk. We waited in line for half an hour killing precious time, but they couldn't help us as their next flight left for Amsterdam at 3:00 p.m. They sent us back to terminal #3 to the United desk as it was their problem to get us out of our mess. Here the que was long, and we waited another two hours before they could tend to our problem.

It was afternoon before they booked us on a flight with Kenya Airways from London directly to Nairobi. The lady was kind and felt sorry for us, so put us in business class. The Airbus was to leave London at 8:30 in the evening. Problem solved. However, we had only seven more hours to kill in the transfer lounge, plenty of time to ponder the fate of our four huge pieces of luggage.

Kenya Airways took good care of us in business class, even gave us carnations with our meals. The seats were wider and more comfortable and leaned far back for sleeping. We had five good hours of intense sleep and woke with the Sudanese sun rising in our window.

It is so beautiful up there with the sun shining over the eastern horizon turning the upper side of the cloud cover into a study of fleecy white with dark shadows. Up there one gets more of God's viewpoint, a new perspective on things.

The pilot greeted us with a "Good Morning, I hope you rested well!" He announced we'd be landing in Nairobi in two hours. Soon breakfast was served. There was a break in the clouds, and Lake Turkana appeared to the left of us, then Mt. Kenya above the clouds further east. Then the Aberdare mountains showed up, and soon we were touching down at the familiar Kenyatta International Airport. It was Sunday morning, about nine o'clock.

Two days later, we went to the airport and found our luggage. The four pieces had arrived on three different airlines. We were grateful to have a fresh change of clothes.

CHAPTER 39

Ogwedhi Sigawa Revisited – October 1992

I n the fall of 1992, before taking up the challenges of teaching at Daystar, EMM sent Vera and I to take another four months of Swahili language study. This time, the venue was the highly reputed *Shule ya Lugha* (language school) at Makoka, Tanzania. This Catholic institution was situated in their beautiful, quiet, Maryknoll Seminary campus on the lovely shore of Lake Victoria, just a few kilometers south of the town of Musoma. We enjoyed the fellowship of living together in the common residence with about twelve other missionaries of different Catholic orders and some Protestant agencies.

During the one-week mid-term break, we had an opportunity to visit our old home and our many friends around Ogwedhi. We accepted an offer to ride to Migori with Sharon Thompson, a Baptist missionary studying with us, who was going on to Nairobi in her little red Suzuki, taking along a fellow student, Father Jim Corrigan, and our teacher, Raymond Dibogo. It was a trip worth remembering.

Of Brake Lines, Dogs, and Driving

Travel plans were put in jeopardy about two weeks before departure, when both of the front brake lines of the Suzuki were mysteriously cut. The maintenance man, who helped Sharon, was sure dogs chewed both of them. Some of us had our doubts that dogs would find a dry rubber and nylon hose, encrusted with dried mud and the odor of brake fluid, a tempting morsel. Nevertheless, the lines were punctured and broken beyond repair. We didn't worry. Two weeks afforded plenty of time to effect a replacement.

However, we forgot we were in Africa, and Tanzania at that.

There were no spare brake lines in Musoma, but Father Joe Healey, the man in charge at the mission, told Sharon not to worry. He would be sending his trusted assistant to Mwanza in a couple of days. He would bring the necessary parts back with him. Several days later, however, we discovered that the assistant went with the relevant serial numbers and promptly disappeared. Without informing his boss, he had decided this was the right time to take his vacation. By the time this reality was revealed to us, the first week had elapsed.

Sharon looked up the serial numbers again, and someone else was sent. He came back with two different brake lines. One fit, but the other did not. Now things were beginning to look desperate. The maintenance man was sent once again to search Mwanza for the second brake line. It was now Thursday. We wanted to leave by Friday noon. He returned in the evening without the line.

That evening, we heard there was a shortage of fuel in Musoma. It looked like we might have to call off the trip. Then, on Friday morning, we heard that a little petrol had arrived, so a friend drove the still crippled Suzuki to town and waited in line for a few hours until they sold him thirty liters.

As soon as he returned, around eleven o'clock, the maintenance man began his work on the defective brake. With no alternative in sight, he decided to block the fluid flow to the one front wheel. We would go with three brakes, and perhaps the missing spare would be found in Kisii, Kenya. Emergency solved!

After lunch on Friday, we set out slowly and carefully with three soft brakes on the long journey to Nairobi. When we reached Musoma, three policemen stopped us. I was driving. Did I know what I had done wrong? How long had I been driving in Tanzania? Well, I had driven around a new roundabout and made a right turn without signaling. That was a chargeable offence. However, they would be kind to me and let me off with a warning this time. We were very grateful and thanked them very profusely for their kindness and promised to do better in the future.

Our journey to Kenya was rather uneventful. The three soft brakes were not too scary, so Sharon decided to continue to Nairobi instead of fixing them in Kisii. We arrived in Migori after 5:00 p.m. Wes Newswanger soon came to bring Vera and me to Ogwedhi.

Home Again

It was nearing 8:00 p.m. when we drove up to the massive new steel gate securing the Ogwedhi Sigawa Project that we had ordered two years earlier. A new young watchman, Joseph, came running to welcome us in.

When we went up to our old house, Winnie didn't even bark to welcome us. She was kept tied behind the house, so people could come to the front door without being intimidated by the ferocious canine guard, that, in her heart, she really wasn't. We were welcomed by Pastor Paul and his sons, then went in and were soon eating at Marian's waiting supper.

After a long visit, we went to sleep in our old bed in our old room. Sleeping at Ogwedhi was always a pleasure except when someone woke us to attend to a desperately or not so desperately sick person or some other emergency. The night was dark and quiet, and we were tired, so we slept well.

Soon we heard the familiar morning sounds: the first distant crow of a rooster, then the chirping of the earliest birds and the bawling of the hungry newborn calf in the barn, vainly calling for the attention of its mother. Then, we heard the shuffling of the night watchman's feet and the clattering as he put away his equipment in the storeroom and left for home. There were also the sounds of the dairy workers as they began their work of bringing the cows in for milking. A nostalgic awakening. It was time to get up, a marvelously beautiful Saturday morning!

After breakfast we took a tour of the project. Our first impression was how much the trees had grown. To think that we planted little seedlings just five or six years ago. Now the place that was barren and open looked like the Garden of Eden!

The Christian Health Association of Kenya (CHAK) had completed the enlargement and reorganization of the little dispensary into a community health center in 1990-91. This upgraded the quality and range of services to include immunizations, mother-child health care, and family planning. They also built two residences for the Community Health Officer and the nurse.

Isaac and Joy Laizer and their family arrived according to the plan, on July 9, 1991. They came as missionaries sent by the Tanzania

Mennonite Church but supported by OSP. They organized and were beginning to implement a community-based health care program.

The repurposed and remodeled goat barn caught our immediate attention. The front was decorated with a fence, flowers, a gate, and a path. The former barn was now a very nice office building. It had four offices and a large room for seminars and committees. Behind it was a little brick cook house where meals were prepared by Yunia. A lot of seminars were held here, mostly in relation to the Community Based Health Care program. Maurice established a library there for a public reading room.

The dairy was going on as usual. Many Maasai were now bringing their milk to OSP to be sold in the Luo community. They hired one Maasai person to coordinate the collection and distribution of this milk. OSP provided him with an office, but he was being paid from a fee levied from the sales.

Osoro was in charge of the welding shop since Caleb was no longer with OSP. The community had expelled the whole Omondi family from Ogwedhi.

Consequences of Theft

Mwanyakiti had broken into Wes's office at the house one night while Wes was sleeping, and Winnie was watching. He removed a glass from the window and reached in with a hoe and pulled out Wes's brown handbag with money and ID and other things. He only got a couple thousand shillings. He very thoughtfully returned the bag with the documents, minus the money of course, by putting it in the unlocked truck cab.

A month or so later, while Wes was in Nairobi, a gang of several men broke into the workshop and made off with one broken motorcycle and a few tools. The guard surprised them in the act. The thieves threw rocks at him and chased him into Pastor Paul's house. Others heard the noise and started to come, so the thieves fled, pushing the motorcycle, and carrying the grinder and a few small tools. The motorcycle was recovered the next day near *Kona Mbaya*, the bad sharp corner about three kilometers towards Oyani.

It was out of working order and no doubt was a disappointment to the thieves.

Fortunately, the two other motorcycles which normally were stored in the same shed, had come home too late that day, and had been locked into the feed room for that evening only.

The spinoff of all this stealing was a deeper sensitivity to security. The elders of the community decided to expel the whole Omondi family from the community, the father, the small children, and even the twenty-five-year-old Caleb.

Did anyone of them remember the many times, over the past six years, that Meshack Omondi treated their wounds, cooled their burning fevers, stopped the diarrhea or malaria that threatened the lives of their babies, listened sympathetically to their complaints, spoke comforting words to them, prayed for their recovery, and gave them or their little ones' medicines for all their ills, often without charge. Now he was to be treated as an alien, an outcast, a thing to be despised and rejected.

Did any of them think of what it would mean to the community or to OSP to remove Caleb, the driver and mechanic, the only one who knew how to service and repair motorcycles, the chaff-cutter engine, pumps, and the solar electric system?

It seemed so ironic. Here the church and community were cutting off their own right arm, the one person on the staff who could be trusted enough to be sent to Nairobi with thousands of shillings, to purchase what was needed. He could always be depended upon to take good care of the vehicle, complete his assignment, and return on time with a careful report on every cent that was entrusted to him.

Did anyone think to remember the many times Caleb arose at night, or went after a long day of work, to drive them or their loved ones the long hours over rough and often treacherous trails to reach a hospital in order that their lives might be spared, even when he was very tired or when the dark trails might be lurking with bandits or made virtually impassable with rain? He was the one they could depend upon to drive the vehicle on any errand, like transporting the bishop, pastors, or board members to special functions.

Now he had been chased from the community like a despised alien and told to return to Tanzania, and that they never wanted to see his face again, all because his brother was a thief! In the thinking of the elders, the defect of having a son or a brother who became a thief more than cancelled out all these memories. With one bad fruit, the whole basket must be thrown out. The sins of one son were being visited upon the father and the whole family.

Old Friends

Ole Sikawa and Noonkipa invited the Newswangers and us to visit their home for lunch. We were given a very warm welcome. Noonkipa had a delicious meal ready, and we had a very nice visit without the need for a translator. Maybe language school was helping a bit. Of course, everybody wanted to know all the news about Kristina. Their boys were using Kristina's house. The compound looked very different since they built a fence around the houses, keeping the cattle away.

When we got home, who should turn up to greet us but Pilista and Peter Otieno! Pilista was a bit thinner than when she worked for us. Because they had no money, they had walked all the way from their home at Luendo, about sixty kilometers away. Pilista's feet were killing her. She was very happy to see us again. She reported that she had received 1,500 Ksh. that Kristina had sent her and had just bought 500 Ksh. worth of maize and other food at the market when a thief snatched her purse with the remaining 1,000 Ksh. in it!

That poor widow had suffered so much at the hands of thieves. So many times, she had opened her home to keep relatives, or friends of relatives, only to find that they had snuck away with some of her possessions. Several times she had her money snatched away while travelling. She stayed in the pastor's home that night, then went to church the next day. She was anxious to return home as she left her house unguarded.

Sunday morning, Peter Otieno accompanied us out to church at Kiloingoni's home. Joseph Sankale and Francis Rikei were there also. The crowd was very small since many of the members joined a new Pentecostal church that came into the area. This was the direct result of gross neglect on the part of the pastor, and the fact that Francis had been away for training for a year.

Joseph had attended the Bible College at Musoma, Tanzania,

for one term. Upon returning, he was very active, moving about preaching in many places, but not building any one congregation. Clair Good had been concentrating on the Siria side mostly. The Wuasinkishu church was experiencing serious decline. Wes and Marian and Maurice concentrated on a new ministry to the soldiers at the Stock Theft Unit camp and at Naiborsoit. Laizer was helping at Ol'Donyo Oretet. The Kuria church at Nyagutu had started to build a block church building big enough to seat three hundred.

During the rest of the week, we visited many of the homes of our friends. The OSP staff had a special lunch in our honor held in the new seminar room they had made in the re-purposed goat barn. One of the homes we could not miss was Magdalena's. She was waiting for us. Her son, Bayenni cooked tea and rice for us. Magdalena had a new three-month old baby boy. He was still as tiny as a new-born.

Magdalena's neighbors, Arami and Parakuo, came over to visit. Their husband had led a Wuasinkishu attack on the Siria several months back. His hostile act earned him an arrow through his arm and into his chest. He was taken to Kilgoris, then flown to Kenyatta Hospital in Nairobi. The arrow was removed. It was almost fatal; the tip of the arrow having stopped only one half-inch away from his heart. Had it missed his arm, it would have killed him instantly. Now, he was at home, so we went over to visit him. He was very happy to see us. He took me out to see his cattle.

We hoped they learned something from that war. The Siria did not want to fight. They begged for peace, but the hot Wuasinkishu would not listen. Three times they came up to fight, destroying several Siria houses. The third time, the Siria ambushed them and chased them back in confusion. Several were struck down with arrows though none were killed.

This time the Wuasinkishu were ashamed and humiliated. Since that time, there had been peace. Everybody could see that the Siria were not the "bad guys." Also, the Moitanik had made peace with the Siria, so the Wuasinkishu were isolated. This almost sounded like an Old Testament story.

One afternoon, we visited Ole Miberre, and some of his Christian neighbors gathered with us. We were served tea, rice, and potatoes. His son, James Kashe, was home too, sick with malaria. He had been working with the city commission in Nairobi. He had made peace with his father some months previously, so he came home every now and then.

We visited with Clair and Beth quite late that night. He was overseeing the building of the first permanent classroom at the Moita school some distance into the interior of Maasailand. It was closed by the government as a health hazard. Two years earlier, the county council had donated 130,000 Ksh. for construction of that new school. The elders managed to eat about sixty thousand shillings before they asked Clair to help them. Thanks to Clair, they were getting at least one good classroom out of that grant.

On Thursday afternoon, Caleb Omondi surprised us with a visit. He had reached Tanzania and had returned already. He told us that his dad was working in Migori, but his young brothers were still in Ogwedhi going to school. He said that two of the community elders approached him privately, suggesting that, if he would give them *chai* (something for tea), they would allow him to stay in Ogwedhi after all. What hypocrites. They even suggested that they could get him back his old job with OSP, if he would pay them something! They were the very ones who were the leaders of the eviction movement.

It would be very interesting to see how they would move to reverse the expulsion, and how they would respond to what Wes had to say. However, Caleb was in no mood to give them a chance. The world was big, and there were other opportunities for a young man of his ability and character.

Saturday morning, we woke up at 4:30 a.m. and left with Wes and Marian who were going to Nairobi to meet family members. They left us at Awendo where we caught a *matatu* for Migori. Vera and I sat down to have a breakfast of tea and cake at the Mombasa Hotel at 6:20 a.m.

We waited until 8:15 when Wilson Ogwada came to meet us. He had lost one leg due to his diabetes and was walking with a pair of crutches. He wanted to talk to me about some plans of his and about why we were not returning to work in the area.

Our conversation was cut short when Sharon Thompson's car pulled up. We never finished that conversation. A short time later, we learned that our beloved ex-chief, Wilson Ogwada, was taken to his eternal home.

We were taken back to Tanzania. It had been a great week, a

mighty fine break in language study, and an opportunity to test what new proficiency we had gained in Swahili. It was a time to renew friendships, refresh memories, and renew commitment to further service.

EPILOGUE

While living in Nairobi and teaching at Daystar over the next three years, I was able to keep in touch with what was happening in the Ogwedhi Sigawa community. Under the wise and dedicated management of Barak Ogola, and the careful oversight of Wes and Marian Newswanger, the project continued to serve and grow as planned.

In July of 1991, Lutheran World Relief committed themselves to partner with OSP for another four years. Water development and the extension programs were to be expanded. Heifer Projects International also contributed to strengthening the veterinarian services of OSP.

The Children's Peace Choir from the Ogwedhi Sigawa Primary School was sponsored to compete at the annual National Music Festival for Primary Schools held in Nairobi. This unique choir consisted of Maasai, Kuria, and Luo children. They all learned to speak and sing in the Maasai language. This choir composed songs of peace, reflecting their common peoplehood which crosses ethnic and tribal boundaries. The choir won third prize.

Wes and Marian Newswanger gave leadership to OSP for five years. Following their departure, the community elders persuaded Paul Saiyua, the local Maasai from Il Pashire, to leave his administrative position with the Sony Sugar Factory to become director of OSP. For the next six years, from October 1996 to 2002, Paul Saiyua led OSP well. At the end of his term, the local politicians took control of OSP from the church and appointed their man as director.

From there, things went downhill. Donor funding stopped. Programs had to be cut. In the interest of sustainability, a large tract of sugarcane was planted under contract with the Sony Sugar Company. However, through corruption, the company failed to harvest it when it reached its prime after three years.

In 2008, control of OSP was given back to the Mennonite Church.

A new board was appointed, and Charles Kantai was hired as managing director. They were struggling to restart OSP. However, without outside funding, they found it impossible to reverse the downward trend.

In subsequent years, Vera and I visited the Ogwedhi community twice. After being away for sixteen years, we, along with our daughter, Kristina, her husband, James Blakely, and four of our grandchildren, Desta, Darius, Jasmine, and Justus, undertook a visit to Ogwedhi in December of 2009.

This visit was arranged with the help of our Maasai friend, Daniel ole Momposhi, who had been a small boy in grade four when we left in 1991. Now a graduate with a degree in community development from Daystar University, he was working for the Central Bank of Kenya in Nairobi. However, Daniel was very passionate to continue with the work of transforming their Maasai community. Being a very friendly, sociable young man, he was invaluable to us in notifying the people and arranging our transport. Also, being well educated, he was able to translate for us with the community members.

In this visit, we managed to visit Ole Sikawa at home, Ole Kitiyia, Daniel Ole Momposhi's home and several other friends. One notable change in this visit was the numerous churches of various denominations which sprang up all over Maasai land. There were at least thirty churches of several different denominations across the Wuasinkishu alone.

Five years later, Vera and I made one more visit to South Nyanza and the Ogwedhi Sigawa community in the Trans Mara Region. We arrived in Migori by bus on February 24, 2014. The recently ordained bishop, Hellon Ogwada, welcomed us and drove us the seven kilometers to his home at Osingo.

Bishop Hellon Ogwada, a twin son of the late Wilson Ogwada, was ordained in place of the retired Bishop Joshua Okello Ouma. He had a "tent making ministry," supporting himself by running a hardware business. Hellon and his family lived in a modern, relatively new, spacious, Kenyan-style house. It was built on the family homestead where most of his brothers also had their houses. They welcomed us to their home with the customary prayer before being seated in the living room where we conversed. A Kenyan dinner was served at the usual Kenyan time which was between 8:00 and 9:00 p.m.

After breakfast, Bishop Hellon's younger brother, Deacons, drove us to visit the retired bishop, Nashon Arwa, and his wife at their home near Bande, close to Muhuru Bay. Nashon was past eighty years, and his wife was seventy-six years of age. We visited for a few hours and had lunch together.

In the mid-afternoon, we drove back towards Migori and stopped at Korwah to visit Joshua and Deborah Okello Ouma in their retirement home. We were welcomed and shown around their rather large farm. Then, we were given an ample dinner, by solar light, after which we took our leave and arrived back at Hellon's place for the night.

On Wednesday, we were taken to the church office in the former mission compound in Migori for a meeting of the Southern Diocese pastors. We were shown a new primary school, dedicated to the memory of Clyde and Alta Shenk, that had 110 children, many of them orphans, from nursery through grade four. The church provided them with breakfast and lunch. They reported that the diocese had twelve parishes composed of three major ethnic groups (Luo, Kuria, and Maasai) and were served by thirty-two pastors and deacons.

Their Migori Mennonite Theological School of Africa was opened in April 2013 to provide basic theological education for leaders in Kenya. It provided two-week courses three times per year when teachers from the Mennonite Theological College at Nyabangi, Tanzania, would come to teach during their holiday breaks.

After the women of the church served us lunch, Deacons took us to Ogwedhi in the Toyota Hilux which belonged to OSP but was kept in the bishop's home. Upon arrival, he gave us the keys, said "Goodbye," and took a motorcycle taxi back to his home. For the next few days, like in former times, I was privileged to drive around Maasailand in an OSP Toyota Hilux.

In the absence of a director at OSP, Pastor David Ole Shaai had assumed supervision. Since David was living on his own farm, the director's house was vacant. Also, the former pastor's house across the lane was rented out to primary school teachers, so David had thoughtfully arranged to provide us with food and lodging in our former home.

We were welcomed by the teachers living next door. One of the teacher's wives had been hired to prepare food for us. We were given "Kristina's room." It had been cleaned nicely but hadn't experienced any refurbishment since the Newswangers lived there. Pastor David Shaai came to greet and welcome us. It was already getting dark, so we gathered with a few elders and friends in the living room, then ate together before retiring. It was good to be "back home."

The next morning, after a traditional breakfast of bread and tea, a group of locals escorted us on an inspection tour of OSP. This included visiting the clinic which was serving about one hundred patients on market days, visiting the primary school which had 775 primary students plus fifty kindergarteners, visiting the fields, mostly planted to sugarcane, and seeing the few remaining dairy cattle. Also, we were introduced to an emerging secondary school in which thirty-two students were enrolled in grades nine and ten. This school was housed in some of the renovated store and office rooms. Each unit, the health center, the livestock, the crop land, the primary school, and the high school, were operating separately on a semi-independent contract. Hence there was no need for a full-time project manager.

That afternoon, we were escorted on a tour of the Ogwedhi market. We noticed that the electric power line had reached the town, and a cell phone tower had been erected.

That being a market day, the place was packed with thousands of people from all three tribes plus hundreds of merchants who frequent such markets. Of interest, it was one of the larger cattle marketing points in Trans Mara Region. In walking among the cattle, I was happy to notice the preponderance of cattle with Sahiwal or Ayrshire blood lines, a mark of the success of OSP's cattle breeding program of twenty-five years earlier.

Another new thing we noticed was the presence of dozens of Chinese motorcycle taxis waiting for hire. The hinterland still had no road system for cars, but motorcycles are versatile enough to go on most paths where cows can go.

On Friday, after having a late breakfast in the home of Francis Rikei, we drove to Enemasi. We found the seven-kilometers road had been graded, and an electric line had been installed to bring electricity to the town center and school. The primary school, which had been started outside under a tree while the first building was being constructed back in 1988, now had 200 students in kindergarten through grade eight, all accommodated in classrooms.

We had a lunch meeting appointment with the elders and friends there in the house of the former missionaries, Clair and Beth Good. A small group of leaders and teachers assembled to welcome us. Among them were eighty-year-old Samson Masake, the real founder of the church at Enemasi, and four primary school teachers who introduced themselves as pastors of several outreach churches. In line with Kenya Mennonite practice, pastors usually supported themselves with other occupations while serving their congregations.

We were deeply touched when they introduced themselves, "We were among those first students who started primary school here, sitting on logs in the shade of the tree while the building was going on." Now they were pastors, church planters, and teachers. The amazing Kingdom of God, as usual, starts with small beginnings. We were blessed.

The land allocated to the church was mostly planted with sugarcane. The mango trees, planted by Clair Good, were bearing fruit, another source of income for the church. The brothers told us the building was much too crowded on Sundays, and they were planning to build a much larger meeting house near the original one with capacity for 500 worshipers. They had already collected about 400 iron sheets for the roof. New primary schools as well as churches were being started throughout the area.

On our return, we stopped in to see Sofia and Rosa, wives of ole Musukeri, now entering grandmotherhood, and our dear friend and original believer and leader, Magdalena. They all seemed happy to see us.

Joseph Sankale and Esther were the parents of four grown sons. They were living and working on their little farm near Ogwedhi, keeping a few improved milk cows and some chickens, and cultivating a few acres of maize, beans, vegetables, and fruit trees. Joseph, now a middle-aged church leader, still served as an evangelist, a preacher, and a teacher. His whole-hearted enthusiasm for the work of spreading the Word of God throughout Maasailand never diminished. He was working with the Berean Church, giving oversight to more than thirty congregations as their main Bible teacher. The little band of Christian believers continued growing stronger in numbers and deeper in faith, and Joseph had a major role in that growth.

On Saturday morning, we visited Barack and Lois Ochanda Ogola. Barack led us on a tour of the God Ngoche Girls Secondary Boarding

School which is just next to their SDA Church and the God Ngoche Primary School. This new boarding school was Barack's retirement project. He was chair of its Board of Directors. It was interesting to learn how this community project was organized and self-reliant. Of course, Lois served us a nice lunch at noon which was not in our plan.

After lunch, we excused ourselves and quickly departed, driving over to the Maasai pastor, David Shaai's home where we had an 11:00 a.m. appointment. We arrived at 1:00 p.m., two hours late. There we had another lunch, visited a bit, and witnessed the birth of a healthy Sahiwal calf. David kept an improved herd. We were impressed with their home and children, a good example of a Christian family.

That evening, we drove back to Migori and spent the night with the retired Bishop Philip Okeyo and his wife in their Migori home. We enjoyed a good visit and wonderful hospitality. On Sunday morning, Philip arranged for a taxi to take us to the bus station where we boarded a bus heading towards Nairobi.

Last Impressions

After not living at the Ogwedhi Sigawa Community Development Project for twenty-three years, our first impression upon our return was the obvious evidence of the ravages of time. Every tin roof was rusted. Old flaking paint and brown spots on ceilings gave evidence of many years of leaking roofs. We could see a thousand needs for repair, including decaying trim, rusty screens, and broken gates and fences. People also, like what we noticed in looking into our own mirror, showed signs of aging: graying or loss of hair, missing or decaying teeth, and spreading middles. Most of all, we noticed how many people were missing, largely through death. The AIDS epidemic had taken a terrible toll on the workforce I used to know.

Our second impression was one of hope, renewal, and growth. Former children had become adults—farmers, university graduates, teachers, businesspeople, pastors, and leaders. Seedlings we had planted were now towering trees providing a canopy of cool shade over the whole yard. A growing town with electricity made it possible to find mobile phones everywhere. A growing market was serviced and enhanced by a fleet of motorcycle taxis. A recently built second sugar factory nearby encouraged a growing sugar industry which was reflected by the prominence of cane fields everywhere. Primary schools and small churches could be found throughout Maasailand. Prosperity was reflected by bigger houses for the few wealthy and better houses, some with latrines, for most of the Maasai.

In reviewing the situation of what had been a very successful and admirable development project, several observations became obvious. On the positive side, all five of the original objectives of OSP were accomplished. Besides the Ogwedhi Sigawa Primary School, additional primary schools were dotting the Maasai countryside. The health center was serving the public. Churches had sprung up throughout Maasailand. The general quality of cattle in the area had improved. The landscape, which had been used only for grazing cattle, was now transformed into a variegated patchwork with various kinds of agricultural crops.

Also, OSP had succeeded in accomplishing its original purpose to promote peace and understanding between the ethnic groups. An atmosphere conducive to cooperation and development was benefiting each of their communities. The general wellbeing of the community had been transformed.

There was a time when the Maasai said, "We want to be Mennonites." In our last visit, we met a few of the young pastors. They represented several different organized denominations. There were a few Mennonite congregations. However, Kenya Mennonite Church had largely failed to build upon the good will of the Maasai people generated by OSP.

Would it be possible for someone with a vision to bring about a union of the scattered different denominational churches? It may not be a part of the South Nyanza Mennonite Church Diocese. It may not even be "Mennonite." However, it could reflect the best of Christian theology, if handled sensitively. Inter-church seminars and conferences could be held for leadership training and fellowship. These could merge into a union of Maasai followers of Jesus Christ, reconciled to each other, and reconciled to God, a Christian Maasai people, a church worshiping in their own language and incarnating Jesus Christ in their obedience and interpersonal relationships, thus transforming their own culture.

Yes, God does love cows, and he loves cow keepers as well. He also loves those who till the soil. May they all be reconciled in his new creation!

> Therefore, if anyone is in Christ, he is a new creation; the old has gone, the new has come. All this is from God, who reconciled us to himself through Christ and gave us the ministry of reconciliation." (2 Cor. 5:17, 18. NIV)

APPENDIX I

Random Thoughts on Counting the Cost

The On-Going Pain of Separation
Borne by the Children

There are certain costs involved in being a foreign "missionary" in leaving the comforts and familiarity of home and loved ones, especially of separation from close family members. For us parents, there was the grieving of leaving our growing teenaged daughters behind in the USA in pursuit of a college education, and the separation from our younger daughters who resented being put away in a boarding school not of their choosing.

For children, this pain is more keenly felt, yet it is often overlooked in the telling of missionary stories. In the fall, 1992, issue of *Missionary Messenger*, a poem was published, a lament by our daughter, Sheryl, as she felt, once again, the pain of our departure for yet another assignment, this time in Nairobi.

Good-bye Again
Sheryl Hansen-Payne

I'm feeling a little burdened today.
Being a missionary kid is not easy.
The constant uprootings, good-byes
And then
the sometimes-painful memories
of each place with its different faces.
The overwhelming desire to hide,
to cocoon myself in each new place,
forcing myself to say hello to some new face.

The shock of standing out in one crowd,
Then drowning alone, in another.

There is joy too:
the renewing reunions,
the excitement of letters,
the extra appreciation when Dad walked me down the aisle,
the added enjoyment of Mom's friendship and company.

But now they're gone—again.
I struggle to keep my tears inside,
knowing that I should let them flow.
There's a sense of something missing:
Do they know how much I loved having them near?
So, I pray to Jesus:
He is always near, and I am comforted.
Love and pride replace the sadness,
Because Mom and Dad are serving him,
I'll gladly make this sacrifice.
-- Dedicated with love to Carl and Vera Hansen

Burned Out

There was also the chronic exhaustion we sometimes felt as our daily overload of work overwhelmed us. Evaluative, and sometimes tempting questions disturbed us, "Was this really worth it?" There were days when unrecognized burnout showed itself in my exhausted mind. One day, I wrote my honest feelings:

> I don't like beggars. I am tired of them. I'm tired of all these poor people making demands of me. I am tired of being looked up to as the "rich man" of the village, the first they turn to when in trouble: "*Bwana, Nina shida sana!*"
>
> I am tired of sharing my limited allowance in "loans" for school fees, medical emergencies, funeral expenses, overdue dowry installments, and so on.

I am tired of being the only one in the village with a vehicle. I've done more than my share of getting up nights and running the rough and dangerous journey out into some unknown bush village to transport some desperately or not so desperately sick person to the far away hospital and getting back in time to start another day of work.

I am sick of owning the one white face in the crowd, of being the target for those desperate for a scholarship, or a sponsor to support them to study overseas, the one, the sight of whom stirs vain hope for a job in the minds of school dropouts and graduates as well as those multitudes of desperate persons, some who have been knocking on doors for months or even years.

I've helped enough. I'm finished. I just want to be left alone for once, to go home and rest, to shut my ears and eyes to the cries of those with endless needs. I just want to settle down in my hometown and get a "real job," have a nice house and a descent car, some quality furniture, and some money to spend on myself and my family for once. I think I am "burned out."

As a recent article in Newsweek pointed out, we people of the rich nations are suffering from "disaster fatigue." We are simply growing weary of forever responding generously with compassion whenever another disaster hits the headlines. There have been so many famines in Ethiopia, so many floods in Bangladesh, so many wars in the Middle East, so many earthquakes in other places, so many hurricanes and tornados at home, and so many refugees seeking to find refuge anywhere. One cannot be expected to solve everybody's problems. Maybe we've done enough. It is time for "somebody else" to take responsibility for the burden.

But I cannot forget. As Daniel Amos' song says, even though I close my eyes, I still see the "Little bitty

beggars with the great big eyes ... still press their
faces to the window ..."

For they got their faces to the window
Pressin' their faces to the window
Little bitty beggars with the great big eyes
I turn the channel but to my surprise,
They still press their faces to the
They still press their faces to the window ...
--Daniel Amos, 1974

The need is still there. Right now, several million starving
Ethiopians are slowly wasting away in a nation impoverished by
drought and famine and the devastation of civil war. Its city streets
are filled with hungry orphans and widows and crippled veterans and
the unemployed who have lost hope, while our storage facilities are
bursting with cheap grain and even our dogs are obese.

Of the millions of Somalis in a nation turned against itself, the
lucky ones are swelling the refugee camps in Ethiopia, Djibouti, and
Kenya. The rest face death by starvation, or by violence as those with
weapons kill the others for the remaining scraps of food. Need we
mention the millions of others, refugees from Bangladesh, Rohingya,
Syria, Ukraine, Iraq, Afghanistan, Haiti, Guatemala, Columbia, etc.
Who will help them? If we, the rich countries are preoccupied with
our own economic depression and "disaster fatigue," to whom can
they turn for compassionate assistance?

I cannot forget. To know is to be responsible. God has called me
to be a "beggar for the beggars," a voice for the voiceless, an advocate
for the helpless. We must not grow weary of doing good. Yet, we
must not allow needs to overwhelm us to the point where we become
fatigued, calloused, and indifferent.

And I remember the words of our Lord: "Whatever you did for one
of the least of these ... you did for me!" (Mt. 25:40 NIV). I earnestly
pray, "God, have mercy! Forgive me for my feelings of self-pity! Help
me to allow your love and compassion to control my attitudes and
actions! Let your love fill me and flow through me to bless those in
despair who are crying out to you in their hour of need."

On the other hand, I also recognize that even Jesus was aware

301

of the danger of burnout and the need for withdrawal. When the persistent demands of the ever-growing crowds for attention to all their needs drained them, he invited his disciples, "Come with me by yourselves to a quiet place and get some rest." Mark 6:31 (NIV)

APPENDIX II

Following the Bitter/Sweet Christ

May of 2024 will mark the 180th anniversary of the arrival of the first Protestant missionary, Johann Ludwig Krapf, on the shores of Kenya in 1844. This serious young follower of Christ came determined to carry the Gospel to the Oromo, a dominant ethnic group which occupied much of Ethiopia and extended deep into the northeastern interior of Kenya.

It would be no easy task. Alone in a strange land, among a people of unfamiliar language and culture; surrounded by strange diseases which earned Africa the label "The white man's grave"; eyed with deep suspicion by slave traders; scarcely tolerated by an Islamic and pagan population completely disinterested in him or his "gospel"; sensing the opposition of unfriendly spiritual forces, Johann Krapf began to comprehend the deeper meaning and the cost of discipleship.

Very much alone, Johann brought from Zanzibar his young wife, Rosina, to join him in his endeavors. The comfort she brought was brief. Three months after her arrival, weakened by malaria, she died in childbirth. He had sadly underestimated that cost! A few days later, also sick with malaria, he buried his infant daughter. How deep he felt the fellowship of the "bitter Christ" with him!

Some seven years later, Johann returned to his native Germany, disappointed and broken in health. Having come to "save" Africa, his only convert was one dying man he managed to baptize in time. Were his efforts, his sacrifice, his "cross" worthwhile? Could he not be written off as a failure? Or perhaps it was a failure of the Christ who sent him, who promised, "I will be with you always, to the very end..."? How do we reconcile the bitter cost of discipleship with the "easy yoke" and the "light burden" Jesus promised those who came to him?

Anabaptist writers sometimes spoke of the "bitter Christ" in sharp contrast to Martin Luther's "sweet Christ" of "only believe"-ism. By "bitter Christ," they had in mind the heavy personal costs Jesus demanded of all would-be followers. It was their way of affirming, "for each, the highway to Paradise must pass through one's personal Golgotha." The "sweetness" of Heaven can only be reached through the "bitterness" of Calvary. A seed must die before a new plant can spring to life. The invitation to discipleship is a call to come and die. A most "bitter" prospect indeed. How sharp the contrast to easy grace, freely dispensed through the sacrament to all the citizenry of Lutheran Princedoms.

Surely, the "sweet Jesus," who "paid it all" so that the believer has naught to do but "only believe," must never be separated from the "bitter Christ" who demands of his would-be follower that "he must deny himself and take up his cross and follow me" (Mt. 16:24 NIV). The "bitterness" and the "sweetness" of Christ must always be kept together in proper perspective. The "bitterness" of Christ's "cross" was somehow "neutralized" by the "sweetness" of his resurrection! And the "bitterness" of our sacrifices and troubles for his sake must be made bearable by the "sweetness" of his presence and the prospect that after our own "cross," there will be a reward of another "empty tomb"!

Our God is a God of purpose. He has big plans for his world and chooses to involve us mortals in their implementation. Jesus did not only go on ahead to asphalt the highway for us to enter Heaven at our convenience, but invited those who are willing to follow with him in the heavy task of roadbuilding. Such an invitation to be thus involved in the Father's business is a great honor and privilege and is also an extension of grace. At great cost, through tears of separation, through many sacrificial and exhausting labors of love, through the pain of persecution, and at the supreme cost of martyrdom, the highway network must be extended until it is accessible to all humankind!

Yes, discipleship has its price tag. To follow the "bitter Christ," one must first count the cost.

One day a young man came to the master teacher, seeking the secret of how to secure his good life eternally. There must be some certain "good thing" to do? Perhaps some coded creed to believe, or magic formula to repeat? Or a costly pilgrimage to take? Surely, there must be some special act of kindness, a heroic deed of outstanding merit worthy of historic mention.

However, Jesus surprised him with an invitation to discipleship, the challenge to take up his own "cross," to separate himself from all of his past, from all that was near and dear to him: his possessions, his security, his inheritance, his community, even his home and family. "Go! Sell everything you have. Give to the poor. Then come, follow me!" (Mk. 10:17-30 NIV).

The young man did a quick mental cost/benefit analysis, and then, "went away sad because he had great wealth." He was not prepared to accept the pain of separation from all that held his heart, plus the exhaustion of long years of self-giving service implicit in following the "bitter Christ." According to his calculations, he had counted the cost and the price was just too high!

It was in that context that the ever-outspoken spokesperson for the little band of "missionaries-in-training" voiced the question that weighed on all of their hearts, the question that resonates from our hearts also: If the price is too high for that calculating man, what about us? Are we the "fools"? "We have left everything to follow you!" (v. 28). Their unspoken question: "What then will there be for us?"

Jesus sweetened the bitterness of their concern, and ours, with words of encouragement and promise:

> "No one who has left home or brothers or sisters or mother or father or children or fields for me and the gospel will fail to receive a hundred times as much in this present age, (homes, brothers, sister, mothers, children, and fields – and with them, persecutions) and in the age to come, eternal life. (vv. 29, 30).

Therefore, for us who have left everything to follow the "bitter" Christ, there is something in it, some compensation for the sacrifices made, some "retirement benefits," in fact, a very ample reward!

We can be sure that no sacrifice we make in response to Christ's call goes unrecorded. No tears of separation from parents or siblings or children drop to the ground unnoticed. No pain quietly endured for Christ's sake will go un-soothed. No disease contracted in the line of duty will go unhealed. No humble deed of kindness, no labor of love, no sacrifice of personal pleasure or surrender of needed sleep on behalf of human need, or "cup of cold water" given in Jesus name will go unrewarded. No persecution born for Christ's sake will go unvindicated, and no drop of martyr's blood fallen to the ground will be left unavenged.

In fact, the "bitterness" will be compensated in "sweetness" one hundred-fold. And that, in some mysterious way, even in this lifetime. And above all this, there is the prospect of "eternal life!"

But, what about Johann Ludwig Krapf and his wife? As he came to terms with the seeming contradiction between his grief and his sense of call, he wrote to the Church Missionary Society:

> Tell our friends that in a lonely grave on the African Coast there rests a member of the Mission. This is a sign that they have begun the struggle with this part of the world; and since the victories of the church lead over the graves of many of her members, they may be the more convinced that the hour is approaching when you will be called to convert Africa beginning from the east coast.

Was their sacrifice worthwhile? And how does our Lord's promise apply to them? They were a part of God's larger scheme and key players in his team. Thanks to them, and the many who followed them, today Kenya is known as a "Christian country." One hundred and eighty years after that first supreme sacrifice was interred on that lonely hill near Mombasa, over 80 percent of the population of over fifty-five million claim some level of allegiance to Christ! Faith demands a long-range view. As the ancient sages encourage us:

> Those who sow in tears will reap with songs of joy.
> He who goes out weeping, carrying seed to sow, will return with songs of joy, carrying sheaves with him!
> (Psalms. 126:5, 6. NIV)
> Or

Let us not become weary in doing good, for at the proper time we will reap a harvest if we do not give up. Therefore, as we have opportunity, let us do good to all people! (Galatians 6:9, 10. NIV)

Other Books by the Author

This is the fourth book in his *The Odyssey of a Family* series in which the author tells the story of his family. In *Pilgrims Searching for a Home,* he recounts the life story of his grandparents who escaped the horrors of the Bolshevik revolution in Russia with their family, only to settle in Western Canada in time to face the hardships, disappointments, and trauma of the Great Depression and the "dirty thirties."

In his second book, *Shaping of a Servant,* the author begins by telling the story of his pioneer parents, their cross-cultural marriage, and continues in an autobiographical form, remembering his growing years in their family in rural Canada. He notes and evaluates the circumstances and events that God used to shape him and prepare him for a life of service. It is the story of the formation of a young man growing in self-awareness, struggling with a sense of divine call. It leads to a romance in which he finds his significant other.

In his third book, *Into Abyssinia*, the author gives an informative and lively account of the first eight years of his and his family's living and serving in pre-revolutionary feudal Ethiopia. It is a story of adventure as a novice missionary couple learns and adapts to a vastly different culture while raising a family in the less developed hinterlands.

All four books are available from **westbowpress.com/bookstore.**

Printed in the United States
by Baker & Taylor Publisher Services